Drop the Armor

Here's to loving fiercely
& leading courageously!
Christine Jewell

DROP THE ARMOR

Release the Past, Ignite Your Faith, and Unlock an Extraordinary Life

CHRISTINE JEWELL

Hardcover ISBN: 978-1-955811-31-6
Paperback ISBN: 978-1-955811-32-3
E-book ISBN: 978-1-955811-33-0
LCCN: 2024900899

First hardcover edition: June 2024

Cover design: Mila / www.milabookcovers.com
Author photography: Elena Gliosca / www.livepixelsphotography.com
Layout and typesetting: Bryna Haynes
Editor: Bryna Haynes

Published by WorldChangers Media
PO Box 83, Foster, RI 02825
www.WorldChangers.Media

To all the Warriors at heart who have been fighting battles their whole lives, whose hearts have been broken, and wounds are still waiting to be healed. May you discover fullness in the barren places and peace in the road ahead.

To the One who has captured my soul, Jesus Christ, and the Holy Spirit, who has breathed life into the pages of this book, equipping me with the strength and courage to share this message.

Praise

"*Drop The Armor* is a must read for high-performing leaders who want to tap into a deeper faith and live in full alignment to who God created you to be! Christine beautifully shares how you can break free from what's holding you back and run full force into the life you were called to live! Her emphasis on the pursuit of what God is calling you to will radically shift how you work. *Every* high achiever who feels stuck in life or business needs to read this book!"

- Kelly Roach, entrepreneur, podcast host, best-selling author

"Only some fights are worthy of your high calling. If it doesn't align with your purpose, it is a distraction. Reading Christine Jewell's book, *Drop the Armor,* will give you victory over the lingering fights of your past and help you discern the present battles necessary to have the life you know you're called to live."

- Neil Kennedy, author, founder of FivestarMan.com

"*Drop the Armor* is a profound read for those navigating the tug between ambition and true purpose. With Godly insight and profound wisdom, Christine leads readers on a transformative journey from the confines of the mind to the depths of the heart. If you're a go-getter, this book is a must-read. Get ready to break down those walls blocking you from the extraordinary life God has called you to live!"

- Dr. Jennifer Blossom, CEO and Founder of Blossom Leadership

"Christine's vulnerability is her strength. Her story is gut-wrenching and so powerful. This book is a must-read for individuals who truly want to live and lead by faith!"

- Brent Pohlman, CEO of Midwest Laboratories

Drop the Armor is a powerful wake-up call for anyone longing to move from success to a life of long-lasting significance. Christine uses the canvas of her own story, stroked with passion and transparency, to unveil a masterpiece that teaches readers how to love, lead, and live with resilient faith that can move mountains. I love how she talks to us like a friend, guiding us to swap competition for compassion and anchoring our actions in an audacious dedication to give God our resounding "yes!" no matter what He asks us to do. *Drop The Armor* is an invitation for us to step out of mediocrity into our extraordinary God-given potential."

- Staci Wallace, business strategist, CEO of Fueled by Fire

"Christine Jewell's *Drop the Armor* is a revelation for the high achiever navigating the complex terrain of success and inner peace. This profound journey from head to heart serves as an initiation, guiding us to shed the weight of past wounds, fuel our faith, and boldly seize the extraordinary life destined by God. It unveils the path to becoming a revolutionary kind of warrior—one who loves, leads, and fights with a refreshing difference. I firmly believe in God's purpose of raising an army of Christ-centered leaders to redefine our journey by aligning things in the right order. This book is a powerful call to leaders grinding it out the world's way, urging them to recognize their emptiness and find true fulfillment. On the other side of this transformative journey lies a life of freedom, fulfillment, and profound intimacy with God. *Drop the Armor* is not just a book; it's a manifesto for a new way of living and leading."

- Brian A. Covey, speaker, author, EVP of Strategy and Development at Revolution Mortgage

"If you're a chronic overachiever who is starting to realize that pain can only drive your ambition but so far, this book is for you. With raw honesty, Jewell invites us into a journey that many of us are familiar with. Out of her woundedness came a drive to succeed that eventually left her isolated, exhausted, and desperately needing a deeper, cleaner energy that would bear better fruit in her relationships, her work, and her spirit. She found it. So can you. There's a redemption story waiting for you, and this book might be your gateway to experiencing it."

- Alex Kirk, lead pastor, Chatham Community Church

Table of Contents

A New Era

Dear Warrior,

A new era is upon us. One where we can no longer play the games of the past. Where total transparency, honor, and trust will be the norm for those who want to live and lead extraordinary lives. Where deep conviction, inner knowing, and devotion will be the fuel that drives us forward, rather than the superficial striving, competition, and chasing we have come to know so well.

This new world will require a new type of warrior—a warrior who is grounded, calm, and fierce with purpose. Who embodies the power that lies within their heart, the leadership that comes from being in service to the Spirit of God, and the inner peace and love that come from restoring the relationship between the masculine and feminine.

This new era will call us to a different kind of battle.

We will no longer feel the need to be in a constant fight against ourselves, against others, or against time, energy, or money. On this new field, our old battle tactics will no longer work. In fact, they will be the very things that throw us off course, distract us, and destroy the relationships we hold so dear.

This new era will require us to *upgrade our weapons*—to use our swords in new ways.

No longer will our swords be used against us. No longer will they be used for harm or domination over others. No longer will they be used as tools for retaliation, reaction, and weakening ourselves as we aim to slay everything in our path.

Instead, our swords will cut through illusions and distractions to destroy past programming and lies that have infiltrated our minds, hearts, and homes. This new sword will be used to cultivate clarity and precision in our thoughts, actions, and words.

This new era will require us to *upgrade our battle strategies.*

No longer will we entertain the enemy's tactics to distract, divide, and conquer us. No longer will we enter into territories unprotected and unsupported. No longer will we feed into the enemy's games.

Instead, we will understand the nature of the battle and therefore engage in new ways, on new fronts, with upgraded strategies that shift and transform outcomes like never before.

Welcome to the new era. I invite you to rise as a new type of warrior. As the king and queen you are created to be.

But first, we must learn to fight different—not as a warrior of the world, but as a Warrior of the Heart.

Learn to fight as a
warrior of the Heart!

Introduction

When I was younger, I had three recurring dreams.

In one, I am flying.

I need to get away from where I am—from this house, this situation, this thing that is trying to come after me—so I begin to eagerly flap my arms. I feel the lift immediately. What a sensation! Emotions are pouring out from inside of me. There are so many that I can't begin to name them all. I just feel them all with such intensity.

It's easy to move this way. I am light, completely free, and it feels so natural. Up here, I can breathe fully. I can hang out here in the air as long as I want. I can move anywhere at any time with no restrictions.

Am I dreaming? I begin to notice that I am inside of a dream and feel myself lowering to the ground as my awareness increases.

I quickly realize I have the power to control myself inside this dream. I don't have to come down unless I want to. I *can* fly. I *will* fly! I stretch my arms out and surge forward, up and away. I am completely open and liberated, my mind clear as I rise above the noise, above the chaos and confusion taking place below me. I ascend higher and higher for an expansive view of the terrain. I can see forever—the lush valleys and crisp mountain peaks spreading out before me, my heart light and free.

If only I could fly forever!

***

In the second dream, I am voiceless.

I sit up in bed, all my senses alert and heightened. It's dark and quiet, but I'm wildly awake at the same time, all muscles tensed. There is a boy in my room. I can feel him and see him. He's older than me, and his stare catches my eye. He doesn't belong here! Is he coming to hurt me? What does he want from me?

Heart racing, eyes wide open, body erect, I open my mouth as wide as I can and scream.

But *nothing comes out.*

No matter how hard I try, no matter how much I push or force the sound, no matter how much I panic, there is no sound, only constricted air. It's as if there's a noose wrapped firmly around my vocal cords and all the words and sound are trapped inside.

I don't understand. *Why is this happening to me? Why can't anyone hear me? Why is no one coming to save me?*

I keep trying harder and harder to scream, to make any sound at all to alert someone, anyone, to come help me, but I am alone, exhausted, and terrified. It is bizarre to be so isolated and scared while, at the same time, knowing there are people out there who could help me.

If only they could hear me.

***

In the third dream, I am stuck.

I am running. There's something so exciting ahead of me, around the corner, just out of sight, and I am rushing toward it as quickly as possible. I'm not sure exactly what it is, but I know I must get there fast. My whole body vibrates in anticipation; my mind is full of awe and wonder as curiosity rushes through me. My heart feels like it's going to explode.

But then—*BAM!*

Just like that, I'm unable to move.

I look down at my legs and notice that I've landed in thick muck. It doesn't pull me down like quicksand, but instead is a heavy sludge that locks my feet in place like Superglue. I look around—I'm so close—and lean forward, straining to lift my legs. But they just will not move!

All of a sudden, I feel a visceral shift from excitement to terror, as if something is now coming after me and I can't get away. I rest for a moment and then put all my force and energy into my right leg. Slowly, painfully, I pry up my leg and set my foot back down a few inches ahead. But now, I have to go through the same effort with the other leg, and I've barely moved at all.

No matter how hard I try, I cannot seem to move forward. After each excruciating step, I seem to remain firmly in place. I am unable to move toward what's waiting for me around the corner, and also unable to escape what's coming after me. Looking back, I feel helpless and hopeless. Looking forward, all I feel is disappointment and frustration. Right here, I am stuck, drowning in the sheer overwhelm of it all.

If only I could be free!

***

All of the above were recurring dreams I experienced throughout my childhood. The circumstances sometimes changed, but the themes were always the same.

As a young girl, I was a dreamer both awake and asleep. I would sit for hours in front of our oven door, staring at the girl on the other side of the glass, telling her how pretty she was. I was a leader, convincing the other kids to join me on great adventures into foreign lands. I had this insatiable desire to escape, to travel beyond my current world and explore what else was out there.

All this dreaming provided me an escape from a childhood defined by strained relationships. My mother was a fearful yet faithful woman. My father was a charismatic overachiever who lived as if life was one big party. The problem was, he was also engulfed by deep loss, which led him to drink heavily. Home was a place of extreme highs and lows, of love bombs coupled with deep neglect. I was lavished with beautiful experiences and world travel, followed by moments when I feared for my life. Each amazing experience came with some level of pain or suffering attached. We moved countries several times, changing environments, friends, and homes during my formative years. I did not know where my roots were. I felt unstable, as if I belonged everywhere and nowhere at the same time. Fight, flee, or fit in at all costs became my daily norm.

When I dreamed of flying, I felt I could lift myself up and out of any circumstance at any time. This dream was so real that, even in my day-to-day life, I was convinced that I could fly. In the back of my mind, there was always the thought that, no matter what happened, "*I can always rise above this and fly away ...*"

While this dream was liberating, the other two were frustrating, terrifying, and incredibly isolating. I wondered why my voice was trapped, why I was alone and scared, why no one came to check on me. I wondered why my feet were stuck, why it took so much energy to move even a fraction of an inch, why I could never get to whatever was so enticing, and why I always felt pursued by something scary.

Over time, these dreams faded away, becoming distant memories that belonged to the little girl inside me. I fought against those deep fears, pushing them deep down inside. I forgot the freedom, ease, and lightness I felt when I was flying.

Instead, I learned to fight. I became a warrior. I put on my armor. I chose my weapons. I decided that nothing was going to get between me and what I wanted in my life.

Until about thirty years later, when I hit a tipping point that changed everything.

I was at a crossroad, a divine appointment. I had fought so hard to create a life I wanted—a life that felt stable and meaningful and loving. But nothing in my life was easy: not my relationships, not my health, not my inner world, and not my business. I was failing at yet another long-term relationship, years after a high-conflict divorce. My body was rigid and tense. I was experiencing extreme physical pain that didn't make sense. My business was struggling, and cash flow was a constant challenge. I felt like I was misunderstood by nearly everyone who mattered most to me. There was constant friction, and I was just so *tired*.

This moment in time—which was more of a season—kickstarted my dark night of the soul and my initiation into a new way of life. In order to have the life I truly desired, I needed to learn how to *fight different*. And that meant learning how to become a different kind of warrior—a Warrior of the Heart rather than a warrior of the world.

I went through a season of deep stillness, stripping away old layers of dead emotional weight. I chose to forget what I had taught myself about what I "needed" to survive, and let go of an identity that was not my own. I renewed my mind, cleared my body of the past, and unlocked my heart so I could finally receive the love I had longed for all those years. I left behind all the things that no longer aligned with the life I was being called toward. I learned to access the voice of the Spirit, get intimate, and allow God to lead me in this dance called life. I gave myself permission to make the leap into a whole new world, beyond the realm of logic and reason.

It was in this winter season that I began to receive a string of beautiful love letters—messages delivered to me and through me like breaths of fresh air. God whispered into my heart. It was as if the very Spirit of God was pursuing me. I felt these words breathing life into my heart and soul through many tears, prayers, morning meditations, hikes in the forest, and climbs on the red rocks of Sedona. I captured the letters in my personal journals without knowing everything they would become. To me, they were the words my heart had been longing to hear, the guidance my lost soul had been searching for to come back home. They became guideposts for me along my journey of healing, rebirth, and rebuilding.

When I received these letters, I was in a co-creative process of birthing a new life, body, business, and relationship. What I couldn't have guessed was that these letters would become the foundation of this book, and of the work I now do with my clients. You'll read a few of them throughout this book; may they inspire and uplift you as they did me.

But there was more.

When the letters came, my dreams transformed.

For the first time in a long time, I felt air under my wings. I felt my body lift and rise out of the noise, out of the collective heaviness I had been engulfed in. The whisper in my heart reminded me, "*You are meant to fly, my daughter. Lift your eyes, take a breath, move your body, and rise above it all!*" Mentally and emotionally, I was flying again. I remembered who I was, what was inside of me, and where my true power and strength came from. I remembered how to rise.

I found my true, authentic voice—capable, dynamic, and full of energy. Where there had once been constriction, now the floodgates were now open. There was so much pouring in and through me! I had a clear message, and my voice became a vessel for God to speak through. I had a powerful mission and felt compelled to share this message far and wide. I found that I was able to run, leap, and dance with complete ease and freedom. Where once there was heaviness and mud holding me back, I was now light and fast, barely touching the ground as I moved with grace and speed.

Yes, I am still a warrior. But today, I am a Warrior of the Heart, not of the world. I have rediscovered who I am at my core. I know without a doubt what I am here for, and can experience the depth and fullness of the life I was *created* for. I am deeply in love with my soul's true mate, a relationship that is honestly the easiest thing in my life. My days are filled with life-giving work that lights my soul on fire. I am doing exactly what I was created for and living abundantly as a result. My body is vibrantly alive, and each day is infused with play and adventure. My heart is deeply connected to God, my Creator.

Today, I love different.

I lead different.

I live different.

And it's all because I learned to *fight different*.

In order to "fight different," I first had to unlearn my habit of perceiving everything in life as an attack or a battleground to prove my worth. I had to unlearn the lies and tactics of the enemy that were keeping me encased in walls of protective armor. I had to stop relying on my *self* as the source of all power, strength, and solutions, and instead learn to depend upon the true Source that gives life to all things, God. I had to lay down my old identity, my old ways, my old stories at the altar, and give Him, the Author of life, permission to come in and create a new thing in me. It was through this act of surrender, invitation, and willingness to trust, coupled with His magnificent love and overwhelming grace, that I have been fully transformed.

Today I operate from a new identity. I stand on a different battlefield and am equipped with an arsenal of upgraded strategies that bring life to all things, rather than the stress and pressure I knew so well for so long.

This can be your story too. This book is your invitation to spread your wings, open your voice, and run beside me. It is your initiation into the path of a true Warrior.

In the chapters to come, I'll share how I went from being frustrated and alone, fighting everything in my life and feeling disconnected from my heart's desires and life purpose, to being a woman on fire, filled with passion, purpose, and love. My hope is that, as you read, you will rediscover the true person inside yourself—that my story ignites something inside of you and helps you *remember*.

The framework I've built within these stories will show you how to *fight different*. This book is designed as a journey from head to heart, and includes an arsenal of strategies and tools to help you navigate the practical challenges of life along that journey. In each chapter, you will find journaling prompts, action steps, and access to bonus audio materials so you can go further and shape this work for your life. You will also find letters from God—the messages that I received during my own

Warrior Initiation—to guide you along the way.

Finally, you will find supportive verses from God's Word, the Bible, throughout this book. I have pulled verses from various translations of the Bible based on which is most resonant in context; these translations include the King James Version (KJV), the New King James Version (NKJV), the Amplified Bible (AMP), the New Living Translation (NLV), and the New International Version (NIV). However, I encourage you to do your own reading and find the verses that speak His Word into your heart most clearly.

By the time you are done reading, it is my intention that you will be both inspired and equipped to emerge as the Kingdom Warrior and leader you were created to be.

So, arise, Warrior, and let the journey begin!

CHAPTER ONE

The Perfect Storm

"When everything is lost, and all seems darkness, then comes the new life and all that is needed."

— **JOSEPH CAMPBELL**

*I*t happened on the weekend of my forty-second birthday.

After a class of heart and hip-opening postures, I found myself lying face-down in Frog pose on the warmed, dark-blue volcanic floor of the yoga studio, and all I could do was sink into the ground and let the tears flow.

Every muscle in my body was rigid and shot through with pain. My hips felt like tight bands were locking the muscles in place, and I was shaking, inside and out. My lungs felt constricted, as if someone was squeezing them, and I could not get enough air through my throat.

Here I was, the owner of a holistic health and performance studio and a super-fit athlete by the world's standards, but my body was screaming. I was physically tense and unable to relax for any length of time, mentally exhausted from fighting the same battles day in and day out, emotionally drained from pouring my heart into one relationship after another without ever receiving the affection I craved, and spiritually crying out for answers and some kind of direction.

It was dark—not inside the room, but inside of *me.*

Was there an escape route, a way forward I was unable to see? I was so empty—and, at the same time, so full that I could not take another thing on. I wanted so much more, and yet I knew there was no way I could possibly hold onto any of it. In that moment, the pain coursing through my hips and thighs communicated what I had clearly been ignoring, suppressing, and pushing through for decades. There was a lifetime of unprocessed emotions shoved down deep into my body.

Whatever we try to hide, whatever we attempt to ignore, whatever we choose to power through will eventually come back to set the record straight—and the results can be difficult to face. My body had diligently held onto my pent-up emotions and suppressed memories until, in a class surrounded by total strangers and two of my dear friends, it all resurfaced in a barrage of tears.

All the pressure from ten-plus years of hustling as a business owner. The early mornings, late nights, and nonstop work weeks. No rest for the weary.

All the regret, anger, and hurt from staying in unfulfilling relationships long past their expiration date and dishonoring my heart's longing.

All the ignored pains of rejection and abandonment from childhood that I locked up in my body and pretended didn't matter.

All that unconscious trauma and tension bubbled up and spilled out on the floor that morning. There was no holding it back. There was certainly no holding it together.

And ... *what was the point, anyway?*

A BREAKDOWN TRIFECTA

On the outside, it seemed like I had it all.

I was an attractive woman with a beautiful body—lean, strong, toned, and confident. I knew how to use it and how to work a room. At the time, I thought I was fully practicing what I preached.

I had three amazing, healthy, and beautiful kids who I adored. I had done everything in my power to fight for them to have a better life. We lived in a house downtown by the lake along with my attractive and athletic partner, also well-known in his industry as a top performer.

I had overcome the hardship of a divorce years prior that left me reeling in financial uncertainty. With no idea where to turn, no money to my name and no guarantee of support coming to provide for the kids, I had leaned in and pursued my longtime dream of opening a fitness studio. We opened the doors with the bare-bones minimum. An empty room, a dozen yoga mats, and a set of weights was all I could afford, so I ran with it. It was profitable out the gate, and business grew steadily over the next few years with a lot of sweat equity, grit, and loads of passion. I built a team, gained loyal clients, and created highly successful programs. After a lifetime of deep financial loss and uncertainty, cash flowed to me, and it felt like I was living a lifelong dream.

I traveled often, and took my kids on multiple vacations each year. I even got to a place where I could afford to put them all in private school and support our lifestyle all on my own. I invested extensively in personal growth, had multiple coaches and mentors, and belonged to the "one-percenter" masterminds. I read all the books. I was part of the "5 AM Club." I knew who God was. I was spiritual—or so I thought.

But on the inside, I was also lost, confused, and in pain. I constantly struggled with thoughts like, "I should be a happy woman! What on earth do I have to complain about? What else could I possibly ask for? Come on girl, what is wrong with you?"

I might look like I had it all, but my body, my relationships, and my business were falling apart—a trifecta that led to a complete breakdown.

My Body

I thought I understood what it meant to be healthy because I was an athlete. The unwavering motto etched into my brain was, "No pain, no gain!" And so, I did what my programming taught me to do. I ran hard, even when I was sick. I took cortisone shots when I tore my ligaments, just so I could compete in the races and not miss out. If I could still run, if I could still push, then I could still win.

More, I internally competed and compared non-stop with myself, other women, and even men. It was incessant. I could not quiet down the competitive programming. I freaked out when my body fat percentage rose above eighteen percent. Regardless of how many times I won a race or landed in the top three, no performance was ever good enough, and the critic inside kept up her vicious cycle of commentary.

"Why didn't you push harder?"

"You could have done more!"

"How are you going to beat that next time?"

I felt so out of control. Here I was, an athlete who should be at the peak of my fitness, constantly in pain and unable to relax and give myself a moment to recover.

My body was screaming. It desperately wanted rest, which I refused to give it. It was craving gentle and nourishing touch, to be fully loved and held, but I was holding it together for everyone else, walking around with a wall of protection around me. Even though I scheduled time for many of the self-care practices I saw all over the internet, I had no idea what it meant to truly love and care for my body. I had no idea how essential it was to listen and cultivate a relationship with this incredible vessel. As a result, my body was tense and on edge 24/7.

My Relationships

Despite the fact that my partnership looked good from the outside, on the inside I felt completely alone, rejected, and full of despair that I had failed yet again to find the love I craved and needed.

Just after my divorce, I met a guy who owned a local bike shop, raced dirt bikes, and was a phenomenal athlete. So, naturally, I invited him to come to one of my triathlon races as a first date of sorts. (Isn't that funny? "Hi! Want to get to know me? Come watch me race!")

I vividly remember him standing on the sidelines that day, about half a mile from the finish line, screaming, "Second place is *first loser*!"

He spoke my language. The passion and game were on! I was hell-bent not only on impressing him, but also on proving my strength and ability to both of us. His comment pushed me enough to win first place that day, and it felt good to prove once again what I was capable of, even if it was fueled by competition and a fire under my butt.

The relationship that budded was one of passion on overdrive; we were like two bulls in a china closet. That initial attraction, so chemical, magnetic, and irresistible, launched us into an eight-year journey of emotional highs and lows, constant fighting, and perpetual games. I loved that man, and he loved me too; I have no doubt about that. But we did not fully understand *how* to love because we were both unconsciously driven by our past pain and wounding. We were desperate to experience intimacy with one another, yet unable to bridge the canyon of misunderstanding and miscommunication between us. The harder we tried, the worse it got. I wasn't ever able to drop the protective walls and open myself up to receive the gift of love I so desperately longed for. I couldn't communicate clearly or effectively. I was consistently fighting to be seen or heard, and failing miserably in the process. I was reliving the same patterns of my past—of my childhood dreams—over and over.

Both my children and his had already lived through our respective divorces and experienced the strain that comes with that. Now, they were involved in yet another round of drama. Of course, they observed and absorbed all the dysfunctional patterns and energy of our unhealthy relationship. The constant fighting, dramatic text exchanges, and long, drawn-out conversations hijacked both of us from being present with our kids. We created an environment of tension and uncertainty in our home. Walking on eggshells and avoidance became the norm.

Even still, we kept trying, kept fighting. We even went so far as to hold a ceremony of marriage in what I believe was a desperate attempt to keep our relationship from falling apart. Maybe, just maybe, we reasoned, if we made the commitment, bought a house, and moved in together, everything would magically fix itself. (Note: *that never works.*) We never did make the marriage union official. We evaded and postponed it. I think we both knew that we weren't going to make it. As the wall of resentment between us grew taller and thicker, we became distant, cold, resentful, and full of blame. It took less than a year before we sold the house and went our separate ways.

You'd think that would be the end, right?

Oh no. I like challenges, remember? I like to fight for things! Nothing worth having comes without a good fight, right? Relationships are hard work—isn't that what we've been told our whole lives? It took two more years of struggle before I ended it for good.

You'd think I would have paused and taken some time off to reflect and heal—but no. I was addicted to having someone in my life, and convinced myself that, next time, things would be different. (Today, we call this "anxious attachment.") Who knew?) So, I immediately began dating someone else, and this guy did seem different. He had done more inner work. He was in the same field as me. He was attractive, grounded, and calm. My kids really liked him. I wondered, "Could he be the one?"

We had a great start, and then everything turned sour. We went from being the perfect match to being the perfect mess in a matter of months—but not before I had hired him as a key player in my business and moved him into my home. The man I thought was going to be a powerful match for me and a solution to the problems of my past quickly became the source of my pain. We began fighting non-stop, seething with misunderstanding. There was absolutely zero passion and little to no desire to work things out. My savior complex was in overdrive as I took on the role of being his boss while also trying to be his development coach, his mother, and his girlfriend. Years of business masterminds and personal development work had me frustrated that he wasn't catching up, taking ownership, and showing up the way I expected him to. I felt like I had an extra child in the house, someone else to be responsible for and look after.

Looking back. I was living out all the classic behavioral patterns of a person who has not resolved the past, and who was letting her deep wounds run her life.

I wondered, "Will I ever be able to experience real love? Am I built for real love—do I even deserve it?"

Aside from my romantic relationships, I was failing in other relationships too, particularly with my children. By this point, I was ashamed and angry at myself for the choices I had made, the disrespect I kept tolerating, and the relationships I was modeling for my kids. I wanted so badly to create stability for them. I had worked hard to provide them with a nice home where they felt loved, accepted, wanted, and safe. Every dollar I earned went toward giving them quality education and access to everything they needed and desired. I helped create joyful memories and took them on amazing trips. We were close in so many ways, yet there was so much more happening below the surface that I was totally unaware of. I was missing key things because I was so distracted with my own life.

What on earth was I *really* showing them? I kept dragging them through my own personal dramas, chasing unfulfilling romances and my never-ending need to get ahead. Now, with this latest relationship, I had opened my home mindlessly to outside influence instead of fiercely protecting their space.

While my heart was in the right place, my mental programming was fueled by fear, scarcity, and a lack of real faith. I had not modeled what self-respect, honor, and love looked like. Despite all my efforts to the contrary, I had created the same atmosphere for them that I had experienced in my own youth: chaos.

I kept wondering, "How do I turn this mess around and give my kids solid ground? How do I create a calm and loving home that will make them feel safe and accepted?"

My Business

My once-successful business was hanging by a thread, with unhappy employees, customers, and business associates everywhere I looked.

I couldn't quite put my finger on how it happened, but things inside my health and wellness studio had shifted in a bad direction. After a nearly nine-year run of profitability and growth, everything had become hard. I was sitting on a mountain of debt from the purchase and buildout of our new location. There were constant issues with the other tenants in the commercial building who were unhappy with the noise and activity that came along with having a wellness facility in the building. Class numbers were falling, and clients became disgruntled as the atmosphere and culture shifted. We could barely keep up with our ever-increasing expenses. I was overpaying team members in an attempt to keep them on staff, but morale was low. A key employee, whom I had mentored and had been with me since day one, left to start her own business down the street, and a chunk of our clients walked right out the door with her.

I felt betrayed on so many levels. I was angry at myself. I was resentful of the business and the work. I felt trapped inside the life I'd built. The business I used to love now felt like a shackle around my ankles.

I wondered, "Why is my dream falling apart?"

And then, "Is this even my dream anymore?"

ADDICTED TO THE STRUGGLE

That morning, as I lay on the blue volcanic floor after yoga class, I felt mentally and physically engulfed, under attack by everything that was going wrong in my life.

And so, I prayed—or rather, I shouted at God, "What the hell is wrong with me, God? Why does everything have to be a fight all the time? Is this going to be my life forever? When will this craziness stop once and for all? What am I doing wrong?

"Help me, please! I am DONE!"

I felt like throwing up. I was trapped inside a life of my own creation that felt impossible to sustain. I was constantly being pulled in competing directions, and it was tearing me apart. There was never enough of me to make everyone happy or to do all the things I felt compelled to do. It was as if I was living in a glass castle that could shatter at any moment, with any wrong move. I was so sick of myself, and so tired of fighting the same battles day in and day out. I was being crushed under the tidal wave of unmet expectations—mostly my own.

I lived religiously by the mantra, "Mindset is everything." I thought that, if only I could only keep pushing toward the future I saw, I would someday get there.

What a crock of B.S.

The truth was, it was never, ever going to get easier, because *I was addicted to the struggle and fueled by pain*. ← Mom + Jennifer

I lived life like it was an unending battle. I constantly needed a mountain to climb or a race to win in order to prove my strength. I was a serial relationship hopper, terrified of being without a man to prove my value and beauty. Even my best friend pointed out how much chaos encircled my world at all times. (God bless her for listening to my stories all those years and holding space.)

Perhaps most crucially, I was enmeshed in the identity I had created to survive my formative years: I was a fighter, and proud of it. Fighting, pushing through, and overcoming challenges was encoded in every cell of my body. It was me against the world, and I would do whatever it took to win.

The problem, however, was that no one ever taught me how to channel my beautiful, powerful "fight" energy in an expansive, life-giving way.

So, there I was, lying in my pool of tears, with a broken body and a broken heart.

I was massively out of alignment—out of integrity with what I believed, valued, and held dear in the core of my soul. It had been time for me to move on for a while, time for me to honor the next season of my life and heart's calling, but I was holding onto the past, desperately trying to control the transition. I didn't want to lose what I had worked so hard to build, and I was terrified of what the future would look like.

Here's what I know today. When we try to control the process rather than trust it, the whole construct inevitably self-destructs. My resistance created the perfect storm in my life, with the trifecta of my body, my relationships, and my business burning to the ground all at once.

Only, this time, I could do nothing to stop it.

Some people call moments like these "dark nights of the soul." Others call it an ego death, or the breakdown before the breakthrough. In every great epic narrative, it's the rite of passage that culminates in a defining battle. For me, this moment was the accumulation of *many* dark nights of my soul, all crashing together into a final storm that would forever change the trajectory of my life. It was a spiritual crisis unlike any other I had experienced.

As I sat there, watching everything crumble, my heart finally woke out of its slumber. I felt my Spirit breathe, and I said, *"No more."* I was tired of fighting. I was done going it alone. I wanted to experience what I knew in my soul I was created to do, who I was created to be. I was longing for more in my life—and after all the years of fighting and forcing, I was finally ready to truly surrender it all.

I did not realize it at the time, but that was the moment I gave God total permission to enter into me. With no fight left in me, I yielded my mind, body, and spirit to His presence, power, and grace.

***

If you've picked up this book, it's because you are called to be a new kind of warrior.

Maybe, like me, you've reached a dark night of the soul, and know that you can no longer fight in the ways you have been. Or, maybe you feel a higher calling—a sense of dissatisfaction with the life you're living, and a pull toward something greater, simpler, and more fulfilling. Either way, it's time to look at what is required to birth a true Warrior.

Warriors who fight for the sake of fighting are many. I was one of them. But in order to accomplish our goals as warriors, we need to fight for a bigger cause, a higher purpose, and an ultimate outcome of love. The ways in which we have been trained to do this in our lives are no longer working, so we need to be reconditioned. The part of us that is addicted to pain and fueled by the constant struggle needs to die for us to be reborn into a different way of fighting, living, and loving.

WARRIOR INITIATION

At the close of each chapter in this book, I will invite you to ask yourself a few provocative questions that will support your awareness as you undertake your Warrior Initiation.

Please spend time with these questions. Journal about them. Bring them with you as you go throughout your day. Awareness is one of the most potent weapons in the arsenal of a Warrior of the Heart. These questions will help you cultivate yours.

- What are the themes or patterns that keep playing out in your life again and again?"

- Have you had your "perfect storm" moment? If so, what was it?

- What is your soul longing for that you have felt unable to achieve?

WARRIOR LETTER #2

I Am Here

(An Invitation from the Heart of God)

Dear Warrior,

I have seen your hard work. I have heard your voice asking for direction, and I have felt your longing for more, even though you aren't quite sure what that "more" is.

I see you. I hear you. I feel you, and I AM HERE.

I am responding to you; I know your heart's deepest desires. The answers and direction you seek are here, the doors you've been looking for are ready to be opened. I come in the form of opportunity. At this moment. I come quietly, discreetly, like a whisper flowing through your ear, a flutter beating faster in your chest, an invitation pulling you closer to me. Can you hear My delicate call? Can you sense My presence moving within and around you?

You've been asking for a long time. Are you willing to receive Me when I offer myself to you? I won't push, force, or demand you to join Me. I will show myself to you. I will call you forth by igniting a spark of excitement within you. I will invite you to join Me on this great adventure.

But, dear Warrior, it is up to you to join Me. It's up to you to go where you haven't gone before. To let go and allow Me to take you there. Opportunity is here, like a beautiful woman passing you by. She comes softly, stays only for a while, and then moves on.

I am here, presenting Myself to you as the answer to your prayer, the clarity to your overwhelm, the adventure you've been craving, the rest for your busy mind, and the key to unlock the next step in your journey, opening the floodgates of an extraordinary life of deep love, adventure, and courageous leadership.

I am here. Will you slow down, will you recognize Me, and follow your heart into the great unknown where freedom, blessings, and miracles lie? Or will you let Me pass you by?

The choice is yours.

I see you. I hear you. I feel you, and I AM HERE.

CHAPTER TWO

The First
Initiation

"The Warrior of Light holds the sword in his hands. He is the one who decides what he is going to do, and what he will not do in any circumstances."

— FROM *WARRIOR OF LIGHT: A MANUAL*
BY PAULO COELHO

We don't begin life as Warriors, but becoming a warrior is embedded in each of us. It's in our DNA. We are hardwired for a rite of passage where we discover that we can indeed survive and surpass the challenges before us. This is an essential season for each of us to go through, moving beyond total dependency on our parents or the outside world for survival and discovering our own identity, strength, and potential. We leave behind the realm of childlike wonder, awe, and innocence and begin to grow into the next version of ourselves as independent men and women. During this time, the outer world shifts from a playground to explore to a battlefield to survive and overcome.

In this passage, our physical, mental, and emotional strength is tested to what feels like our max. New skills are learned and mastered as we develop ourselves relentlessly in an effort to stay alive, manage what's at hand, and prove we are worthy of belonging. It's the first time we are forced to be disciplined and persevere as we endure what seems one hardship after another, climbing each mountain as it presents itself. We shed tears, build mental and physical muscle, and experience deep pain and burning desire that drives us forward. We "earn" the accolades, and also the scars that will tell the stories of our past. It is here that we discover who we think we can trust, and who we can't. It is here that we learn who has our back, and who will stand beside us. It is here that we also become hardened and build walls of protection. Our hearts get broken, sometimes shattered, and armor begins to thicken like a fortress around our hearts, bodies, and even our spirits. Things are locked away inside, never to surface again.

Early in our lives, we develop certain "anchors"—initial pieces of information that we take on as truths and hold onto. These anchors shape the nature of how we view future information and, in turn, how we engage with that information on our personal battlefields and in our battle strategies. We all have different anchors, and they can be both positive and negative; they can act as lifelines so we know how to find home and don't float away, or they can keep us locked in unhelpful places, unable to move.

In this chapter, we'll look at how our anchors develop, and how our negative anchors create stories and distortions that ultimately keep us fighting the wrong battles for the wrong things.

HOME AS THE FIRST BATTLEGROUND

My childhood home was a battleground hidden behind the veil of a seemingly perfect life. Sometimes this battleground was tumultuous, filled with strife and violent attacks on my nervous system. Other times, it was eerily peaceful and filled with laughter, stories, and gatherings of friends and family. There were multiple realities happening simultaneously.

In one version of my reality, I had a life filled with endless adventure, opportunities, and everything I could ask for. After I was born in Lancaster, California, my parents bounced around—Brussels, Paris, Zurich, and Copenhagen—before landing in Italy. There, we lived in a beautiful home just outside of Rome overlooking rolling green hills, rustic buildings, and begonias as far as the eye could see. I cannot remember wanting for anything material that my heart desired. Though our home base was Rome, we continued to travel the world, and the exposure to new cultures and environments anchored my appetite for adventure.

For me, this was anchor number one. *Life is an adventure. I must be on the move at all times or I will miss it.*

We regularly ate delicious local fare in fancy restaurants, establishing my palette for the finer things in life. My mother and father entertained often, filling the garden with neighbors, relatives, the sweet aroma of grilled meats, and bustling activity. Growing up in Italy allowed me to experience true joy, passion, and vitality. The wine flowed, and laughter and play were a normal part of life. Time felt optional.

Another set of belief systems were anchored in me: *Life is about living, not working. Life is abundant and good things are everywhere. I deserve to have a beautiful life.*

Having been born and raised in the small village of Avellino, Italy, my mother, Anna Maria, was exactly what you'd imagine an Italian momma to be. She was a nurturer from the beginning, unwavering in her devotion to her family. I can honestly never remember a time I felt unloved or unwanted by her. It brought her so much joy to see us thriving. She was patient. She was kind, beautiful, compassionate, and graceful. She showed me, and has continued to show me, what unconditional love looks like. I often consider her the best gift God has ever given me.

My father, Stephen, was a highly driven, charismatic man relentlessly committed to performing at the top of his field. He was an incredible provider and self-made success who overcame the odds stacked against him as a young boy. He was an adventurer at heart who would often sweep me away for Saturday dates at the lake. (At that time in Italy, kids went to school on Saturday mornings, so this rule-breaking was a little taste of the American Wild West!) To me, my dad represented hope, opportunity, and adventure. Much of the time with him I felt like I was on a fantastic ride. It was exhilarating, thrilling—even dangerous, because he liked to play on the edge. Once, in Switzerland, he placed me on a luge, sat behind me, and pushed us off down the hill. I thought I was going to die as we sped down with the snow whipping around us. I was terrified, but at the same time, I knew he had me. On our boating days, he would let me sit on the bow as we flew over huge swells, with no life jacket on and nothing securing me other than my hands on the wet metal railings. While Mom prayed to God to keep us safe, Dad would drink his beer, and I'd laugh my heart out as the boat slammed up and down in the waves.

Yes, my addiction to adrenaline was fueled early on.

My dad was wild, affectionate, adventurous, and charismatic. He had the best stories. He had a strong personality and was committed to doing whatever it took to provide for us. And I, without a doubt, was Daddy's girl. He was my hero and I *loved* to perform for his affection. The more I did to show him that I, too, was adventurous, athletic, and driven, the prouder he seemed to be of me. I lit up when he bragged about me and celebrated my achievements. My looks were also a point of pride for him. The more beautiful I became, the more recognition I received and the more I felt loved by him.

In this version of reality, I was given plenty of room to explore, to be free, and to be myself. I was lavished with affection and knew I was loved. I got to laugh, sing, climb on things, and disobey *a lot*. I felt unrestricted and encouraged much of the time. I was a bit of a wild spirit from day one.

Life was *good*.

And then, there was the darker side of life, the one we hid most of the time. I was ashamed of this confusing and painful part of my experience that no one acknowledged or talked about. Worst of all, I never knew when the shift was coming.

Sometimes, my father would come home angry and violent. He would stumble around, his eyes red and bloodshot, spewing hateful words. He would fall into fits of depression for days and become emotionally and physically unreachable, retreating into his own world. The voice that showered me with compliments and told fun stories now became the voice that frightened me the most. His pent-up rage erupted from him like a volcano, often when we least expected it. The same hands that held and protected me became aggressive and violent. They were now the hands that threw furniture across the room, lunged at me, and aggressively went after my mother and brother. I began to worry for Mom's physical well-being. Was he going to hurt her? Was she going to be able to stand up to him? Yelling and screaming became a normal mode of communication, followed by silence and avoidance, and all of us pretending everything was fine when it clearly wasn't. I would hide in my bedroom to avoid my father's wrath, trying and failing to drown out the fights from the other room. I remember taking my little brother into my room and telling him stories to calm him down. It was frightening, not knowing if my dad would burst in or if it was safe to come out. I often cried myself to sleep with worry over my mother and brother.

The same man who celebrated life so deeply also hated his life. How could both these realities exist at the same time? And yet, this contradiction was at the center of all of our realities. I never understood how my dad, who had everything he could ever want, could be so angry, cynical, and resentful. Weren't we enough? Why wasn't he happy with us? What was so wrong with him, with us? My heart broke for him, for me, for all of us, every day.

One night, when I was five, chaos broke out well after my bedtime. I woke up to a frenzy of people running about. I don't really remember much other than the feeling of chaos in the air. Something was wrong! The neighbors burst into my room, helped me get dressed, and put my shoes on so they could take me to their house. But why? Why were we getting dressed to go out at night?

Meanwhile, an ambulance took my father and mother away. So much more confusion in the air. Where were they going? Were they ever coming back?

I learned later that Dad had overdosed on pills.

He did not die that night, though it wasn't the first time he'd attempted to take his life. I am not sure to this day whether he actually wanted to die, but looking back I can see that his suicide attempts were desperate cries for help. There was a little boy trapped inside him who was feeling alone, scared, and abandoned, and who had never been seen or appreciated for who he really was.

For me, that night was a defining moment. My five-year-old self decided she was no longer safe. She no longer had a protector and could no longer trust her father—or any man, for that matter. It was con-firmed inside every cell of my being and body: my greatest protector was unreliable, and I had to look after myself. A bond that I thought was unbreakable had been shattered.

A new anchor was in place: *I am unsafe. My environment is not safe. People, even the ones that love you, are unsafe. I am unprotected. I am my protector and my own source of safety from now on.*

The seeds of abandonment were dropped in and given the fuel to come alive. My thoughts and experience that night put in place a new operating system that would run many areas of my life from that day forward, even if it didn't manifest fully until much later in life.

As we will discuss later in this book, abandonment wounds are not new. They have run their course in humanity since the beginning of time. Abandonment is one of the original core wounds that all humans experience at some level. I believe it is ultimately there to bring us back home to God—to our original design of sacred unity where we find our source of security, protection, and peace within and in Him rather than in the external.

At five years old, however, I had no understanding of or context for any of this. I only knew that I was unsafe—and that no one could ever make me feel safe again.

RITES OF PASSAGE

Nearly every culture around the world has a way of marking the developmental changes throughout a person's life. There are rituals and rites of passage to initiate young men and women into adulthood, and to mark the end of one era and the introduction of another.

At their most basic, all rites of passage are characterized by three distinct phases: separation (leaving the old/familiar), transition (a time of testing, learning, and growth), and a return as the new version (incorporation and reintegration). Most often, these also involve some sort of ritual, mentoring, testing, or ceremony. The common themes are intention, preparation, testing, and celebration.

The purpose of a rite of passage is not only to celebrate a milestone or accomplishment, but also to prepare the individual mentally, emotionally, spiritually, and physically for a new role or season of life. It is that aspect, more than the accomplishment itself, that really prepares us to show up for life from moment to moment.

In tribal and warrior cultures, there is a distinct moment where the boy leaves his mother's arms and father's protection and sets out alone to discover who he is and what he is capable of. Will he have the capacity, courage, strength, and skills to hunt, to protect himself and the tribe, and to provide for his future offspring? Will he have what it takes to survive alone in the wilderness?

In such a rite, the participant leaves a boy and emerges a *warrior*.

A warrior knows there is a battle worth fighting. He is willing and ready to sacrifice his own life to defend others. Only then is he suited for the tasks of adulthood, like protecting and providing for a family.

Of course, these initiations were a product of simpler times. In our Westernized world of convenience and consumerism, we have lost this tradition for the masculine. There is much writing on this subject suggesting that, as a result, most boys today bypass this essential state of the masculine journey, resulting in a wake of men who don't know who they are, don't trust their instincts, and are not prepared to lead effectively.

While some cultures certainly have similar initiation ceremonies for women, there are already natural rites of passage that nearly all women go through, perfectly planned by our Creator. There is menstruation, the celebration of womanhood. The minute a female is able to reproduce, she is no longer a child biologically, but a woman. Many cultures, religions, and tribes have rites of passage to celebrate this transition from girlhood to womanhood and to prepare the young girl emotionally, spiritually, and mentally for this new season. However, in Western culture, menstruation is often treated as something to be ashamed of, minimized or trivialized as an everyday occurrence instead of being celebrated and acknowledged as a monumental occasion in a girl's life.

With pregnancy and birth, a woman's body and heart are taken through a natural rite of passage again. The moment a woman gets pregnant, she instantly becomes a nurturer, vessel, and protector of life as life is forming inside her. With the birth of a new life, her survival instinct shifts from self-preservation to preserving the new life that she carried in her womb for nine months. For women who choose not to give birth or are unable to, this rite of passage is available in any creative endeavor that brings life into the world—such as music, art, business, or the creation of community. The feminine births life into all things and is, by nature, a nurturer.

There's no doubt that, in today's world, the majority of people grow up without an honorable rite of passage. Instead, the workplace and the home have become the training grounds where men and women prove themselves and determine their worth, often without any guidance or higher perspective. The drive to accumulate wealth, status, and recognition is embedded deep within us, but we now find ourselves isolated and alone—disconnected from ourselves, one another, the core of our original design, and the Spirit of God. This leads to struggles such as divorce, addiction, and violence, which then create the breeding ground for the cycle to repeat itself.

I believe we will always get what we need in the end. God designed us that way; ultimately, He is a God of process, evolution, and refinement. It is impossible to go from being a child straight to being a confident, secure adult who can provide, protect, and love fiercely without first becoming a warrior. A warrior knows how to survive, protect life, multiply resources, and move forward courageously under the influence of pressure and fear. We cannot become Kings or Queens of our own castles and kingdoms without first understanding how to be Warriors of the Heart who fiercely protect their people and are equipped with the skills, strength, wisdom, and discernment to lead through hardship.

The warrior path is one place where our natural rite of passage has been distorted. In lieu of an intentional and ceremonial rite of passage that properly prepares us to honor the journey from child to warrior, we have been forced to make up our own. This "making up" is often fueled by a need for belonging. Many of us today have grown up disconnected from a masculine role model who can take us through this passage effectively. As a result, boys and girls become warriors overnight without any solid support, grounded principles, intentional preparation, or real purpose to guide them. Often, they're just copying how they see others acting—older kids who they idolize, celebrities and influencers pushing lifestyle choices, or other forceful personalities telling them what success looks like. Or, perhaps they are thrust into the masculine role of protector, emotional parent, or provider early on at home due to a physically or emotionally absent parent.

We all get a rite of passage, alright. But in my opinion, it is often a far cry from what God intended for us. Instead, it is one that worldly programming has selected for us, and therefore it is *incomplete*. It is where we develop our negative anchors and false beliefs. It is where we buy into a lie as truth. It is where we allow our past pain to begin running our lives and block us from the life we ultimately long for. This has left warrior men and women with unhealed wounds, hardened battle scars, and closed hearts. Empty, directionless, and questioning our worth, we anxiously and unsuccessfully strive to fill the void inside.

My dad was a warrior. I was a warrior. But neither of us really understood, in the end, what we were fighting for.

THE FIGHT IS ON

My father's drinking got worse. The canyon between my parents got wider and deeper. The love I witnessed between them as a little girl transformed to mistrust, and fear overcame my mother. We stayed in Italy for a few more years before they decided to move back to the United States. Perhaps, my mother thought, if he were back on home soil, my dad would heal. But that was not the case.

After the move to Florida, my mother found herself an ocean away from her tight-knit family with no external support system, immersed in a brand-new culture and language, and caring for two small children and a husband who was increasingly angry and unpredictable. She wasn't filled with light and laughter anymore, and although she tried not to show it, I could see the heaviness and worry she had been carrying for years.

She no longer trusted my father, and I didn't blame her. Betrayal was rampant and he was unsafe to be around. Women were rolling in and out of his life; he didn't bother to hide it. He was addicted to external hits of validation. Addicted to women, porn, alcohol—anything that would give him temporary reprieve. It became unbearable. We walked on eggshells, everyone's nervous system on high alert wondering which version of my father would walk through the door each day. Chaos, drama, and fear oozed in the atmosphere, and Mom's peacemaking efforts accomplished little.

While today I can only imagine the cage my father was trapped in, at the time I felt violated as a woman and betrayed as a daughter. I wasn't sure whether to love feminine beauty or hate it. I began mistrusting all women in my life and distanced myself from other girls. The relationships I did have with girls my own age were fleeting and superficial, a pattern that would continue for decades. I had no sisterhood bonds or supportive girlfriend groups. It seemed like all other women could offer was endless competition over guys, catty attention-seeking, and ridiculous drama. In my eyes, women were weak, insecure, backstabbing, and honestly, a waste of my time. So, I decided to surround myself with guys instead. This helped in some ways; I could separate myself from that "weaker" feminine energy and feel some sense of masculine structure around me again.

I got to a place where I refused to let any of the darkness at home show on the outside. I had zero tolerance for negativity or negative emotions and became relentless about being Miss Optimistic—energetic, confident, fun, flirty, strong, and happy at all costs. I even earned the titles of "Class Flirt" and "Most Spirited" in a class of six hundred students. I learned how to use my feminine energy to my benefit; by using my charm, I was able to make others around me light up and win their favor with ease, all while getting what I needed (which was often attention). I loved this feminine part of me and hated it at the same time. It felt fake, but also powerful in some twisted way. Today, I know that this was, at its core, a battle strategy of manipulation and control. The very thing I was trying to run from was the same "weapon" I was using to keep myself safe.

At home, I was still begging my father to stop drinking. To not kill himself. To leave the other women. To be the fun, loving man I had once known. "Just stop," I pleaded, but he paid no mind. The claws of addiction were just too strong for me to compete with. Only a miracle can change the heart and soul of someone who has fallen into the hands of addiction. Only they can choose to get the help and support they need to fight the *real* fight within.

During my last year of high school, Dad lost his job, and we subsequently lost the house. Overnight, my parents were divorced, and Dad was no longer living with us. Overnight, the furnishings in the house were liquidated to pay off my father's debts, and I went from being a senior student living in a four-bedroom house with a pool in a respected golf course community to a girl sharing a bed with my mom in a two-bedroom apartment. I had sabotaged my relationship with my high school sweetheart of two years and spiraled into a year of partying and promiscuity. I went from celebrating my admission to Florida State University and planning my dorm decor to dropping that dream to stay close to home. My mother worked the night shift on the prayer lines at church to make ends meet. We were getting food from the church. My brother stopped wanting to go to school. Dad fell off the face of the planet and was nowhere to be found.

There was no help. It was just me, Mom, and my brother, abandoned and unsupported.

The anchor that had been dropped when I was five now sunk deeper into my heart as the evidence that life was unsafe kept stacking up to support my story.

I was so *angry*. Angry at my father, and at how his actions had flushed away life as I knew it. Angry at my mother for allowing all of this to go on and putting up with him for so long. Angry at men in general for being unreliable and untrustworthy. Angry at women for being doormats and sex objects. I was embarrassed and resentful beyond measure. Determined and fueled by my rage, I refused to allow myself to be heartbroken, and instead made the decision to fight my way forward and be strong at all costs. I built a huge wall around my heart in order to protect myself and embarked on a journey of *fierce independence*. There was no way I would allow *any* man to treat me poorly, ever. In fact, there was no way I would allow myself to depend on another human being for anything!

At seventeen, I moved into my own place with my new boyfriend and never looked back. I needed to support myself fast, so I learned the art of sales and upselling by waiting tables. By the time I turned eighteen, I had a brand-new car and was putting myself through university. I also learned how to use my beauty and charismatic nature to get what I wanted. One of my gifts is influencing and leading others. I do this through my energy and my ability to read others, so I always knew who I could charm. I believe our gifts show up early in life, but we first learn to use them in dysfunctional ways, fueled by deep fears, pride, and misunderstanding. We don't yet understand how to harness and use our gifts in expansive and creative ways, let alone use them to glorify God.

The home that had been my battleground for so many years was behind me. I felt like I had my act together, and I had no tolerance for those who weren't showing up and driving hard. I was a fighter, fully prepared to kick butt and take names along the way. I was strong. I was independent. I was optimistic.

I *was* going to become successful, and I wasn't going to fail.

Ever.

THE SPELL WE'RE UNDER

The root system for the high-achieving warrior was firmly implanted within me. "Unsafe" and "Don't Trust" had been anchored, and I was living according to those beliefs. I had officially bought into the survival programs—the lies and distortions of this world that rule over us until we choose to break free from the spell, complete our initiation, and come back home to our original, God-given design.

The lies and distortions created by our early experiences and living in survival mode are funny things, because there is some truth in them. There is evidence to support their validity. As you read the list of common distortions below, you may still resonate with them. I get it. Therefore, I invite you to consider that there is more here than meets the eye. Most distortions and deceptions are composed of truth filtered through a clouded lens of painful experience. This lens skews truth into untruth. Therefore, if any of the following statements feel true for you, I urge you to look deeper at what they are fueled by and what they have compelled you to fight for in your life.

The Lies and Distortions

- **I am unsafe.** I have to watch my back at all times. I can't trust anyone or anything.

- **I am alone.** I have no one to support me or fight for me.

- **I am unloved**. I have been rejected and betrayed. I am unwanted.

- **I am the source of all things.** It's always going to be up to me. I make things happen, and I am 100 percent the creator of my reality.

- **I am what I do.** I must prove I have what it takes to be loved, to be worthy, to be successful.

Can you relate to any of these? Would you add anything else to this list? Take a pause right now and write your own list down. Put those lies and distortions out there. Lies lose their power when they are exposed!

WARRIOR INITIATION

Get out your journal and answer the following questions:

- When did you begin your initiation from child to warrior? *at 4½ n 5*

- What were the familiar patterns, stories, anchors, and distortions of your childhood? *Fights, Yelly Screams, curss, things flying thru the air — fear*

- What programs did you pick up that are still ruling your life today? *Isolation escape* *hurt distrust*

- How have these programs served you? How are they no longer working? How are they actively causing harm to you right now?

CHAPTER THREE

What Are
We Really
Fighting For?

"The ultimate battle is for the soul, but the battleground is in the mind—for whoever rules the mind controls the heart, and the heart is the gateway to the soul."

— **CHRISTINE JEWELL**

*F*rom a young age, we follow a path laid out by those who "know better." We are programmed to follow the blueprints and systems of society and the world's definitions of what success, love, belonging, growth, and significance look like. We are indoctrinated into *what* to think, not *how* to think. We are taught to believe a specific version of right and wrong, truth and untruth. We are taught what we should want, and when we should want it. We are taught what "successful" people do and don't do, what "smart" people do and don't do, and how to label and give meaning to everything in the world we live in.

We are trained in schools, legalistic systems, religious institutions, clubs, and associations—nearly all organized, centralized, and highly-controlled structures—to ignore the deep longings of our hearts and set aside our God-given intuition to follow the supposedly logical and "smart" pathways set out for us. We look up to and follow our well-intentioned parents, our teachers, and the experts, many of whom are pawns of the system themselves. We become enamored with promises of the future. If we just follow the program, we think, one day we'll get there. Maybe there is a nice house on the other side, enough money in the bank to make us feel safe, a family who will finally accept us and show us the affection we crave, or the job title or position that would finally make us feel worthy.

If we just do as we're told, we'll eventually get there.

We'll make it.

Wherever *there* is. Whatever *it* is.

We are taught to chase what we don't even truly desire. These aspirations are camouflaged for us in seductive wrapping, screaming, "This is it! *This* is the thing you need, the thing you should want, the thing that will make you happy. If you just follow the program, you will have a great future."

Those who don't go along with the storyline are left with the impression that life is going to be very hard for them. Isn't it always the ones who speak out, who think differently, who ask the unpredictable questions and challenge the system—isn't it always they who are pointed out, labeled, and ultimately told there is something "wrong" with them?

Combine that tension with the pathways imprinted in our psyche and nervous systems from our individual traumas and adverse childhood experiences, and you've got the perfect recipe for a misaligned life.

We all have experienced trauma, loss, or pain along the way. This isn't "special," nor is it wrong. While our circumstances may have been unique to us, the deep grooves of unresolved shame, guilt, fear, and anger that directly impact how we view ourselves and the belief systems we operate from are *not* unique. Trauma, loss, and pain are part of the human experience. However, when we don't know or learn how to face the pain and work with it, we attempt to avoid it at all costs. We shut the doors to what's inside our hearts, and get to work executing on what we've been told to do. We become relentless in the pursuit of the next goal, accolade, or achievement. We need to prove ourselves over and over again. We become warriors fighting for the wrong things.

We become "warriors of the world," fighting the good fight for the causes we've been sold. We push down and ignore what we really think and feel. We avoid listening to our hearts and souls as we unconsciously train our ears to follow the external noises, which get louder and louder with time, drowning out the voice of our innermost being and that of the Spirit until they're nothing but faint, foreign whispers. We follow the program that makes the most logical sense instead of questioning if we are doing what is in integrity for us.

The driving force behind so much of our striving is our deep-seated need to avoid reliving the pain of our youth. Fear, rather than love, has unconsciously become our fuel, our source, to get ahead. Yes, even for those of us who think we broke the mold.

For so much of my life, I was hell-bent on doing it my way. I thought my way was going to be different. I was wrong. I was still operating according to the same old program, only now it was dressed up in a different label and branded as fierce independence. Inside, I was still chasing the same stuff, driven by the same core wounds and faulty teachings.

THE "PERFECT" LIFE

At twenty-one, I was fully convinced that I was ready to build the life of my dreams.

I moved in with a man ten years older than me just months after meeting him. I was obsessed with the illusion of safety, security, love, and the "right" future I'd been chasing since I left home at seventeen. He represented it all. He came with promises of a good family whose parents were still together. He owned his company (or so I thought). He drove a Range Rover. He spoke like a visionary, was athletic, and had a thirst for adventure. He checked all the boxes for what I thought I needed and wanted in a husband.

But before long, the cracks started showing. The business ran out of funding and was dissolved overnight. The Range Rover got repossessed. His family stopped talking to us, and not a single person on his side of the family attended our wedding two years later. I was devastated, caught up in a whirlwind of confusion, wondering what on earth was going on.

That was just a foreshadowing of our next eight years together.

Despite our rocky start, I tried hard to build the perfect life I envisioned. We were a blended family: his two young children from a previous marriage lived with us full-time, and were soon joined by three healthy children of our own. Our first child came within two years, our second two years later, and our third two years after that. It quickly became a full house buzzing with all the excitement of a young family and the push to get a new business off the ground and grow it.

There were many moments of happiness along the way, but our relationship, the new business, and our entire life had been built on a foundation of quicksand. There were a multitude of lies, avoidance, and false promises from the beginning. Piles of borrowed money and debt accumulated to fund our new business and lifestyle. We made many purchases we couldn't afford. Relationships with our extended families were strained, causing constant tension and division inside our home. Trying to keep up with the demands of the outer world while still maintaining the appearance of having it all together became too much. We were living in a glass bubble without any solid infrastructure; one wrong move and the whole thing would shatter.

By the time I was thirty-one, I was exhausted, bitter, resentful, and completely alone. My husband was now traveling most of the time. I was a stay-at-home mom with five children, and even though we lived in a huge home in one of the nicest areas of town, we rarely had funds in our bank account to cover simple expenses like groceries. Everything was borrowed or owed.

That year, I began an affair to escape my reality, which became the catalyst that ultimately ended my marriage. I'm not proud of the way things went down. The truth was that I did not have the strength or courage at the time to address my situation head on. Rather than admitting that my plan for my perfect life had gone sideways and protecting the things that actually mattered, I looked to an outside source for comfort and affection, and it tore my whole world apart.

Alone with my three young children, ages three, five, and seven, I was hit with the reality and urgency of my situation. No one was coming to save me. No one was going to provide for us. Up until this point, I had helped with my husband's businesses on the side, but had been completely dependent on my husband for financial support. My separation and divorce was a battle filled with financial and emotional games that tested me to my limits. Everything I thought I had built over the past ten years came crashing down around me.

As a result of some incredibly poor decisions in the divorce settlement, I found myself without a home, a car, or any source of income. It was the most terrifying place I have ever been. I *had* to find a way to provide for myself and the kids while maintaining some sense of physical, mental, and emotional stability for all of us.

Every day, I told myself, *I cannot lose them. I cannot be weak at this moment. I cannot fail them.* My only choice was to armor up and find the strength to keep moving forward.

I found myself reliving the same anger, isolation, and fear I'd felt when my dad left us. I was terrified of the future—and at the same time, remembering, *I've been here before.* I knew what it was like to lose everything and bounce back. I had survived then, and I could do it again. But this time, there was so much more at stake.

My mantra became: *I. Will. Not. Lose!*

Two paths lay before me. I could go into the "safe" corporate world, commute into the city, and hardly see my kids in exchange for a predictable paycheck. Or, I could take a leap of faith and open my own business. This was my chance to do what I loved and be more available for the kids, but it came with no guarantees that it would even work, let alone pay the bills.

It was a *hard* call. I had a huge responsibility to my kids, and it seemed so logical to seek a steady paycheck. But my soul was unsettled with that option. And so, terrified and determined, I sold my wedding ring for $4,000—just enough to pay the deposit on a leased unit where I could realize a dream I'd kept tucked away for years.

That's how PUSH!FIT Studio was born.

What a perfect choice of name.

PUSH, Dear Warrior

Push forward.
Push beyond what you can see is possible.

Push your body.
Push your comfort zone.
Push past all this BS.
Push, girl. Just push. It will be fine on the other side.

I put those words on the walls inside and outside my fitness studio, and lived by them for the next eight years. "Push" became a way of life; it became my identity.

And it worked ... at first. Within my first year, we went from starting with zero to breaking six figures. Then that doubled and tripled. The studio was rocking, new clients were coming in easily, and we were consistently voted the best fitness studio in the area. I slowly hired a great team, and we all thrived doing what we loved. Moreover, I had some sense of order in my life again. There was enough money to support my kids and for us to enjoy life together. It seemed like things were flowing just right. I had trusted myself and the process, and listened to my heart—and things were good.

What more could I ask for, right?

But the taste of success was enticing, and soon I wanted *more*. More growth, more structure, more money, more time off, more influence. I soon hired a business coach and a team of experts to help me scale the business. They had better systems, the right knowledge, and all the stories to prove their success, so it seemed like a smart move.

I remember my first live event with that group. At the registration table, they were handing out burgundy t-shirts to all the attendees. But some people were getting different shirts, black ones with "VIP" emblazoned on them. Throughout the conference, I kept noticing this hierarchy. There were tables for the regular attendees, then there were the VIP tables. There was a luncheon for the regular attendees, then there was the VIP lunch in a closed room by invitation only. I later found out there was even another level, Platinum, and that those people got all the VIP access plus exclusive trips to amazing locations.

The bait was set. I was hooked.

I made a decision that day. *I am going to get to Platinum. I am going to be a Platinum client. I am going on those ski trips. I am going to be in that room, whatever it takes.* So, I went all in, working hard to implement everything they told me to do, restructuring everything I had created.

I pushed harder.

WHAT WE THINK WE'RE FIGHTING FOR

As with most who chase the dream, I thought I was fighting for a better future for myself and my children. One of stability and certainty, where we would never have to worry about money again, and where we would be positioned to say yes to opportunities without hesitation or fear. I thought I was fighting for growth, and to make clear to my children, my clients, and myself that when you put your mind to it, nothing can stand in your way or knock you down—that we, and we alone, are the creators of our destiny!

I thought I was fighting for my kids' future. I thought I was fighting for my team. I thought I was fighting for my clients. I thought I was fighting as an advocate for health. I was *pushing* us all to become our best selves and to create a better life. I felt this call deeply in my heart. I was certain I was pushing for all the right things.

Maybe you're fighting your own version of this battle right now. Your journey has been well intended. But at some point, you lost yourself in your mission.

Here's the truth: somewhere along the line, when we push too hard and too fast, we lose sight of what we are fighting for, and the fight begins to feel different. The objectives shift, our focus gets thrown off, and we lose our way. It doesn't happen overnight; rather, it happens so slowly you don't even realize it. When we are conditioned to keep pressing forward, we zoom right past the small signals that tell us, "Something's not right. Something's not working."

Everything in my life started to feel heavy and chore-like, and it became increasingly challenging to access the joy I once had for the work and our clients. I went from loving what I did to resenting it. I was also having a harder time feeling good in my body. Where once I had been flexible, fluid, and light on my feet, I started to feel weighed down, tense, and rigid. Each day, I left the studio exhausted. I was putting on weight for what seemed like no reason. Running became harder, and I found myself nursing one injury after another. I went from craving my workouts and leaving them energized to dragging myself through them and struggling to keep my energy up for the rest of the day.

Frustration became my emotional home base. I became irritated and impatient, and would snap at my kids for the simplest things, which in turn made me feel guilty and judgmental about myself as a mother. I was having a harder time communicating clearly with my staff, and became frustrated when they didn't execute tasks at the level of my expectations. I had so much to celebrate and be grateful for, but I was a hostage to the never-ending gap between where I was and where I thought I should be, where my peers were. My mind constantly reminded me that I should be further ahead by now. As a result, my inner fuse got shorter and shorter. I felt like a hamster stuck on a wheel, running the same loop for eternity.

The truth was, all that frustration was really my disappointment with myself.

I was used to winning at what I put my mind to. I was attached to the timelines I had set, and angry when they didn't succeed as planned. When you consider yourself a high achiever and have succeeded at most things, any stall in progress can feel like a major setback and failure. Not overcoming the challenge at hand feels like you're losing a war. I was a type A personality, a D/I on the Disc Profile, a Quick Start on the Kolbe Assessment—I did all the personality tests, and as far as I could tell, I was not living up to my potential. Patience wasn't anywhere on my radar.

The clear vision I'd had for a better life was overtaken by the noise jabbering incessantly in my head. There was always one more thing to do, and while I could shut down the to-do list for an hour or so during a workout, prayer, or journaling session, it would return the moment I plugged back into real life. I would wake up throughout the night and every morning with a sense of unease and anxiety. The inspiration and creative fuel that once drove my desire was overtaken by obligation, and the boundless energy I'd once felt in my body was drained by constant battles and putting out one fire after another. The race against time was on nearly 24/7.

Now let me be clear: it wasn't *all* bad. There were many moments when I would tap into that well of inspiration and clarity again—mostly when I would step away to attend retreats, live events, mastermind weekends, or just take a vacation. That space provided me the room to breathe again and recalibrate my system, but I had no idea how to sustain that clarity and spaciousness once I came back to the daily grind. I was always escaping just to get a moment to myself and catch my breath.

Here's what was really happening. I had many typical high-performance habits in place—morning routines, sleeping optimization, meditation, a community of other high performers around me—but I couldn't move forward freely because I was letting certain things in my life hold me back, and procrastinating or hesitating on decisions that would actually move the needle.

My intimate relationships were completely out of alignment, but I was terrified to be alone.

There were staff I needed to let go, but I was too worried about what people would say, and feared letting down the people who depended on me.

There were programs and systems in my business that needed to be overhauled or ditched altogether so I could step away from the company or sell it, but I was holding tightly to the old, familiar, and reliable, afraid of not knowing what was next. Afraid of the uncertainty.

Grasping. Holding on. Fearful. Even when I knew it was well past the time to let those things go, I couldn't. It was as if I was paralyzed.

So many decisions that I was making (and not making) were from the frame of scarcity, fear, and loss. I needed a shift in my business, but there was no way forward through the same old PUSH. What had gotten me here was the very thing now making me miserable. I needed to slow down and truly pay attention to my body, but I was terrified of what would happen if I did. Would I get fat? Would I get slow? Would I lose my drive and ambition?

I often found myself wondering, "If this really is my path, why on earth do I feel so exhausted, disconnected, and alone? Do I even want all this anymore?"

My spirit was dull and disconnected. I wasn't dedicating the time and space to listen to my heart and grow in my spirit. I wasn't training myself to connect to the Heart of God, to listen to the instinctual wisdom of my body and the intuitive guidance of the divine intelligence that is always present if we allow it in. I hadn't trained myself to go deep inside to the inner knowing that resides inside all of us.

It was time to unlock my hardened heart, infuse life into my tired body, and tap into the depth and well of my soul. It was time to *trust*. To trust myself at deeper levels and lean into the support and guidance of the amazing God who created me in the first place.

I was feeling the call deep within my bones. It was time.

WHAT WE'RE ACTUALLY FIGHTING FOR

It's always easier to see clearly when looking back on ourselves from the other side of the wilderness.

Today, I can clearly see that I was fighting for all the things I am, we are, ultimately designed for: love, connection, worthiness, growth, and purpose. I was fighting to create and contribute to a better life for myself and others. What I didn't grasp in that season was that I had gotten caught up in a distorted view of *how* to get there. As a result, I was fighting in all the wrong ways, for all the wrong reasons. As so many of us do, I had bought into the idea that if I accomplished more things, gained more things, made more money, or made something of myself, *then* I would be more loved, more safe, more at ease, and more able to make an impact. This is a slippery and dangerous program that has too many of us fighting for money, status, titles, significance, approval, and accolades.

But what are all those things really for? In the end, if we keep chasing these things, we end up selling our soul and compromising our most sacred values in order to get our needs met.

It's important to pause and ask the questions:

- What are we actually fighting for?

- At its core, what is all this daily hustle about anyway?

- Am I in alignment in this relationship, business deal, position, or situation?

- Am I living in integrity to what I hold valuable and sacred?

- What needs to be adjusted immediately to open up the flow of life force for me now?

There is a passage in scripture that reminds us to check in on what exactly we are chasing: *"Do not store up for yourselves treasures on earth, where moths and vermin destroy, and where thieves break in and steal. But store up for yourselves treasures in heaven, where moths and vermin do not destroy, and where thieves do not break in and steal. For where your treasure is, there your heart will be also." (*Matthew 6:21, NIV)

Are we chasing treasures that can be taken away in an instant? One stock market crash, real estate crisis, economic downturn, pandemic, divorce, medical scare, legal battle, key employee leaving, or competitor coming into town can send all those precariously stacked dominoes crashing down around us.

What if instead, we were storing up treasures within ourselves that infused more life into us, into others, and into this world?

When it comes down to it, what we're really after is to *experience.*

To *feel*. To feel happiness, love, connection, peace, joy, inspiration, and freedom. To feel alive in every cell and fiber of our being. The beautiful thing is, those feelings we are working so hard to tap into are available to us, right here, right now, at this very moment. No chasing or craziness required. The moment I gave myself permission to not only recognize this, but to accept and live by it, was the moment everything began to reorganize itself in my world.

Poetry began to flow through me as I reconnected with my heart and the Spirit of God. Some emerged in the form of the Warrior Letters I've shared throughout this book. The messages I received in this season forever changed me, and I hope they will touch your heart as they did mine.

A BOLD DECLARATION

A few months after my "perfect storm" moment that I shared in Chapter One, I signed up for a series of live events to work on myself and my business in new ways.

The first event was Unleash the Power Within with Tony Robbins. I thought I was there to "get my life in order." During the event, we were taken through a powerful reflection tool called the Dickens Process. This process is based on *A Christmas Carol,* where Ebenezer Scrooge is visited by the ghosts of Christmas past, present, and future. Through a long exercise, we were instructed to envision our lives in five years if we kept up with the same pattern of struggle and beliefs we had been looping through. The picture was grim and disheartening. Then we went further, ten years down the road, twenty years, and finally to our last days where I was well into my nineties. I did not hold back. I knew if I kept entertaining the belief that I was alone in the world, eventually I would end up that way—old and alone, with no one to love me. I knew if I kept fighting against everything and everyone, my entire life would be a series of exhausting battles without any peace.

I had already experienced my dark night of the soul. This, however, was the moment I gave myself full permission to do whatever it took to not walk down the path I just saw. I made the decision to restructure my specific beliefs and inner operating system with no idea how it was going to play out.

Weeks later, I attended my second Tony Robbins event, Business Mastery, thinking that I was there to get my business in order. Ha! It's funny how divine appointments work. What we think we need is never actually what we need. In a definitive moment, Tony called me to stand up, and I took the microphone in my hands. Boldly, I declared in front of a crowd of 2,500 people, "I am one hundred percent done with being Miss Independent and depending solely on myself for everything. This is killing me. I am tired, and I can't do it alone. I am ready and committed to move from the place of fierce independence to one of *interdependence*."

In order to experience the love and life I craved, I would have to open myself up to depending on others, and ultimately to fully depending on God instead of myself as the ultimate authority. I would have to put my proclaimed "faith" into action. I would have to learn to trust in completely new ways, more than just myself. To trust others. To trust God's way forward, rather than the world's. To trust the journey and stop trying so hard to anxiously control every detail of it.

At that time, I did not realize the weight of that bold, public declaration.

When we make a decision to change something, our subconscious gets to work orchestrating how we will execute it. That is a whole other level of commitment! This, dear Warrior, is where the fun begins. I believe this moment of declaration is when we give God the green light to step in and begin equipping us to receive what we just claimed as our own.

I thought I was at that business conference for my own agenda, to get my business in order. I didn't fully get it for a while, but what I was actually there for was to make that declaration out loud, in front of the entire audience, and to feel it in every fiber of my being as my "new normal." God will use any circumstance or means to get to us; when He does, there is an indescribable knowing and strength that washes over us. We know that life as we knew it is over. Something has shifted. A door has just closed, and a new one has opened up.

That moment, which I call a Divine Appointment, was the beginning of my transformative journey from PUSH! energy to pull energy—from reactive to proactive, from survival-based thinking to prosperity-based thinking. Instead of pushing and forcing everything in my life, I began to be pulled by something greater. Instead of constantly reacting and being fueled by the shadows of fear, I began leading by the fire of inspiration in my heart. I went from the familiar past and feeling trapped and obligated into a new future where I could experience true freedom.

On top of it all, although I had no idea at the time, a miracle and answered prayer was already taking place. As I spoke that bold declaration into the room, into the universe, and to God himself, my future husband was sitting just a few rows back from me, recording the whole thing on his phone! I'll share more about that journey later in the book, but as I write this chapter, that same man is sitting across the fire pit, smiling at me. What a wild and beautiful ride it's been.

LEARNING TO FIGHT DIFFERENT

Dear Warrior, my intention is that this book becomes a Divine Appointment for you—a definitive moment that changes the course of your life forever. If you are ready to step beyond the chaos, confusion, and loneliness of the path you're on, you are in the right place. We are always being positioned for something greater to make its way to us, if we are willing to walk through the door when it presents itself.

Making the leap into a new space requires us to learn to fight and engage differently. In my own quest for a new battleground and a life worth fighting for, I discovered a pathway—a system for transforming life in all areas. It's the same pathway that transforms my clients' lives each and every day, and supports them to become Warriors of the Heart and fight for what truly matters in their own lives.

Let's look at the life-changing process you're about to undertake, step by step.

Step 1: Shift Your Allegiance

The first order of business is to get things in the right order. To get out of your head, back into your heart, and connected to the Spirit to receive clarity. Are you willing to step away from the noise of the world, stop putting your material goals on a pedestal, and choose to come back to the ultimate Source and Author of life?

Step 2: Embrace the Unknown

When you decide to step into a new space, it will feel and look foreign, unfamiliar, and even terrifying at times. Here, you will be called to go inward. You must learn to see things through new eyes and open your ears to hear what you could not hear before. Embrace the spirit of adventure as you move away from the worldly lens into that of the heavenly.

Step 3: Drop Your Armor

Your old ways, methods, pains, resentments, and lack of forgiveness created dead weight and thick walls keeping the very things you long for out, blocking the flow of life that longs to fill you, support you, and move through you. This is the place where I will invite you to drop the baggage of your past, lay down your protective armor, and release the weapons you once used to get ahead, but now are the very things being used against you.

Step 4: Unlock Your Heart

You cannot receive the life you long for if your heart is hardened, mistrusting, or closed. Here, you will learn how to open your heart back up, explore the deep seated desires held inside, and make room to embrace what is meant for you and only you. What you have been seeking has been seeking you—but in order to receive it, your heart must be open, willing, and have the space for the new to enter.

Step 5: Remember Who You Are Created to Be

Here, you will peel away the veils and layers you have bought into with regard to your identity, and truly remember who you are created to be. Physical reality is only one version of "home," and it has held many of us captive in an identity that is not truly our own. It is time to get clear on who you are not, and who you truly are. You will do this by reclaiming your God-given identity.

Step 6: Know Your Enemy

When you become aware of the tactics and strategies that the enemy uses to pull you off course, discourage you, depress you, and ultimately enslave you to the world systems, you will no longer get baited into battles that distract you from your purpose. Instead, you will be equipped with Kingdom strategies to shift your focus and channel your energy into that which supports life, multiplies the gifts within you, and opens doors to victory.

Step 7: Understand the Nature of the Battle

Not all battles are what they seem. If you only see surface-level problems, you will keep fighting for surface-level solutions. When you learn to see beyond the surface and engage from a different vantage point, you will be able to lead with wisdom and discernment rather than reactivity. You will recognize the right strategy at the right time to deal with the real issue at hand.

Step 8: Upgrade Your Weapons

At this point, you will no longer be engaging in surface-level play or bringing the same old tactics to the table, exhausting yourself in the process. Instead, you'll enter the playing field Spirit-led rather than ego-driven, equipped with new eyes, new ears, and a whole new set of tools and weapons. Get ready to upgrade your arsenal with weapons that help you build the future you desire, and weapons that move mountains where there was once resistance and stagnation.

Step 9: Cultivate Trust

This is the place of ultimate devotion, and in turn, ultimate freedom. Here, you finally realize and acknowledge that you are not alone. In this step, you will learn the arts of surrender, obedience, trust, and discernment. You will gain a new perspective on divine timing, guidance, provision, and opportunities.

Step 10: Practice Discernment

Here you will learn how to cultivate and lead with discernment. You will discover how to be led—when it's time to wait, when it's time to move, and when a whole new strategy and outlook is required. You will establish what it means to be a protector of the things that matter most, to be a Warrior who loves fiercely and maintains the integrity of the whole. In this stage, you will put in place the physical, emotional, and spiritual boundaries required to preserve what it is you are here to steward, build, and multiply as a Kingdom Warrior.

Step 11: Rise Up and Claim Your Assignment

By the end of this journey, you will feel a renewed sense of purpose and life force rising inside you to lead differently and love fiercely. This is your moment to boldly claim your new identity, clarify the mission at hand, and create your Warrior Manifesto so you can lead from a place of integrity, freedom, and a heart that is fully alive and on fire!

***

I trust that this journey will help you fly high, discover your voice, break free, and dream again—just as it did me.

So, Warrior, are you ready for the journey? Are you ready to do what it takes to receive more life, more love, and more freedom than you could ever ask for, desire, or imagine?

Let's get started.

WARRIOR INITIATION

- What have you been fighting for your entire life?

- What are some familiar ways you have tried to achieve success, love, status, or purpose by your own means?

- How successful has this been for you? How sustainable is it moving forward?

- How do you know, without a shadow of a doubt, that it's time to "fight different"?

WARRIOR LETTER #3

No Other

Dear Warrior,

No other human can "make" you happy.

The more you expect them to, the more
disappointment you will experience.

No other human will ever make you feel "good enough,"
qualified enough, or wanted enough.

The more you expect them to, the more emptiness
you will feel.

No other human will ever be able to make you feel "safe"
enough, all of the time, in all circumstances.

Not your husband. Not your wife. Not your lover.

Not your mother, father, kids, friends, or colleagues.

Storms happen.

(Every day.)

Stuff gets old.

(And not fun anymore.)

People get sick.

(Unexpectedly and unplanned.)

The world evolves.

(And we can't keep up.)

Businesses crumble.

(Even empires we thought would last forever.)

Money comes and goes.

(That's why it's called "currency.")

Status and significance are fleeting.

No person,

No thing,

No amount of anything,

Is designed to "make you" anything other than
who you are.

Only your Maker can answer these questions.

This is an inside job between you and God.

And until you get that ...

As long as you keep searching outside of yourself for the
answers ...

The void will remain.

Once you fill that with what it's designed for?

Intimacy.

Connection.

Trust.

Patience.

Abundance.

Peace.

Freedom.

Strength.

Energy.

Clarity.

Become the norm.

Not the exception.

Not just fleeting moments available at someone else's whim or will.

So, what is it you truly desire and have been seeking?

I guarantee, what you have been seeking has been seeking you.

Just not in the way you think, nor in the place you thought you'd find it.

The only way to "it" is through the heart and into the Spirit.

Are you willing to take the inner journey?

Life as you know it will never be the same.

On the other side, a whole new world awaits you.

CHAPTER FOUR

Shift Your Allegiance

"No one can serve two masters. Either you will hate one and love the other, or you will be devoted to one and despise the other. You cannot serve God and be enslaved to money."

— **MATTHEW 6:24 (NIV)**

Ask yourself honestly: *who and what runs your life?*

When we worship things of the world, we become puppets of the world. We become slaves to our businesses, schedules, and other people's opinions. We become slaves to the things we have built or created—they literally consume us and take over our lives. Where once there was joy and excitement, we find ourselves operating from pressure and underlying fear. We pretend we are in charge, but when we dig deep and get honest with ourselves, it's plain who and what is really holding the reins—

And *it isn't us.*

What we think we are in control of is actually controlling us.

We think we are large and in charge, but really it's like we are holding the leash of a very big, very strong dog. The minute we let go of the leash, that dog will bolt! In order to keep it under control, we must attach ourselves to it, or it to us. It does not come or stay out of free will. We certainly have not trained it to come when we call, and it doesn't want to sit in our company with ease. The truth is, the dog is the master, and we are the ones on the leash. We are stuck holding on, and we can't let go, or else.

It's funny when you think about it. In such an arrangement, there is no trust and natural order. There is only control and attachment. That is the very opposite of love.

Before you get all worked up, I'm not here to tell you that money is evil, or that the ambition to succeed is wrong. I believe we are designed to grow, create, and enjoy life abundantly in all areas. Rather, this chapter is about unearthing what, exactly, is driving us, and deciding whether it is time to shift our driving forces. In doing so, we create a new way of operating altogether.

In this chapter, you will develop a new understanding and aware-ness of three things:

1. Who and what has actually been running your life, and who and what you *want* to serve instead.

2. What tools, idols, and resources are, and where they might be creating imbalances in your relationships to money, other people, your body, and other aspects of life.

3. The choice, power, and freedom we have been given by birthright to opt into living from a sense of richness, purpose, and intentional choice every day.

I believe most people feel dissatisfied and unfulfilled in life because they are consciously or unconsciously worshiping and chasing the idols of this world. Like the dog owner described above, they are chained to the very things we have been given as resources, tools, and vessels. Instead of assisting them, these things now dominate them, consuming all of their energy and attention.

We were created to be masters and stewards *of*, not slaves *to*, money, time, other people, our bodies, our relationships, our stuff, our influence, and so on. But somewhere along the line, things got distorted, and we became disoriented. We bought into the idea that we can't live without certain external things— some special inside knowl-edge, a certain relationship status, a title or achievement to define us. In turn, we put objects, money, people, status, and experiences on a seductive pedestal that we can't look away from. It is the same process of manipulation, seduction, and distortion of truth that originated at the beginning of time, when a fallen angel wanted to play God.

We forgot that we are called to become the masters of the tools and resources we have been entrusted with. We forgot that God, the Creator of all things and the Source of all universal intelligence, is ulti-mately the origin, root, and giver of all things that are life-giving. We bought the lies that God is in something or someone else. Or, perhaps, we bought into the idea that *we* are the ultimate Source of all things, only to find ourselves crushed when we can't create or manifest everything we want in the time frame or manner we desire. Both ideas can keep us trapped in a world of inner tension.

Here's an example of how this works.

Over the course of my life as an entrepreneur, I've joined many business masterminds. If I'm honest, I joined several of these because I did not trust myself, my process, or my decisions. I was comparing myself to others, trying to rush the timing of things, and seeking someone to tell me what to do and show me the way! In my mind, the people leading these groups were where I wanted to be, but since I wasn't there yet, they must have better tools, systems, and networks than I did. Maybe they even had access to some secret wisdom and knowledge I could only guess at.

None of these things are wrong in and of themselves. In fact, it is absolutely essential to have teachers, mentors, coaches, skill development, and tools so we are equipped to navigate key situations. We are not meant to go through life alone and unsupported, especially when we are in a big growth period! We can bypass a lot of hardship if we are willing to seek guidance and get help along the way. However, there is a dangerous trap in the "hero worship" mentality that often pervades the athletic world, academia, coaching, and religious/spiritual spaces. As I sat in those rooms listening to various gurus tell people "The Way," I watched their students put them on pedestals and treat everything they said as ultimate truth instead of checking in with themselves to see what resonated.

There were times when these teachers made logical sense, but in my gut something did not sit well with me. Often, I left these meetings feeling worse about myself than I had going in. Instead of coming out with more clarity, I left with greater confusion. Instead of feeling more in integrity with myself, I left doubting my ability to trust myself and do things my unique way. I would fall into comparison, and an increasing sense of frustration would set in.

Worse, when I tried to implement these gurus' "successful" methods, often I would get resistance and pushback from my team and clients. After hearing the latest marketing tactics suggested by my coach, one friend told me, "I feel like my soul needs a shower." These systems did not align to what I truly believed and valued. They were driven by scarcity and fear, and my sense that I needed to look outside myself for the answers I wanted.

Long story short, I had made these people the *source* of my business success, rather than *resources* to assist in my journey. I put so much faith in them—in their words, their methods, and their hype—that I became disconnected from my inner GPS. In the end, this never works.

Today I know that, if someone is claiming to be the source of all my answers, I can be sure they will soon become the source of all my problems, too. I am discerning about the strategies, advice, and tools I choose to implement. While I value great coaching, mentorship, and counsel immensely, I am highly intentional about running whatever information is given to me through my own filter—a process I will discuss later in the book. I refuse to hire or collaborate with anyone who tells me there is only one way (their way) to do things successfully.

I truly believe that each of us has unique gifts and ways to "do" life and business. When we fully embrace this, and allow the One who created us to guide us, we experience alignment in our mission and new levels of prosperity across the board. The tools we think we need are rarely the tools God uses. There are many resources available to support us in our journey. The key is learning to discern what is for us, and what is not.

AWARENESS

As Dr. Wayne Dyer famously said, "When you change the way you look at things, the things you look at change." We can't change what we don't recognize and are blind to. We can't begin to solve a problem without an awareness of what created it in the first place. Most often, the reason we are stuck is because we keep trying to solve the wrong problems!

UNPACKING LANGUAGE

Source is the cause, the point of origin at which something begins its course or existence. It is the author or one that initiates, the inception that causes the thing itself to come into being.

- Who/what is the Source for me?
- Who/what do I draw my strength, inspiration, peace, comfort, and identity from?

A **tool** is a device or instrument that aids in accomplishing a task; one that is used or manipulated by another.

- What tools have I been entrusted with?
- Am I the master of these tools or are they the master of me?

An **idol** is an image or form without substance used as an object of worship; a false god, or one that is adored, often blindly or excessively. An idol is anything that replaces God.

- What have I been putting on a pedestal that is not the ultimate Source and giver of life? In fact, they might be the very things that are siphoning life force from you right now.

The first step in any change or transformation is always awareness. Awareness happens in the moment our eyes are opened to a new vantage point or reality. Something hits home inside us, and we know that this message was just for us. That "a-ha!" resonates and vibrates through our body and we finally get it! What we were blind to before suddenly becomes the obvious, clear as day. We wonder, "How did I not see this before?"

We cannot experience a new reality until we are aware that it exists in the first place, and that it is therefore a possibility for us. For example, I absolutely love to travel, and I would like to say I am a well-traveled woman. At the same time, I don't know what I don't know. Many places I've visited weren't even on my radar until, suddenly, they jumped out at me from my phone screen or the pages of a travel magazine. Suddenly, I couldn't imagine *not* going there—and before I knew it, I was buying tickets. Once the awareness is there, it demands to be explored.

As we will unpack in the next chapter, we are divinely created to embrace the unknown. Yet, for most of humanity, the unknown is a terrifying place. All this talk of awareness and adventure might sound fun and exciting, but with it comes the possibility that a truth we don't like will hit us between the eyes and force us to confront it. When that happens, we can't stick our heads in the sand anymore. Once we are presented with a truth, we can't pretend it doesn't exist. We can't hide from it any longer. Additionally, with new awareness comes a new sense of responsibility, or response-ability. Not only do we feel the weight of the responsibility, we are also now equipped with the ability to respond. But how will we respond to this new information or insight? Will we continue to hide from it? Will we face it and do something about it? These are the questions awareness brings forth, and also the reason why many people prefer to remain unaware. For some, it's better not to know—to carry on in ignorance and therefore have no obligation to do or change anything.

There are many reasons why we avoid opening our eyes, but fear is at the heart of all of them. It's not uncommon for me to get calls from both men and women who were blindsided when their spouse came home one day and said, "I want out." All of a sudden, their reality looks very different. The question, though, is: is this *really* a shock? Or were they just pretending things were fine and avoiding the real issues this whole time? Sometimes this shock of awareness is the best thing that could happen to the couple. For the first time, they are forced to deal with their past, have meaningful conversations, and clean up their relationship. For others, it's too late.

Unfortunately, this lack of awareness and chosen ignorance is highly prevalent in homes where there has been abuse and in environments where there has been injustice—not just among the key players, but also in the people around them. Perhaps it's because we feel helpless or hopeless. Perhaps it's because we feel ill-equipped to do anything about it. Perhaps we just don't know how to solve it, and haven't sought out the tools to engage differently and create something new. But, inevitably, there comes a point where truth surfaces and demands to be dealt with.

Awareness is the tipping point to a new reality. It is the first step in setting ourselves free from the old and creating something new.

The second step, once our eyes have been opened, is to *choose different*: different thoughts, different emotional drivers, different actions, and therefore, different outcomes.

ALLEGIANCE

Who is your master? What is your allegiance to?

We may say our allegiance is first and foremost to our faith, our marriage, or our children—but is it? Peace resides where we are in harmony. When our allegiance is to the wrong things, an inner civil war ensues. We find ourselves constantly unsettled.

When I speak of allegiance, I mean *that to which we have attached and devoted ourselves at some level of our being*. It is the thing (or things) that have captured our mind and heart—the things we are loyal to and will do anything for.

If we want to examine what matters most to us, and where we have put our allegiance, we simply need to take a good look at our lives. Our lives don't lie. Our schedule doesn't lie. Our bank accounts don't lie.

Oftentimes the people closest to us are the greatest mirrors to show us the things we cannot see or refuse to accept. What gets the first and best parts of us? Where and how do we spend our time, money, and energy? These things reflect back to us what we have put at the forefront, and where our true allegiances lie.

Let's go through a few key areas of your life and unpack your allegiances.

Money

Money can be such a powerful force. Who and what do you give your money to?

The world's currency is money, and so it's not surprising we have been programmed to equate money to safety and security. As with all things, there is some truth to this. We require money to purchase food, shelter, and provide for many of our basic needs. Unless you come from a culture where bartering is the norm, money is in fact a source of security. The question though becomes: how much do we actually need to feel safe and secure inside? How much money is enough? Can there ever be enough? It's funny how the more we make, the more we think we need.

Money is simply a tool. It is up to us how we choose to view it, use it, and engage with it. It is a currency—and like a current, it is meant to circulate. So, are you circulating it for good, or are you hoarding it? Are you using your wealth to contribute *to* the world, or simply to fill an appetite inside that can never be sated?

If you lost all your money tomorrow, would you no longer feel intrinsically safe? Would you go into full-on freakout mode? Would it be impossible to access peace, love, and joy? Does money truly hold that much power over you? Is it an ally or an adversary—a collaborator or a dictator?

I have known several multi-millionaires who have piles of money yet constantly live in a state of fear. They are fearful that they will lose it, fearful they haven't made enough, fearful that someone is going to take it. Like the vicious dog on a leash, it demands all of their energy and attention, and never lets them relax. The fear of potential loss—or of just having less—drives them to be controlling and manipulative of everyone and everything around them. We all know someone like that, don't we?

Money is a means to trade and circulate things. It's a vehicle, not the source. It has value because we give it value—and that value isn't even a constant. Physically, money is just paper, or numbers on a screen—it has no inherent worth unless we collectively decide it does. Just look at Bitcoin prices in the last few years. Look at the stock market. They rise and crash all the time, and yet people keep expecting them to stay the same—to offer stability and security. I recently saw a picture of Russian families in WWII burning piles of paper money to keep warm. The value of their money had dropped so much that its only worth was as something to burn. Isn't that ironic?

There is a common misconception about money being the root of all evil. One place this misconception comes from is the faulty teaching from Matthew 6:24 (quoted at the start of this chapter) and 1 Timothy 6:10.

Let's look at 1 Timothy 6:10 (NLT): *"For the love of money is the root of all kinds of evil. And some people, craving money, have wandered from the true faith and pierced themselves with many sorrows."* According to this passage, the love of money, not money itself, is the root (cause) of all evil. It's amazing how often that one piece has been omitted and how it drastically changes the meaning of the passage. Second, let's look at the use of the word "money" throughout scripture. Money is an English word often used to translate the original word used, *mammon*. Interestingly, *mammon* represented an entity or spirit that was the source of greed, wealth for evil, a worship of wealth and riches. In Hebrew, the word *mihamon* is a contraction of *mi*, meaning "from," and *hāmōn*, meaning "accumulation," and connotes wealth or money. During the Middle Ages, Mammon was personified as a demon of wealth and greed, the prince of Hell, and was linked to many pagan gods.

What the Bible is actually telling us is that those of us who claim to serve God cannot put the endless pursuit of money above our love for and pursuit of God. God is Love personified. Mammon is Greed. Love and greed cannot co-exist.

Money is not evil; but love of and obsession with money as the Source of life corrupts us. The idea of money as a source of happiness cages us. Many kingdoms rise and fall because of greed—but greed is separate from money. Blaming money for people's misaligned actions is like blaming the sword instead of the warrior who wields it.

So, let me ask: how much power does money have over you? Does it rule your days and nights? Does it occupy most of your thoughts? Does it influence your every decision?

There was a time in my life where, immediately upon awakening, I would check my bank account—as if money would magically appear or disappear overnight. I would check in again multiple times per day. I knew every account balance, incoming sale, and projected sale. I had three young children to support on my own, and no help on the horizon. In addition, I had a team of staff who depended on me for a paycheck every two weeks, mortgage payments on our commercial property, huge tax installments, and endless other obligations. The pressure was legitimate, but ultimately, fear and anxiety, rather than faith and ease, were running the show. Of course, there's nothing wrong with knowing your numbers. It's essential to stay on top of things and plan accordingly. But there is a difference between managing the numbers so you can be proactive and letting the numbers manage *you* even while you sleep!

Money had incredible power over me—a power I willingly gave it. Like any other addiction, I was only satiated and at ease with a given amount for so long. Soon, I needed more in order to feel the same sense of safety and comfort. Every time I hit a goal, there was always a bigger number just out of reach, and I immediately wanted it. I also had a hard time when money exited my life for any reason. Whether it was paying bills, investing in new equipment for the business, or donating to a cause, I felt panic when it slipped out my grip. At the root of this was the fear that I would not be able to support or sustain the people in my life. I had seen my family gain and lose everything as a child. I went from living in a beautiful home to having nothing overnight, not even grocery money. I knew just how quickly a financial picture could change, but I was stuck on the part of the story that focused on loss— and that was what kept me enslaved to and obsessing over gains.

Realizing that I had made money my God was the first step in shifting my allegiance and re-evaluating from *what* and from *whom* my certainty and safety comes. I realized that, no matter what physical things I possess, the ultimate source of my safety and security will always come from within, from God, and not the external or physical world. I have experienced a world of peace and a world of misery, regardless of how much money was in my life at the time. I know without a doubt that when my heart is in the right place—when I lead from a desire to serve others, give generously rather than hoard, and be grateful for all I have already been given—I am blessed, often more abundantly than I expect. When I'm in that state, money flows to me; I don't have to chase it.

A beautiful representation of this wisdom can be found in the story of King Solomon. The Bible tells us that God appeared to Solomon, who had just become king, in a dream. God invited him to ask for anything he wanted—anything at all—and it would be granted to him. Solomon responds,

> *"Now, Lord my God, you have made your servant king in place of my father, David. But I am only a little child and do not know how to carry out my duties. Your servant is here among the people you have chosen, a great people, too numerous to count or number. Give your servant a discerning heart to govern your people and to distinguish between right and wrong. For who is able to govern these great people of yours?"* (Kings 3:7-9, NIV)

pray like Solomon!

Wow. He could have had anything at all—flashy new palace, thousands of horses, great riches, even to be the most loved king in the land—but instead, he chose wisdom and the ability to lead his people well. How many leaders would have asked for more wealth and success? As a result, he became known as the wisest man who ever lived. He was sought out by people and rulers the world over for his wisdom and understanding, and amazed people with his vast depth of knowledge. Even today, the Book of Proverbs is often referred to as the Book of Wisdom.

Not only did Solomon become the wisest king to ever live, he also was a man of wealth and honor beyond measure. By modern estimates, his net worth may have been nearly two trillion dollars! There is not a single man or woman alive today who can match that level of wealth and wisdom. I would consider it wise on our part to meditate on Solomon's writings on finances and success. Many can be noted throughout the books of Proverbs and Ecclesiastes. One in particular relates to our love for money:

> *"He who loves money will not be satisfied with money, nor he who loves abundance with its gain. This too is vanity (emptiness). When good things increase, those who consume them increase. So what advantage is there to their owners except to see them with their eyes?"* (Ecclesiastes 5:10-11, AMP)

This speaks volumes to me about checking my own heart. When my heart and intention are in the right place, prosperity flows. When we move from a heart of service rather than a heart of greed or fear, and use tools such as money to serve well, lead well, and bless others, everything we need and much more is provided unto us.

Secondly, I chose to embrace my relationship with money and material things from a Kingdom perspective: everything I need and require will be provided to support the vision given.

I am *not* the source of this abundance; I am simply a vessel that is either positioned to receive it, or not. It is always circulating around me. Even if it exits, I have the ability to regain and increase it in the same breath. The healthier my relationship is to God, the Source of all things, the less power I give to material things, and the more ease I have around them, for they are no longer the source of my confidence, certainty, or strength.

Matthew 6:33 (AMP) says, *"But first and most importantly seek (aim at, strive after) His kingdom and His righteousness [His way of doing and being right—the attitude and character of God], and all these things will be given to you also."* This gives me such peace. When my heart is focused on the right things, everything else is provided to me. The more I lead with love, with appreciation for what I already have, and with a heart of generosity, the more resources flow toward me and through me, and the more I am positioned to receive and steward those resources well. When I take my eyes off those things and focus on "getting" worldly things, that's when I experience the most anxiety, the well dries up, and life gets harder.

So, ask yourself, "How do I respond when money comes into or out of my life?" It's a quick but eye-opening question to assess how much power and energy you give to the arrival and exit of resources such as money.

Time

To what and whom do you give your time and energy?

I can't count the number of times I've heard, "I don't have twenty minutes to meditate/ pray/go for a walk/get that workout in." Or, "Once this is over, *then* I'll have time to take that trip with the kids/do that project/take care of my body." It's a never-ending when/then cycle.

It's amazing what we will say yes to without realizing that we just said no to what really mattered. Or how we will say "not right now" until the situation is an absolute necessity or on fire. We wait to plan intentional time together until someone has had the affair, threatens to leave the relationship, or worst of all, passes away. We wait to pray until we have exhausted all other options and find ourselves desperate, on our knees and begging for an intervention. We fail to rest or listen to our bodies until we are forced onto our backs by an injury or illness.

We rush. We cram way too much in. We put things off for a better time that will never come. We jump at every email and notification on our phones but ignore signs and signals from our bodies and loved ones that tell us we are getting wildly off course. For example, if we ignore the nudge that we are tired during the day, but refuse to slow down and step away from our desk for a nap, we might push forward, drain yet another coffee, and dive into another call. But, as we get more exhausted, our mind gets cloudy, our fuse gets shorter, and things begin to take three times as long to complete. Suddenly, because we were not willing to take a ten-minute micro-nap or a twenty-minute walk, we end up wasting three extra hours and piling on a whole load of tension.

The truth is, *we are always choosing.* Every day we are choosing, consciously or unconsciously, who and what we will serve—who and what is master over us. Every yes is also a no. Every no is also a yes. Every decision is a reflection of what matters most to us.

So, it's time to become more aware of how you actually spend your time. What captures your attention and gets first priority in your day? Are the things that matter most to you even in your calendar? How much time do you waste scrolling on your phone or binging shows on your favorite streaming network, while at the same time saying, "I have no time"? Do you say yes to everything and everyone because you are terrified of rejection? Is your calendar infused with things that bring you joy, connection, vitality, and fulfillment? Do you even know what those things are? Or is your calendar jam-packed from morning to night with things that add complexity and stress, and suck your energy?

Many people I work with have forgotten what brings them joy because they stopped paying attention. When I ask them, "What do you truly enjoy, and when was the last time you did it guilt free?" they often stare at me blankly.

Time just *is.* No matter how we define it, measure it, or attempt to control it, it marches on. Rather than trying to leash it and make it obey, we can observe it, experience it, and play with it. A powerful shift happened for me when I began saying and believing, "I have all the time

I need for all the things that matter." The question then became, "What matters most to me right now, and *how will I choose to experience this moment?*"

When you shift your allegiance away from the pressure-cooker of worldly time and begin to have a more eternal view of time, the clock and other people's agendas are no longer your masters. Instead, you learn to experience time differently. You realize that you are always choosing to experience a moment. You learn how to understand timing and seasons. You understand the concept of divine timing, divine order, and divine appointments, and stop trying to force everything into a limited timeline. Later in this book, I will unpack this topic further, upgrade your view of time, and give you actionable steps to work with time instead of against it. For now, though, I just want you to get clear on where your loyalty has been, and what has been controlling you.

Today, or tomorrow morning at the latest, pull out your calendar. Go through a typical day and check in with yourself. What have you been pursuing? Who or what is the master of your time?

Then, make a list of the things that light you up, bring you joy, and add life to you and those around you. What would you love to experience more of? Add those to your calendar right away. Make your calendar a living document of your joy, rather than a jailer. If you don't respect and honor your own time, you can be certain no one else will either.

People

I spent years attached to the opinions of others. Most people I know struggle with this, too.

There was a "public" version of me that everyone outside my inner circle saw. To them, I appeared confident, capable, successful, and totally driven. People often told me they wanted my life. This was my outward persona. We all have one. It's that version of you that you bring out when you're in public, on social media—when it's game time. That version, identity, or persona has been conditioned in us. It's the personality that allows us to experience the connection, attention, and even significance we crave. As if on autopilot, that persona turns on the minute we are around other people.

Then, there was the life I led inside of my intimate relationships—a totally different life that defined so much of my (low) self-worth.

In my marriage and with my family, I could not bring myself to fully express myself without feeling judged, or ask for what I wanted and needed without apologizing or feeling shamed. Something as simple as going out for a run or a bike ride became a big deal. I worried that others would say, "Why do you have to go? Why now? Can't you do it later when I'm not around? Don't you think you've worked out enough this week?" This inner back-and-forth was pretty much the norm any time I wanted to do something for myself or improve myself in any way.

I bounced from one extreme to another, sometimes multiple times a day—from people-pleasing, avoidance, and dancing around other people's moods, to getting angry and going into fight mode. It was a wild ride. I only truly felt like myself when I was on a trip, out in nature, or in the company of other men and women who had purpose and were focused on a greater mission. But that version of me would disappear the moment I came back home to my partner and family.

The one place I wanted to be seen and loved more than any other was the place I felt least safe to be me.

What happens when your spouse doesn't respond to you the way you'd hoped? When someone you care deeply about disagrees with your point of view or refuses to accept your feedback? Are you constantly anxious about being judged, minimized, or confronted?

I often work with couples who are desperately seeking to heal their past and create an amazing relationship with their partner. They want to cultivate deeper connection, trust, and intimacy in their relationships. The trouble is that many of them have placed so much significance on the perceived success of their relationship that they end up completely distraught when the other person is disappointed or disagrees with them.

I have heard from multiple men and women I have coached, "I am a wreck. I can't think straight. All I do is worry about what he/she is thinking, doing, wanting. Or what I am going to come home to."

I ask them, "How much of your bandwidth—your mental, physical, and emotional energy—is going toward trying to anticipate, control, or analyze their behavior and the outcome?" Most of them say 80 to 90 percent or more. That's a lot of our creative life force dedicated to something we are not capable of controlling.

One couple in particular had immense love for one another, and their desire to make the relationship work was extraordinarily strong. The problem was that they were constantly at each other's throats. They felt offended by what their partner did or didn't do, defended themselves for their every decision, and constantly attacked each other in anticipation of a fight. They were two warriors on opposing sides of a battlefield. It was painful to observe and more painful to be in the midst of. They had placed such high expectations on themselves and each other that they were constantly setting themselves up for disappointment.

When we place someone on the seat only God is capable of holding, and we give them power over us, we are doomed, and they are doomed. No human can fill those shoes. No human is perfect. No human can say all the right things, read our minds, and meet all of our needs 100 percent of the time. We come into relationships full of hopes, desires, and expectations, only to be crushed when the person we chose can't live up to them. This happens in romantic relationships, business relationships, friendships—you name it. The problem in these situations isn't that the other person is wrong or bad. It's that we are expecting another human to be God to us, and for us.

I am happy to report that things totally turned around for that couple once they came into this awareness. Where they were once an entangled mess, enslaved to one another in an attempt to affirm their worth and strength, they are now two individuals who can recognize their human limitations and embrace God as the Source of their identity. They are now committed to showing up, serving, and supporting one another in new ways. By redefining what support and caring for one another looks like, as well as releasing the grips of control, new life is being breathed back into the relationship.

Take a moment to reflect on the following questions: *How much power am I giving others to "make" me feel a certain way or define my worth? How much bandwidth would I regain if I was no longer consumed by others' opinions?*

Your Body

Our bodies are miraculous. They give us form and allow us to move through the world. They sustain us and are constantly working for us. However, most people have a complicated and disconnected relationship with their bodies.

In a world where every ad, show, movie, and social media reel features filtered and curated versions of life, it's easy to constantly judge yourself or compare your body to everyone else's, even when you know (cognitively) that those expectations are unrealistic. And while the media is partially to blame, the truth is that dissatisfaction with your body is signaling something on a deeper level. If your happiness is tied to your physical capabilities or appearance, you will never feel at ease in your body, no matter how much weight you lose or how many times you beat your top time in a triathlon.

So, what sorts of expectations are you holding yourself up against, and who (or what) is telling you how to meet them?

During my years as a fitness professional, I witnessed so many people, especially women, enslaved to a number on the scale. It was heartbreaking. If the number went down, they were confident, happy, and successful. But if it went up, even for a day, they were a failure. It didn't matter what else was going on in their lives; the fact that they were menstruating or going through a difficult time with a toddler made no difference. Their idea of the "ideal body" was sacred. If only they could achieve it, *then* they would *finally* feel confident in their skin and be able to do anything. This ideal became their master.

We know how this story goes. These people would lose fifty, eighty, or even one hundred pounds, but while there were absolutely physical and health benefits to this accomplishment, nothing fundamental about who they were changed. Whenever they looked in the mirror, they would still see an insecure, unsettled, incomplete person staring back at them.

Perhaps your inner unease pushes you to dissociate from your body. Feeling that you aren't good enough, or that your life is missing something, is uncomfortable, so you reach for whatever distracts you from that feeling. My father was enslaved to alcohol for his entire life. While he often put on a facade of having it together, I have never known him to be free in his mind or heart. This led to him misusing his body, looking for that quick fix and instant gratification. For others, this might look like a steady diet of comfort foods that taste great but then leave you feeling sluggish and undernourished, prompting the cycle to continue.

For me, this inner dissatisfaction manifested as an excruciating and strict running regimen. I idolized athletes who hit certain times and won races repeatedly. I pushed myself to prove I had what it took to be on their level—it was the only thing I saw as success, so if I could perform at that level, then surely I too would be successful. My training schedule was the master of me, but all that training didn't ease my heart. It only led to more training, more conviction that achieving the *next* goal would bring me happiness.

As a culture, we spend most of our time avoiding or ignoring the signals that our bodies send us. Most people are walking around in physical bodies riddled with exhaustion and disease due to poor food choices, alcohol, caffeine and other stimulants, overworking, over-medicating, not resting enough, or any combination of these factors. Dis-ease manifests when something is out of order within us. Whether it manifests as unrealistic expectations about what you think you should look like or lifestyle choices that run you into the ground, if you do not treat your body like the vessel of communication, execution, and receivership it is meant to be, it will begin to break down. My dissatisfied women clients remained chained to the scale until their inner workings were reconsidered. I remained laser-focused on pure runner perfection as the only worthy goal until I shifted my perception.

It is all an internal game, my friends.

What is your allegiance to? The best way to find out is to take away that thing you think you can't live without. What if there's no scale anymore? No booze? No sugar? No scoreboard? No race to compete at? It is not that these things are bad, but they are *things*. Just like money, time, and other people, they only have power over us if we grant them that power—but when we do, they become remote controls that move us and make us feel and want. When you become aware of what has a hold on you, you can decide to flip it, and become the master of the tools in your life once again.

We do this by remembering *who* created this incredible body you get to live in, and *what* it is designed for. Your body is a vessel meant to help you experience the fullness of life and execute your dreams and visions. It is a sacred temple, and a channel to receive inspiration, guidance, love, wisdom, and so much more. It is a precious, beautiful, self-healing, and strong ecosystem that is perfectly designed to work *for* you—as long as you stop working against it.

Your body—no matter what it looks like—should be a reflection of your strength, joy, and love for your life. When we are at home in our bodies, we are at ease. We are confident in our own skin, not always trying to change the external. We are relaxed, flexible, and mobile rather than tense, rigid, and full of inflammation. We are rested rather than exhausted. We are tuned-in and responsive, rather than disconnected and suppressed.

Your Heart

When we look inside our hearts, we will find what we treasure.

The problem and the opportunity here is that not many are willing to dig deep enough to find the riches within. Instead, they play at the surface, pursuing anything that makes their heart jump momentarily.

Before you can get to unlocking your heart's full potential, you need to understand the things your heart has been trained to want. So, let me ask you, what captures your heart and ignites your desire to move forward? Then get out your notebook and put those things in two columns: material things, and things that last and give life meaning.

You can hardly go online without hearing someone scream about self-love and self-care, but as long as we continue to expect that things and other people will fill our hearts, our hearts will remain devoted to the idol called *Self.* Self-preservation, self-protection, self-love, self-gain. The focus is always the Self. The question constantly running through our minds is: *what about ME?*

How many times have you gotten what you thought you wanted, only to discover it was not what your heart truly longed for? Maybe you were really excited about getting a new boat to hit the lake on the weekends. But was the boat what you were really after—or was it the status, meaning, and adventure? Ultimately, you aren't going to get that from any material thing, no matter how good it feels for a moment. Superficial things are fun, but they quickly lose their luster, and we need to collect more and more *and more* of them in order to feel satisfied. Eventually we get to a point where we may be sitting in a beautiful home with our picture-perfect partner, toys in the garage, boats for the lake, money in the bank—and yet, we are still empty and bankrupt in our hearts. Just because we have the money does not mean our hearts will feel at ease. Just because we are in a relationship does not mean our hearts will feel safe and loved.

In the end, the boat, the house, and the wealth are all just tools we use to experience the feelings that are our true end goal—love and fulfillment. The not-so-secret secret is that these feelings come from the heart, and are always available to us. They should, in fact, be our starting point, not our end point.

So, how did we get so lost?

Some of us are living life with hardened hearts. Some of us are living with hearts that are numb and disconnected, unable to feel from years of protecting our backs at all costs, pressing forward in warrior mode, clawing our way to our goals no matter the cost. This may be due to past resentments, disappointments, unmet expectations, or unresolved and unhealed pain. Regardless, if we are honest with ourselves, we will realize we have been enslaved to our unmet expectations, false illusions, or flawed ideals. We find ourselves servants to the approval and acceptance of others who are unable or unwilling to give us what we think we need from them. In our foolishness, we think we are in charge, when in reality things and people still hold the power over our hearts, and we are operating under the fear that we will lose those things or people.

If you are a slave to fear—fear of being rejected, fear of not being seen as the best, fear of failing or losing it all—then you are not free to fully give and receive love.

There is a difference between prudently guarding your sacred heart space and locking it up for good. There is also a difference between having a heart that is open to receive life and goodness and one that has the doors flung open to anything, without discretion. So, is your heart a fortress with no windows or doors? What would it take to let down the drawbridge and step out into the sun?

For me, it's been a journey to come back to an open heart that is here to love others, to experience fully, to share dreams and visions, to give in a spirit of joy, and to receive freely. To get here, I had to drop the armor around my heart and let my heart touch my life unguarded. This was a huge piece of my Warrior Initiation, and one I'll guide you through later in this book. For now, though, take a moment to feel the immense weight of the unnecessary attachments you have been dragging around. Move into a place of awareness. Ask yourself, "Who and what is holding my heart strings? Is my heart guided by inspiration or desperation?"

And, ultimately, "What do I want my heart to be in service to?"

Your Home

If you want to know who you serve and what has a hold on you, simply look around your home. It won't take you long to figure it out. What is it filled with, and what is the motivation behind those things? What's on your bookshelves? In your garage? Crammed in your attic?

Our attachment to the stuff we have, the deep sense of meaning and purpose we give to all of it, the fear of throwing something out or letting go ... it grips some of us. Do you know anyone who just collects more and more and more stuff, until they can barely move in their own home? I get it. But at what point does our security and identity lie in our things?

In my first marriage, we lived in a relatively high-end neighborhood with gorgeous homes, deep lots, and plenty of space to pour money into landscaping and theatrics. Again, I'm not saying there's anything wrong with having a beautiful garden, a hotel-like swimming pool, or the ultimate playground in the backyard. Those are all fun! The problem is when we become fixated on the next thing we *must* have in order to keep up with those around us. This was the case for us in that neighborhood. As soon as someone put in a swimming pool, it was if it set off a row of dominoes. Before you knew it, everyone on the street was getting one, each more lavish than the one before. The conversations at most neighborhood gatherings centered around the latest home upgrade or purchase. The FOMO was real. At this point, our love for making our homes a place of rest, connection, and love slowly got overtaken by an obsession for keeping them magazine-worthy for others.

We must ask ourselves, is my home a reflection of what I believe a home is designed for, or has it become a money pit and source of stress for me? What is it that makes a home a home? Yes, it's what we fill it with, but it's also more than that. It's a reflection of our priorities.

Today, I have a beautiful home in a gorgeous neighborhood. We have a great community, but the focus for us was to create a place of "gravity" for ourselves and others. We named it Gravitas—a safe haven where whomever walks through our doors can feel welcomed, accepted, and at ease, a place where each thing we bring in is intentional. The focus is first the atmosphere we choose to create through the words we speak, how we handle conversations, what respect looks and sounds like, what sounds we fill it with. Yes, we also work hard to keep it clean and in good order, but the focus is not on accumulating more stuff.

One definition for "idol" is "a likeness of something, a pretender or imposter." The key word here is *likeness*—it's not the real deal; it's a copy, something made to resemble, mirror, or imitate something else. Whatever we have been fixating on, obsessing over, chasing, and hoping for, it's *not the real thing*.

DECIDE, DECLARE, AND ACT

Here is the beautiful thing: at any given time, you can decide to shift your allegiance, your loyalty, and your devotion. You can decide who and what you serve. You can choose to become the master of the tools you've been given without idolizing or chasing them.

The three steps to shifting your allegiance are:

- Declare
- Decide
- Act

Once you do these three things, you will be ready for the next step in your warrior's journey.

Decide

Once you have awareness, you are in a position to make a conscious *decision*. Will you continue down the path you were walking previously, or will you decide to do it differently going forward?

It's amazing what happens when we come into a full *decision* in our heart. There is an instant rising of strength in our bodies where, just moments before, there was indescribable weakness. Instantly, the fog that was creating so much confusion and disorientation lifts; a weight immediately falls away from our chest and shoulders. We can see again. We can breathe again. We feel the expansion in our bodies.

We are lighter, stronger, freer, and more empowered because, in that moment, we pulled our power back inside our vessel. We came back to ourselves and became infused with an even stronger, super-natural presence within us. I believe that any time we say yes to life, yes to peace, yes to getting things in the right order, we send a message to God to meet us—and He will. The decision is step one.

Declare

As you've seen, we can be ruled by that which gives life, or that which takes life from us. When you decide to shift your allegiance away from the objects, things, and ideals this world has been seducing you with, it's important to simultaneously make a bold declaration to serve something greater. Your life, your energy, is a gift that has been given to you. How will you receive and use this gift?

The spoken word is powerful. It creates life. It brings forth blessings or curses. Speak boldly into the atmosphere. The key is to declare, out loud, what you will give your precious life force to. In doing so, you reclaim your energy (life force) and become the empowered master of the time, energy, money, and things you have been entrusted with.

These things are not really ours. They come and they go. We came from the dust, and when we return to the dust these things will have no value; they are only tools and resources to help us flourish and multiply, borrowed for a time and a season.

When I go back to our definition of *Source*, it brings me to my point of origin. What am I derived from? Who was the Author or Creator who brought me into existence—and for what purpose did He do so? There is only one place we can go to get these answers, and that is our Creator Himself, the Source of all life. What does God have to say about who you are? What have you studied and learned about the true Heart of God? If you believe you are made in the image of God, this is a great place to start.

Do it now. Decide, and make a bold declaration, aloud, at the top of your voice.

Below is a simple and extremely powerful framework you can use— not just one time, but regularly, even every day. Feel free to modify this as you see fit, and add what you are inspired to add. I also have included my own personal declaration below the framework so you can feel the potency and energy behind this statement.

DECLARATION

I, [your name], decide and declare that I am no longer a slave.
I am no longer ruled by _____
(Ego, pride, fear—fill in whatever is on your heart and be specific!)
Effective immediately,
I shift my allegiance to and serve only _____
(That which gives life and adds life unto others,
to God as my ultimate source)
Let it be so.

***

I, Christine Jewell, decide and declare that I am no longer a
slave to the programs and ways of this world.
I am no longer ruled by other people's opinions, by fear of loss,
by useless distractions, or the endless pursuit of personal
significance and gain.
Effective immediately,
I shift my allegiance to serve God, the Creator of life
and all that is life-giving.

I obey the calls and desires placed deep in my heart
by the Spirit.
I move forward in courage, in service, and in faith,
trusting that the path has been laid before me, and all I
need—and so much more—
will be provided in perfect order, in perfect timing.
Let it be so.

Action

It's inevitable: the moment you make a bold declaration out loud, opportunities for action will present themselves to you. Some call this the Big Leap, the leap of faith, or the testing ground. Whatever you call it, this is your first devotional checkpoint. If you don't pass this test, you have not yet shifted allegiance, and will keep repeating the same mistakes until you gather the courage, strength, and faith to lean in and move forward.

The moment you decide to take action, everything changes. It is both terrifying and exciting at the same time. You can't possibly know what is on the other side because you haven't been there yet. There is no roadmap. You are about to make a leap into a new reality.

In *The Chronicles of Narnia: The Lion, the Witch, and the Wardrobe*, there is a pivotal moment when the youngest of four siblings, Lucy, follows the call of her curiosity and goes through a door in the back of a wardrobe while exploring a professor's house. Many people wouldn't explore a wardrobe for fear of getting stuck inside what is likely a dark, claustrophobic, scary place. Instead, Lucy leans in to explore. Instantly, she is dropped into another world, and life is never the same. The magic of Narnia opens before her and her siblings, and they begin the journey to fulfill their mission.

This is the essence of the Hero's Journey, which plays out over and over in books, movies, television, and theater. *The Matrix* and *Star Wars* are well-known examples of plots that utilize the Hero's Journey framework. What's important to note is that, in all of these sweeping tales of heroism, there is a moment where the hero must *choose* the quest and take action to begin on his new path. Neo must choose the red pill or the blue. Luke Skywalker must choose to leave the only home he's ever known to rescue a princess he's never met. King Arthur must pull the sword from the stone before he can ever know his own strength, calling, and purpose.

These moments of choice are where all the movie magic begins. But when our lives hang in the balance, it's not nearly so much fun. Taking that step into the wilderness without seeing any light in the distance, that leap of faith without fully knowing there's anything to catch us ... it's scary. There's a reason these heroes are "chosen ones." If everyone were brave enough to take that kind of action, we wouldn't need warrior heroes to look up to.

So, ask yourself, "What is my walk through the closet/red pill/Jedi moment?" It does not matter how big or how small your action is. What matters is that it's a complete interruption of your normal patterns—a disruption of familiar routines and behaviors that requires a new level of trust, courage, and faith.

If the above question is too broad, focus on the one thing you know you've been ignoring or putting off, or have been fearful of doing. Perhaps it's saying yes to something you want to do more of. Perhaps it's saying no to someone you want to please. You may have this insistent feeling, like a bug buzzing around your head, and you know it is not going to go away until you do something *different*.

Deep down, there is something that's been nudging and calling you. How do you answer that call, *effective immediately*?

I worked with a client who talked about delegating his email for years. Week after week, managing his email sucked his time and energy away. Instead of being connected to his vision and making plans to lead others, he was reacting to pings and notifications and leaving every workday feeling defeated by his never-ending to-do list. He knew it was a problem, but he was stuck, frozen by the fear of letting go of control, of trusting someone else, of opening his schedule for something more. When he released his allegiance to control and busyness and hired an assistant to manage his inbox, it was a game-changer. His company grew almost overnight. He reclaimed his visionary time, and also his joy and energy.

The worst thing you can do is sit in hesitation, overthinking and analyzing, trying to figure out a way around action. The mind loves to create complexity and keep us in the chaos and drama of things. We love to try and barter and negotiate with God. But hesitation is disobedience to the Spirit, and will ultimately trap you between two worlds. Action is required at this moment. You know what to do. Now, just do it—as soon as possible. Preferably today.

More often than not, our minds will try to make a case against change. But you aren't here to do the same old things in the same old ways. If you were, you would never have picked up this book! The Holy Spirit speaks through clarity, not confusion. The only thing left to do now is move. Take action. Be swift. Be bold, and breathe. Your word is like a sword, and the cut has already been made through your bold declaration. The old is no longer; this one action, taken in faith, will open the gates in the most magnificent way.

A whole new world awaits you on the other side.

WARRIOR INITIATION

Awareness

- Who or what have you felt enslaved to, unable to put down, or unable to walk away from?

- What have you made the source of your strength, significance, or self-worth? What has been the well you go to?

- When you look at your life, what do you see you have valued and held as treasure?

- Have you been leading from a place that is life-giving, or life-draining?

Decision

- What clear and life-giving decision will you make today?

- What will you choose to no longer be enslaved by?

- What will you eliminate or set boundaries around?

- What will you choose to prioritize instead?

Then, make the declaration.

Action

- What one specific and uncomfortable action are you convicted to move on right now that will require courage and faith?

- What will be lifted once you move on this?

- Have you written and spoken your declaration? Speak it out boldly and repeat it daily as you work through this book. Repetition builds muscle. What we speak, we create!

CHAPTER FIVE

Embrace the Unknown

"Adventure is out there, waiting for those who dare to take the leap."

- JOHN ELDREDGE

March of 2020 was a time in history many will never forget. The sudden onset of a new and deadly virus brought government-mandated lockdowns and more unknowns than anyone could count. Life as we knew it drastically changed overnight.

At the time, I still owned my brick-and-mortar studio, PUSH!FIT. However, it had been weighing heavily on me for about a year, and I was exhausted from constantly trying to press forward on my own. Then, I got the news that we, and all fitness studios in our area, had to shut down operations for an indefinite amount of time. I had staff on salary plus a ton of overhead, and the burden was so heavy. While I had known for some time that I was being called in a different direction, I just couldn't bring myself to move on and trust the inner guidance I was receiving, so I tried to come up with ways to pivot the business.

At this time, an opportunity came up for my partner Mark and me to go to Arizona for a few days. With airports barely operating, we made the eighteen-hour road trip during a time when most people were terrified to leave their homes. The last thing I was going to do was lock myself inside. I knew I needed to move, to get out there. Little did I know that this was just the beginning of a wild adventure.

After three days in Phoenix, I felt the pull to go to Sedona, one of my all-time favorite spots. The town was desolate. Hardly anyone was out on the trails or roads. I found a cute bed and breakfast that was normally $400 per night for just $50 a night. The pull of the red rocks was so strong, and I felt this deep sense that I just needed to stay a while longer. I told Mark I would not be driving back with him and instead chose to extend my stay.

What was originally supposed to be three days turned into nearly a month. I *thought* I was heading to Arizona to create a bunch of content, try and figure out how to keep cash flow coming and pivot PUSH!FIT in a new direction. But God had other plans. Instead of being in massive creation mode, I was in deep rest mode. It was all I could do to muster the energy to pray daily, take long hikes, nap, journal, and serve the clients I was coaching remotely. I invited God to take over my agenda, and surrendered the need to make sure I was making enough money and doing enough to stay ahead.

I told God, "If you are truly the one who meets all my needs, and I don't need to constantly prove myself, I will go there with you."

It was the beginning of what would be nearly a year-long journey of deep rest and recalibration of all areas of my life and business. In the moments when most of the world was panicked and locked inside, I began flourishing again. I had this incredible adobe villa all to myself and the amazing Colombian proprietors cooking for me each day. I gave myself the gift of resting as much and as often as I needed—and in that rest came insight after insight, revelation after revelation. As I gave myself time and space to just be, without needing to constantly be doing, I began to write and sing more. At the time, I did not realize this would become the raw material for my new coaching programs, and ultimately this book! I was called to release so much of the weight I had been carrying emotionally and spiritually. And on top of it all, my income nearly tripled.

In the midst of all this recovery and growth, my body was still experiencing waves of massive discomfort—not only from the pain I'd been living with for so long, but also from the craziness of what was going on in the world. The lockdowns. The unknowns. Being separated from my teenage children while they were in Canada with my ex. The completely new rhythm and pace of life I was dropping into. The visceral discomfort was real, hence my need for so much rest. My body was going through its own process, while my spirit came alive and life around me began to reorganize.

What on earth was going on? What changed?

What changed was that *I was suddenly doing everything differently.* I gave up needing to know it all, to map it all out, to have evidence before I moved on anything. Instead, I embraced the unknown as an adventure and refused to shut down from fear. I chose to move toward that which was life-giving. Instead of trying to protect myself, I focused on opening myself up, which allowed me to receive spiritually, emotionally, physically, and financially.

I embraced deep rest, a foreign concept to me. Sleeping as often and as much as my body needed felt wonderful. Instead of heeding the guidance of the experts to shift my business, I chose to deepen my communication with God and get my guidance directly from Him. I no longer entertained the voices that said I should be doing things a certain way. Instead, I chose to go where I was being led. For the first time in my life, I learned how to follow instead of leading all the time. It was a radically different perspective.

There's an old saying: "If you want to go fast, go alone. If you want to go far, go together." I will add, "If you want to experience the extraordinary, go with God."

Since the beginning, mankind has been seeking wisdom and counsel from the spiritual world in order to navigate the physical. There is much written about this already, but I will say that there is an innate knowing in all of us that there is a reality and a force beyond what we can see. I wanted to understand how to create something new, and for me this could only be done by inviting God, my Creator, back into my life.

The Holy Spirit is called the Mighty Counselor and Great Comforter for a reason. He provides direction and peace in the midst of uncertainty. I believe the places where we are forced to encounter the unknown in our lives are perfectly designed to bring us back into connection with our Creator so we can live out the expression and purpose He has designed for us.

MADE FOR THE UNKNOWN

As I've shared, I'm a bit of an adventure junkie.

Every winter, I challenge myself to ski new mountains and glades. In the summer, I look for water adventures, mountain bike parks, breathtaking hikes, and new places to visit with my loved ones. In business, I've experienced the fastest growth by putting myself in rooms where I felt completely out of my league or making bold declarations and taking risks before knowing how it would all pan out. In my relationship, deeper connection and intimacy are forged in the depths of the most vulnerable moments or new experiences together.

In other words, these leaps weren't created by doing the same old routines.

I'll bet it's the same for you, too. Why? Because *we were made for the unknown*.

We are designed for adventure, both physically and spiritually. Biologically, our bodies light up whenever we experience newness and novelty. Our hearts race with anticipation. As blood flow and life force increase, a blend of fear and excitement kicks in. Blood rushes to our limbs to help us navigate our terrain better. Our eyes widen to take it all in, and every sense in our body turns on. We are fully in our bodies, feeling everything around us in a heightened state that is known as *flow state*. Numerous studies and books have been written on the topic of flow state, and it's linked to heightened performance, growth, and fulfillment. I've been there many times; I'm sure you have, too.

Adventure and novelty also affect our brain plasticity. In an article published in *Science Direct* titled, "Unexplored territory: Beneficial effects of novelty on memory," author J. Schomaker shares that, when we are in unknown territory, our capacity for memory and learning increases so we can remember landmarks to find our way back home. Quickly learning where to expect danger and where to find rewards has long been crucial for the survival and growth of humanity. It literally expands our capacity and threshold to not only protect our homes, but also to move forward, settle into new lands, and overcome new challenges. Theta waves—the creative brain waves that get us dreaming, imagining, and setting off on new visions—increase when we engage in new activities. Children experience the most theta wave activity in the first seven years of life; we can come back to and cultivate a state of childlike wonder when we expose ourselves to situations beyond our daily "normal." This openness, as much as the new experiences themselves, is crucial for our growth and ongoing fulfillment.

Beyond the biological hardwiring, we are also "soft-wired" for adventure. Our hearts and souls crave the unknown. They crave adventure, and when we don't get it in healthy doses, we often resort to unhealthy and toxic ways to mimic that ignition in our hearts and souls. Think about what happens at the beginning of a new relationship: it feels as if your heart is going to explode right out of your chest! It's so exciting. So new. You don't know every detail or every step of the way. You don't have the whole lay of the land before you. You are simply filled with possibility and promises. Or, consider the first time you traveled on an airplane, immersed yourself in a new culture, or even watched a movie where the hero goes on an epic adventure. You probably felt a "high" and a sense of greater possibility for yourself. This is a great thing, and can spark tons of creativity and inspiration for you.

But if we keep doing those same "new" things over and over, it doesn't take long before predictability breeds boredom. When we are bored, we're stagnant, and disconnection takes place. We blame it on our partner, on our business, or on the new thing itself, and go searching for something else to excite us. Unfortunately, lack of "newness" is a common reason for many affairs. We can have the best of all worlds if we become more aware and intentional about curating moments of depth, adventure, and healthy, life-giving challenges in our daily lives.

Something within us is awakened in each moment of discovery. Something inside of us grows as we overcome that challenge. A new level of confidence sets in. A new level of strength is found. New awareness unfolds. We develop not only our physical skills but also our mental and emotional ones. Playing in the great unknown literally strengthens, equips, and develops us more than our comfort zone ever could.

BACK TO OUR ROOTS

Most cultures and religions share a similar backstory of how man and woman were created. They were formed in the unknown and life was breathed into them by a greater power. Out of nothing—no-thing— they became something. The void, darkness, or wilderness that terrifies so many in the modern world is the very place we originated from and were formed. In the Biblical origin story, Adam was created out of the dust of the earth, and Eve from the rib of Adam, bone of his bones, flesh of his flesh. It's no wonder we crave reconnection with our primal nature: there is a sense of bringing us back to our roots. I feel this every time I am in nature. Not only do I feel at home, but I also get to be in the adventure with something much greater than me, as if I am being guided. I believe that, at our core, each of us longs to get back to this home and be in the adventure—not alone on an island, but connected to something greater than ourselves.

On mountaintops, we come face to face with our true selves and God. In the deep quiet of the forest, we can hear the whisper of the Spirit speaking to our hearts. In our darkest moments and most terrifying experiences, we find super-natural strength and courage to rise above the situation. There's a *knowing* inside us that allows us to press forward when things don't make logical sense. It's in unknown environments that we can experience the fullness of life. We feel more. We see more. We discover more. We embody new levels of consciousness and a new normal is established. One thing I have come to know is that God is a God of process. He is more concerned with our character than our results or our comfort. He will invite us into challenges and seasons of leaning into the great unknown in order to stretch us, draw us closer to Him, forge our character, and develop us into men and women who can steward well the thing He is preparing us for.

When we activate faith and allow the Spirit of God to work in us, we allow ourselves to come into union with All That Is, the Source of life itself.

We cannot escape this intelligent, divine call and design within each of us. When we try to ignore, avoid, and escape our design, chaos ensues, and a slow death begins. When we become disconnected from our own spirit and that of God, we begin to feel isolated, alone, and adrift.

Perhaps you know exactly what I am talking about, or perhaps you are struggling with this a bit. You might be thinking, "I am not sure I have a lot of adventure in my life," or, "Not me. I don't like the unknown. I prefer comfort." Either way, I invite you right now to get out your notebook and make a list of the last five amazing experiences you've had in your life. It doesn't matter how far back you have to go. If you want to make this even more potent, write down the last ten. When have you felt totally alive, excited, and turned on about life? When was the last time you had a breakthrough moment or a season that catapulted you into a new reality? Jot those moments down and bring them back into the here and now.

Now, let's get real. Those moments are awesome *in hindsight*. But how comfortable were you while those moments were playing out? How predictable was the situation? How much information did you actually have? Were these moments the result of your own doing or planning, or was there something greater at work in you and around you?

I'll bet that, if you pause to put yourself back in these moments, you will find that these things were true:

1. You were not comfortable.

2. You did not have all the answers at that moment.

3. It was both terrifying and exciting at the same time.

4. On a visceral level, you knew you were not alone. Something greater than you was at work, and you were along for the ride.

What connects these four truths about amazing experiences? They are all about getting out of our predictable, safe, and comfortable place.

The Illusion of Comfort

We have bought into the idea that comfort will make us happy, when in fact it just makes us passive, disconnected, fearful, controlling, dissatisfied, gluttonous, and dis-eased. This list may sound aggressive, but stay with me.

The word "comfort" means "to soothe, pacify, or give solace to." So, once again, the question becomes, "What have I been seeking comfort from, and why?" I believe the goal so many are chasing is to feel ease in the midst of chaos, and peace in face of uncertainty.

The first thing to realize about comfort is that material and external things only offer a sub-par and fleeting version of it. When a small child is crying, a pacifier may comfort them momentarily, but only as long as the pacifier is in its mouth. The moment it's gone, unease sets in, and a temper tantrum ensues. True ease, on the other hand, comes from within, and peace is a state we can experience regardless of the external situation.

Remember how I was obsessed with constantly checking the balance in my bank account? The problem was not a lack of money coming into my life. The problem was that I developed an *idea* that what I had was never enough. I had plenty of cash to pay our bills and for my family to do the things we needed and wanted to do. I was rich by the world's standards. But the more comfortable I became, the less satisfied I was with what I had, and the more fearful I became of losing it. No amount was ever enough.

What mind games we play with ourselves!

This was also true in my previous relationships. The more I obsessed about creating a comfortable and safe life with another person, the more controlling, anxious, or fearful I became. In my first marriage, we had a beautiful home in a gorgeous neighborhood. We took vacations and went out to nice dinners. And yet, there was a restlessness inside each of us, and a restlessness inside our marriage. There was no ease, even in the midst of a life of "comfort." The moment we bought one new thing, it was on to the next.

My restlessness came from seeking comfort in the wrong things and never finding it. The opposite can also happen when you put so much weight into something or someone that they become the source of comfort for you. As I mentioned earlier, if we remain too comfortable for too long, it can become a breeding ground for complacency. When you get "settled" and comfortable with another person, you often stop exploring and growing together like you did at the beginning of the relationship. When you think you're in a good spot, it's easy to start going through the motions, lose motivation, and settle in. The days become predictable as the external takes over your schedule. Soon, you stop being intentional about what you want to create. Then, the bad habits start creeping in. Perhaps you start drinking a little more than you know you should. You and your spouse start complaining and criticizing each other rather than celebrating each other. You get bored with the routine, lose your sex drive or passion for life, and start looking for something to fire you up again. Maybe you borrow more and more money to satisfy your own or others' demands for greater comfort and security. Maybe you avoid making tough decisions to avoid puncturing the "comfort bubble." Maybe you hide the whole truth to keep others happy. Before you know it, your life has been infiltrated with habits that make you unhealthy, sick, and passive.

None of this happens overnight. It's a slow process of misalignment and disconnection from that which is life-giving. At first, it's like taking a shortcut to our desires, but eventually it leads us to make the wrong things into our idols. Before long, the very thing we went to for comfort and security begins to make us sick.

I'm not saying routine is a bad thing. It takes routine and repetition to build skills and gain strength. However, when routine becomes mundane, it also becomes ineffective. Rather than deliberately engaging with our chosen tasks, it's as though we are on autopilot—living life without experiencing it. Awareness is the key here. With awareness, we will know when it's time to mix things up and interrupt our stagnant patterns.

Let's do a quick exercise to demonstrate this.

Make a list of the last five things you *thought* would bring you comfort and make things better for you or those around you. Was it the latest iPhone upgrade? That new outfit, or the pair of shoes you couldn't walk out of the store without? Winning that argument? Putting that certain amount of money in your retirement account?

Now ask yourself, did it do the trick? And if so, how long did that sense of comfort and peace last? If you continue to sit in this place of "comfort," how excited about life are you?

A "comfortable" life, dear Warrior, is the most dangerous place to live. It will slowly drain the life out of you until you become a shadow of the man or woman you are designed to be.

Let's consider for a moment that we could be wildly uncomfortable, wildly alive, *and* wildly at peace *at the same time*. What would life look like then?

What Is Your Fear Response?

Maybe the question above made you prickle with anxiety, doubt, or even fear. How could you possibly be uncomfortable *and* peaceful at the same time?

Humans have an innate fear response for a reason. In the most primal sense, the reptilian part of our brain is designed to heighten awareness and produce a surge of energy when we are faced with potential danger. This was important when our ancestors faced predators and needed to be able to whip into action at the slightest provocation. But even though we don't face threats like that on a day-to-day basis anymore, our bodies still react the same way when we're confronted by difference, conflict, and fear.

We know there are four main responses to fear:

1. Fight—"I will beat this!" Like a bull in battle, sometimes we go in for the attack when challenged. We yell, we scream, we throw punches (sometimes literally), and pull out every weapon we have got in our arsenal. This is the land of most warriors. We are trained to fight, and we will fight to the death. Sometimes it works—but other times, we just end up wounded and exhausted.

2. Flight—"I'm out of here!" Sometimes we run away from scary things. This can look like ghosting someone you're having an argument with or dropping out of a project in the midst of a challenging phase.

3. Freeze—"I just can't go on." Sometimes we are paralyzed with indecision and are unable to move forward. This might manifest as a deer-in-the-headlights feeling, a blockage in creative flow, or shooting down every solution that others present. It also looks like complete exhaustion and a collapse of energy.

4. Fawn—"I will diffuse this." Sometimes, when we are presented with a dangerous person or situation, we try to appease or please it. Instead of running from the lion, we try to pat it on the head. This is a common response for warrior women in combative relationships; they try to minimize the danger by controlling it.

All of us have done some (or all) of the above when faced with stressful situations, and most of us have a favorite fear response to which we default. However, there is a fifth response that happens when we flip the switch on our relationship with the unknown, and begin to lean into the knowing that we are no longer alone.

5. Faith—"What don't I see? What are you doing here, God?" This is the response of a Warrior of the Heart, and it requires a choice to completely release the attachment to what we are afraid of and what makes logical sense, and instead put our faith in the things we cannot see. This evolved level of awareness says, "There is more here than meets the eye. Let me get curious and explore what this is actually about, and how I can move through this in a new way." This way of reacting will not come naturally; it requires willingness, a new heart, new eyes, new ears, and most of all, new rules of engagement (which we will unpack in upcoming chapters). When we can do this, we activate our warrior spirit and temper it with childlike wonder and an adventurer's heart.

As you cultivate a greater sense of awareness, you also cultivate a greater ability to choose how you respond. We can choose to let fear rule us, drive us, and direct us, or we can lean in and choose wonder and excitement over anxiousness, curiosity over fixed thinking, and faith over fear.

I often use the analogy of standing in line for a roller coaster. You can stew in misery, drowning in fear and fixating on the worst possible scenario, or you can get excited about the wild ride and focus on how incredible you will feel after the experience. When you release the fear, you will enjoy the ride more. And, with that accomplishment, the next roller coaster will be a lot less terrifying and perhaps even something you look forward to!

BRING ON THE ADVENTURE

I have met many people who, well into their adult years, have never been on an airplane. Many say they just don't have a desire for it—they are comfortable at home. When they finally do get away, the experience can go one of two ways. It can be too overwhelming, terrifying, or uncomfortable, and send them running back into their familiar "safe zone." Or, it can ignite a fire of curiosity and an insatiable appetite to do more, see more, and experience more. Here's the thing that's consistent for both parties, though: once you've seen what's out there, you can't unsee it. Once you leave your familiar bubble, you will realize how much more is waiting to be discovered.

Last year, two of the women who attended my retreat had never traveled alone in their lives. They were both apprehensive at first, not knowing what to expect from either the travel or the retreat—but they both came and played full out. I was honored to see them step *way* out of their comfort zones and experience life-changing growth as a result. Recently, one of them shared that she'd just returned from a week-long solo trip to the beach where she road tripped eighteen hours by herself and had the time of her life reading books, hanging on the beach until sunset every day, and getting more intimate with God. As I write this, she is on another trip to the mountains of Colorado with her sixteen-year-old son! Adventure is now a way of life for her, and she is beyond lit up at the way the world has opened up for her.

Physical travel isn't the only way to bring more adventure into your world. You might feel called to put yourself out there in other ways—like cultivating a new skill set that feels awkward or unnatural to you, talking to complete strangers for no reason, or challenging your long-held assumptions about life, truth, and the nature of the universe. For me, writing this book was a perfect example of this kind of adventure. If I'm honest, writing is one of my least favorite ways to communicate. It has been a labor of love, challenging me to be present and focus over and over again. Speaking on video or audio comes easily and flows for me. Taking this project on, by the prompting and direction of the Holy Spirit, has really stretched me!

Another past client of mine, Karen, was an avid and passionate musician. As a hobby, she loved playing the classical guitar, attending conferences, and playing in concerts. In her "real" life, she was a pharmaceutical consultant and speaker. Then, after decades as an expert in her field, she came into my office, sat in the chair, and said, "I want to play music. I am so tired of doing this job I've been doing, but I don't know how to make this transition or what it would even look like!" She was terrified, and there were many unknowns. But, a shift had begun in her, and shortly thereafter she made a bold declaration to shift her identity and step into the next season of her life: effective immediately, she would introduce herself as a classical guitarist rather than a pharmaceutical consultant. She had no idea at the time how this was going to go, or what response she would get, let alone what would possibly come out of this—but she did it anyway. Today, she is living the best of both worlds, leading a movement in the industry to use "music as medicine." She is still speaking on stages, but now her talks are infused with music, industry-disrupting content, and her passion for her work. She is a sought-after expert in a brand-new space that blends her passion, gifting, and expertise.

When we move into the space of the unknown, anything is possible. New experiences both invite and pull us into the space of imagination and trust, where we can go inward and open ourselves up to receive the support, guidance, direction, and connection we so deeply long for.

This is how we begin to experience and establish a new normal.

A NEW VANTAGE POINT

In order to get out of our old patterns, we must gain both a new vantage point and also a new internal set point—a new level of understanding that becomes embodied and automated in our nervous system.

There is an old Chinese proverb that says, "I hear and I forget. I see and I remember. I do and I understand." In other words:

1. What you are told, you forget.

2. What you see, you remember.

3. What you experience, you *understand*.

When you immerse yourself in the new, everything inside of you rearranges itself according to this new understanding and way of relating to the world.

We have been told things for our entire lives. We've sat in classrooms and listened to teachers telling us what to think. We've sat through church services and listened to the pastor or priest telling us what it means to be a good person and live a Godly life. We've listened to podcasts, read books, and studied with teachers who told us the "right" way to go about getting what we desire. We have accumulated copious amounts of information—and, as a result, we, too, claim to "know" things. The truth is, we have a lot of head knowledge, but not a lot of embodied knowledge, aka earned wisdom. Some of us might even have letters behind our names and stacks of degrees, but that doesn't always equate to real-life experience.

Many people walk around claiming to be faithful believers in God. They say they are led by the Spirit and have all these spiritual rituals in place—but the minute they walk out of church, they come unglued. They start fighting with their spouse in front of their kids or stressing about the bills that need to be paid. They then spend the rest of the week complaining (lacking appreciation), worrying (praying in reverse), and blaming the external world for why they can't move ahead. This applies to the "spiritual but not religious" crowd too. I have been in countless yoga classes, meditation sessions, and retreats with people who are all bliss, love, and light until they get cut off in traffic or someone doesn't agree with their philosophy. Then, watch out!

What comes out of us when we are squeezed speaks volumes about our character. Head knowledge without embodied wisdom equals weak character. The truth is revealed when the surface cracks.

At PUSH!FIT, we specialized in weight loss. A lot of people came in overweight, stressed out, and looking for a quick fix. When we would talk about nutrition, sleep, stress reduction, and other good habits, they would inevitably say, "I know, I know, but ..." They loved to tell me what they *knew*.

My answer was always the same: "You don't *know*, or you would be *doing*."

None of these people needed more information. They simply weren't *acting* on the information they already had. As a result, they never got to have a new experience and embody their "head" knowledge. What they considered knowledge was just a bunch of information they had been accumulating but not putting into practice. This left them repeating the same experiences over and over again, like their own personal *Groundhog Day*.

Here's a hard truth: *what you truly "know" is what you act on consistently*. Awareness is the first step, but without action there is no integration and certainly no embodiment, which means you will never experience a new reality. When we truly begin to embrace the unknown, we choose to act on our new ways of experiencing. As a result, we develop a new level of understanding.

THE INVITATION

The challenge—or rather, the invitation—is to open our eyes to see and our ears to hear more than just the superficial, the surface level, or the physical.

Adventure is nice when we go alone. It often gets better when it's shared with the right people. But it goes to a whole other level when we choose to bring God, the ultimate Source of life and all that is life-giving, into the equation.

I have taken many solo trips in my life. In the past, however, I operated much of the time as a lone wolf. When I got away, it was usually because I was escaping from something, or running either from or toward something on a mission to conquer whatever I was up against at the time. I have also embarked on many business ventures by myself, plunging headfirst into the unknown. Trying to figure it out all on my own, I often forced my agenda on everyone around me. When obstacles presented themselves, I would activate my worldly warrior within and fight my way through it. But although I was able to dig deep and find the willpower to press on, I also felt terribly alone and unsupported.

I don't believe we are meant to experience the great unknown alone. As humans, we are created to go into the unknown together. It's why every great hero has a sidekick. It's why cowboys run together, and warriors unite. It's why movies like *The Patriot*, *Braveheart*, and *Gladiator* speak to us. It's why love stories take two people through battles and challenges together. There is an unbreakable bonding that happens when we enter into the unknown with someone else. Then, when super-natural support comes to meet us, a whole other level kicks in. The darkness no longer feels so daunting when we know we have a hand to hold. Fear no longer has a grip on us. We can pause to breathe, or rest, or sleep without the fear of losing everything or being eaten alive because we know something greater has our back. The road no longer feels so long and arduous when we have the encouragement to press on. In the moments when we can't see clearly, there is a whisper that reminds us what to focus on. Where there was confusion, there comes clarity and assurance.

Today, I embrace the unknown because I know I am no longer alone. I regularly book week-long solo cabin stays in the mountains so I can write, explore, play, and recover. I also make it a habit to take quick weekend getaways to recalibrate my focus and vision, and day trips to replenish my energy stores. My time in Sedona made clear to me my need for deep rest in certain seasons. The wilderness calls me back whenever it's time for another bout of self-discovery.

THE UNSPOKEN AND UNSEEN

Between 80 and 90 percent of human communication is nonverbal. That's quite a revealing statistic. It's no wonder people argue so much about what was said and not said.

Being in a new space invites all our senses to tune in and turn on. Just as we must pay attention to body language, tone, and other factors to communicate fully, when we seek adventure as a tool for our expansion, we can no longer pay attention only to surface-level things. We must look for the truth behind all things. We can no longer see people, situations, circumstances, or solutions at face value; instead, we need to open ourselves up to multi-layered, multidimensional reality, and ask, "What else?"

"What else is going on?"

"What else am I missing?"

"What else is being communicated here?"

This is how we begin to move into the realm of infinite possibility.

Once you activate a willingness and set the intention to see, hear, and experience your life differently, things will begin to present themselves to you in a different light. This, I can guarantee.

I used to see the world only through the lens of my individual ideas, past wounding, and life experience. We all do this—and, to some degree, we will continue to do this throughout our lifetime as long as we are human. It's called projection, and it not only limits our ability to see but also puts a huge wall of resistance between us and others. Operating from this place without awareness makes it nearly impossible for us to truly understand one another, connect at deeper levels, and receive the experience of something *different*.

In order to move beyond our projections, we have to step past the superficial and ask God to give us the eyes and ears to see what He sees—in essence, to see people and situations through their own eyes, and His eyes, rather than just our own. This is how we activate compassion and curiosity, and begin the process of enjoying a fuller range of life.

Imagine an oak tree for a second. What do you see? You're probably envisioning a massive, sturdy trunk with branches and leaves spreading out across an expanse of grass. But is that all the tree is? What lies beneath the surface—beneath our range of vision—offers quite a different reality. The vast network of roots spreading out under the ground often matches the height and width of the tree above. What we thought was one size is actually double or more what we see. There are millions of channels for sap and nutrients to move beneath the bark of the tree, transporting nutrients from the root system to the leaves and branches. This, as much or more than the sun and rain on its leaves, keeps the tree alive. In fact, here is a whole underground ecosystem working together in perfect harmony—and it's all just out of sight.

If that holds true for a simple oak tree, just imagine how much else lies below the surface of life that we have yet to discover? Let us not be foolish: what meets the eye at first glance is not all that exists. Beyond the realm of the physical, logical, and linear lies a multidimensional reality that contains depth and richness beyond our current understanding.

God, the one who knows you by name and formed you uniquely, the Creator of this amazing universe, wants to bring us back to this place—our true home, where the physical and the spiritual come together to work in perfect harmony. The place where we adopt new eyes and new ears, and operate by new laws. The beautiful thing is that it all exists in the here and now, waiting for you to tap into it.

If you're feeling scared or unsure, I get it. Discussions like this one awaken the skeptic inside of us who is always looking for hard proof before moving. But now is the time to decide if you will be led by God and moved by His Spirit, or led by fear. When you find the flavor of excitement that the unknown offers, you can open yourself up to experience and receive what you were created for all along.

In order to truly embrace the unknown and move from fear into faith, there are six critical steps I have found to be consistent and essential.

Six Steps to Turn Fear into Faith

I invite you to pause on each step and meditate on the passages provided. Reflect as to what comes up for you.

Set Aside Control and Fear

Do not waste your time being anxious or fretful. Instead, choose to look forward to this season with excitement and anticipation of where God is going to take you. Imagine putting on your adventure gear, which includes an adventurous mindset that will help you be flexible and adaptable, as well as a heart open to the unexpected and unplanned. For this journey, we pack light; the heavy stuff that's been weighing you down must be left behind.

Meditation: *"Who of you by worrying can add a single hour to his life?"* (Matthew 6:27, NIV)

Come Back to Childlike Wonder

There is something extra special about taking kids on adventures. They have a way of seeing what we can't see. They delight in even the smallest things, and light up at a moment's notice. You, too, have this ability; it's what comes alive in you when you are in the presence of children. Allow that childlike wonder and belief to become your new normal as you move forward. Choose to be delighted as a child of God, for He wants to show you marvelous things, if you are willing.

Meditation: *"Jesus called for them, saying, "Permit the children to come to Me, and do not hinder them, for the kingdom of God belongs to such as these."* (Luke 18:16, NASB)

Slow Down

When we move too fast, we don't receive the depth or richness of an experience. So, stop skimming, and train yourself to experience life at a new pace. This can be uncomfortable, but if you want a different experience, you are going to have to interrupt your current patterns—and that includes the pace and speed at which you think, talk, move, and react. So, speak slower. Listen slower. Focus on one thing at a time. Set the intention to experience more depth.

Meditation: *"They who wait for the Lord shall renew their strength; they shall mount up with wings like eagles; they shall run and not be weary; they shall walk and not faint."* (Isaiah 40:31, NASB)

Be Present. Be Here Now

Many people on this planet are either hypersensitive or numbed out and desensitized because they are rooted in a fear response to the external and their nervous system is on high alert. Either way, they are not physically present, not grounded. As you actively and intentionally become more aware, you will become aware of all your senses and begin to calm down and notice more. So, next time you take a walk, engage your senses: sight, sound, feeling, touch, and taste. What do you see and hear beyond the surface? What can you tune into beyond your physical senses? Can you feel your own presence and the presence of God in you and around you?

Meditation: *"Be Still, and Know that I am God."* (Psalm 46:10, NIV)

Lean In and Have Faith

You can choose to be led by fear or by faith. Faith extends beyond your own self to the Source of all things. Having faith means inviting the ultimate Creator and Author of all life itself to dwell within you. Once you connect with His ever-present, limitless well of love and life, you will encounter a level of presence, protection, and guidance unlike any you've experienced before.

Meditation: *"Truly I tell you, if you have faith as small as a mustard seed, you can say to this mountain, 'Move from here to there,' and it will move. Nothing will be impossible for you."* (Matthew 17:21, NIV)

Take it One Step at a Time

Learn to be gentle with yourself. Practice grace. You didn't learn to walk or ride a bike overnight. You didn't master the skills you have today overnight. It took patience, practice, and time—and this process is no different. Train yourself to be humble and gentle not only with others, but also with yourself. Consider it all practice. After all, these micro-moments will be the ones you talk about later. The journey is what makes the adventure worth living.

Meditation: *"Always be humble and gentle. Be patient with each other, making allowance for each other's faults because of your love."* (Ephesians 4:2, NLT)

WARRIOR INITIATION

- What has your relationship with the unknown been?

- Can you recall a time when you embraced the unknown and leaned in with openness and faith? What was the outcome?

- In what areas of life have you fallen for the illusion of comfort?

- Which one of the six steps above is resonating most with you in this season of life? What can you implement or work on today in this one area?

CHAPTER SIX

Drop the Armor

"Walls built for protection can also become our prisons. Only by facing our fears can we truly set ourselves free."

— **THE KNIGHT IN RUSTY ARMOR**

*P*icture an amazing medieval castle. It is an impenetrable fortress, dominating the landscape, and it was built for battle. Magnificent in its day, with sky-scraping turrets and imposing walls, it is now hidden behind a forest of overgrown thorns. Behind the exterior lies wall upon wall—layer upon layer of protection to keep out what is dangerous, what is painful, what may cause harm. It guards against the enemy or anything that could possibly turn into one. Nothing dares to enter or even come near these gates. There is nothing inviting here. It's cold. It's hardened. It has lost its beauty and luster. At the same time, the protection is so thick that it locks everything deep inside. There are catacombs, dark tunnels, and corners that have not been visited in years.

And inside ...

Little girls and boys cower in corners with terrified looks in their eyes, barely breathing, hoping they won't be seen, and at the same time desperately seeking a strong hand to pull them into the light. People who once laughed, sang, danced, and made love, now mindlessly walk through their days with a blank stare on their face. Wandering, and at the same time, wondering; nostalgic for a time long past, or hoping for a future that only becomes dimmer with time.

These walls also guard a warrior, his appearance hardened, his body rigid. He has been fighting for so long just to prove himself that fighting has become his only nature. He has fallen for trickery and manipulation under power-hungry, controlling lords in the past. He has been burned and stabbed by those closest to him, learning that no one can truly be trusted. He must watch his back at all times. But now, he has battled his way to a deep, dark place in the castle, and there he remains. He locked himself up to avoid the people and pain of his past, the potential of having to face yet another disappointment. He locked up who he was long ago so that he could survive the battlegrounds, the wounds, the bloodshed. He has become numb. Desensitized. Armored up. No more than a machine going through the motions.

The long, cold hallways and dark, still rooms also hide a young woman with many dreams and a bright future ahead of her. But her heart is broken by unresolved issues, unmet longings, and too many jabs from others that left their mark on her body and soul. She continues to look ahead with the strength of a fierce lion, but inside there is a waterfall of tears begging to be released. She is terrified and wildly fierce at the same time. She cannot and will not let that water run free, for it will be the death of her. So, each day, she swallows the tears, hides herself behind the protective walls, and shuts the door to her heart so that she can survive.

WHAT'S YOUR ARMOR?

You probably aren't locked up in a castle, and you probably don't walk around in chain mail, but we all wear armor. We think it is our strength, shielding us from the pain of the outside world. However, more often, this armor is made of layers of unresolved, unhealed trauma and pain that we've hardened so we can hold ourselves together.

Our armor is the anger we never allowed ourselves to fully feel, express, or heal. It's the unprocessed grief that occupies the abyss of our heart and organs, waiting to be seen, felt, and moved out of our system. It's the bitterness and resentment that has built up over the years of swallowing our words, putting ourselves last, and giving more than we received. It's the pain of rejection we felt when we were told we weren't loved anymore, were stupid, didn't make the cut. It's the deep fear of inadequacy we've been hiding from and overcompensating for. It's the shame from the past abuse. It's guilt and remorse from all the terrible decisions we made, everyone we hurt along the way. It's the lies we bought from others, and all the ridiculous rules and judgments society forced onto us. It's layers and layers of memories, fears, and beliefs that have been passed down from generation to generation and are now stored in our bodies, unaddressed.

Unspoken. Unresolved. Unprocessed. Unhealed.

To sum it up: our armor is all the stuff that is *not ours to hold onto any longer.* It's time for us—for me, for you—to break the chains of the past by putting down these layers of armor we have consciously or unconsciously picked up and put on along the path of life.

There comes a very specific point when we realize that what got us here will not get us to where we want to be. In fact, what got us here is now the very thing that is gripping fiercely at our hearts and our feet, disconnecting us from our faith and the courage to step forward down a new path. It is the very thing causing us to recycle the past, re-invite the same battles into our lives, and create struggle after struggle.

Since you've come this far along the journey, you have already made the decision to walk through the door and begin to fight differently. Maybe you can even see the road before you, but before you know it ... *BAM!* You feel the weight of your past creeping in like a heavy shadow that washes over you, blanketing everything in darkness, filling your head with chattering noise that you can't seem to shut up or shut out. Your physical body may even feel paralyzed, unsure of where to go in this vast new landscape.

You simply cannot move forward and sustain any real momentum while still carrying your old armor. You may take a few labored steps forward, but you'll soon be faced with a decision. If you make that decision armored up, you will only end up recycling the past. And each time this happens, not only do the same conflicts come back just like the last time, but in my experience, they compound and multiply.

If we engage life with a distrusting and hardened heart, only betrayal, hardship, and disconnection will make their way to us. If we engage expecting to be disappointed and rejected, rejection and disappointment follow, just like a boomerang. As the saying goes, "If all you have is a hammer, everything looks like a nail." I would suggest, then, that if all you have is your old armor, everything looks like the same old battle.

Our actions are initiated by what's inside us. You cannot get cherry juice by squeezing a lemon. Everything matters: our tone, our energy, and our body positioning all communicate whether we are open or closed. If you are armored up, you are walled up, closed off, defensive, and unreachable. Ralph Waldo Emerson summed it up succinctly: "Your actions speak so loudly, I cannot hear what you are saying."

A client who was trying this approach recently told me, "I feel like I take two steps forward, then five steps back, trying to hold it all together so it doesn't burn down *again*."

The one thing I have consistently noticed in myself and others is that the longer I try to hide behind my armor, the more I suffer under the weight of it. Everything begins to drag. Things take longer than they need to, and they become *way* harder. Soon, everything feels forced—like a battle. Or worse, like a charade. A reenactment. It's never authentic.

My dear Warrior, this suffering is *optional*.

The end of suffering begins with putting down your armor. Over time, you will gather up a new, lighter version that will protect you spiritually and energetically while also allowing love and blessings to permeate and infuse your entire being.

In this part of the journey, you will come face-to-face with your current and past identity, which is where you get your sense of safety and security. You will be asked to put things down and trust the process. It will take slowing down massively, learning to breathe and regulate your nervous system, and going deep within when you feel like searching everything outside of you for relief. It will take devotion and faith, and it will be uncomfortable at times, but you will feel so much lighter, clearer, and free on the other side. One day, you'll look back and wonder why it ever took you so long!

In this chapter, we'll unpack four key areas where we armor up— physical, emotional, mental, and spiritual—and what they might look like for you. This is by no means an exhaustive list, and whether you are experiencing one of these things or something else is coming up, it does not mean there is anything wrong with you. These are simply signals from God meant to get your attention and redirect you so you can open yourself to love again—to life again.

TRAUMA TAKES A TOLL

As you read through the list of armoring tactics below, you will realize that most, if not all, of these are trauma responses on a spectrum. Traumatic events leave an imprint in our psyche and our body. Sometimes, that looks like a splitting off and complete dissociation with that memory; other times, it is so embedded that it develops a deep belief system. These moments and memories create maps inside and outside of us.

Traumatic events do not always need to be life-altering. Sometimes, they are a simple look, an accident, or an offhand comment that hits us in a tender moment. We are not here to measure the severity of our traumas, simply to notice that our amazing bodies have held onto something that is now looking to be healed, processed, forgiven, loved on—perhaps for the first time ever—and then released. Often, healing begins the minute we give our walls and wounds a bit of love by bringing them to the surface in a safe place without entangling with them again or becoming consumed by them. When we create a space for our trauma and acknowledge it, we can lovingly communicate with it and choose to change our relationship with the events. When we keep fighting, hiding from, or refusing to accept the past, we continue to relive it and recycle the same patterns.

That said, I want to be clear that this is not a book on trauma recovery. If that is something you'd like to explore, or you don't feel safe doing the work I'm recommending without additional support, there are many great books, tools, and highly equipped practitioners out there to aid you. You can find a list of resources at www.dropthearmorbook.com.

Physical	Emotional	Mental	Spiritual
Acne, rashes, or hives	Anxiety	All or nothing mentality	Disconnection or disassociation from God
Addictive tendencies, particularly to substances or sex	Apathy		
	Conflict avoidance	Beliefs that others are the enemy	Fundamentalism
Chest pain or stabbing aches	Confusion or disorientation	Blaming/victim consciousness	Hardened or closed heart
Increased heart rate and body temperature	Depression	Consistent thoughts that are unwelcome, distressing, or irrational	Hiding behind notions of love and light
	Disconnecting/ disassociating		
Intense physical arousal	Emotional outbursts (emotional dysregulation, yelling, blaming, attacking character)	Fixed beliefs about self, the opposite sex, situations. ("They are wrong/I am right")	Refusal to face any darkness
Migraines			Spiritual blindness
Neck and back pain	Fear of intimacy	Judgmental thoughts	Using theology, dogma, or religious ideals as a protective wall
Numbness, especially in sexual organs	Feeling unsafe in relationships/ environments	Toxic positivity	
Shortness of breath/ breathing disorders		Violent thoughts	Lack of spiritual acknowledgment (agnosticism)
	Inability to access joy or feelings of love	Irrational or self-harming thoughts	
Sleep disturbances			
Stomach upset/ nausea	Judgment		
	Shame		
Tense muscles			
	Unaccepting		
Tight fascia			
Weight gain			

The body keeps a tally of our experiences. Physical ailments—as far as I have witnessed in my twenty-plus years of working with clients in the health, wellness, and nutrition space—almost always have mental, emotional, or spiritual roots. Therefore, you might be armoring up in more than one of the above areas.

Here are two examples of how armor can show up:

Example 1

From the time I began dating in high school, I quickly attached myself to relationships and went all in. I anxiously clung to whoever showed me the most affection and attention. But all it took was one mistake—one call that was not returned, one text that was not responded to in the time I deemed appropriate, one invitation not extended, one night when my partner fell asleep and didn't call to say goodnight—and I would lose it.

No joke. I cannot tell you the number of times that those simple events activated my abandonment wounds. Immediately, my heart would race, my body temperature would rise, my mind would be inundated with irrational thoughts and jealous accusations, and my entire system would be flooded with fear and anger. My body's hormones and chemicals would scream, "Shut this down and run before you get hurt! End this first, before they can!"

I would feel this huge wall come up inside me. The stabbing pain I felt in my heart would turn ice cold. I would literally block the "offender" (after sending a barrage of ridiculous messages attacking their character and telling them how incompetent they were). I am embarrassed to admit how explosive I would become at times. Once I calmed down, I would then quickly switch into fix-it mode. Or, I'd jump into the next "relationship" that provided the sense of attention and attachment I desperately wanted—until it all happened again.

Given these behaviors, it was no wonder that I kept attracting unreachable, uncommitted, emotionally unavailable men whom I could never seem to "get through to"—at least, not until I left them. Then, their worlds seemed to come unraveled. Suddenly, I was all that mattered to them—but by then, I had moved on to the next guy.

I can write this today without swimming in shame—but *wow*. There was so much unconscious programming and unresolved pain surfacing within me, and my way of dealing with it was only causing more of it. Now, I can look back on that younger version of me and see her, love her, and laugh a little with her. She wanted to be loved and give love so badly. She longed to be held. And, she had work to do to heal the part of her that still felt abandoned by her father.

When I gave myself the gift of getting raw and real about my armor, learned to put it down, and began to accept and honor the past, I no longer needed to fight in my relationships. Today, I am in the most emotionally grounded relationship of my life. Yes, we love each other. We long for each other. We need each other. However, we are *not* the source of love, identity, or all our needs for each other. We source love first from within, so we can pour into one another.

Example 2

I remember vividly the moment Shayla came into my life. She was radiant in so many ways, and I could feel her huge heart shining through her gorgeous blue eyes. At the same time, a shadow dimmed those eyes, and there was a rigidness in her body and tremble to her voice that spoke of her long relationship with pain. Life had offered her plenty of physical, mental, and emotional challenges to forge her armor.

I was honored when she raised her hand to start dropping it. As she took her first steps into this new territory, she could feel the weight of her past wanting to pull her back into that familiar, guarded place. She became aware of it, and did the work to move through removing those layers gently and lovingly.

She told me later, "I came to a point in my life where everything felt as if it was imploding—like I was stuck in a hole. I would dig and scratch at the sides but never could get enough leverage to emerge from it. I remained trapped in the dark, drowning under the weight of my armor. Many years of traumatic experiences combined with the unconscious patterns I developed to survive them added layer upon layer onto my body and heart. There were layers for protection, layers for acceptance, layers to prove and defend my worth.

"I masked it all with alcohol and pushed my body to the max to prove I was 'strong.' But my body started to fight against me. I was viscerally uncomfortable 90 percent of the time, but continued to take on more than I had capacity for. I was seeking a feeling of worth or value, like that would magically fix it all. In reality, I was just packing on more weight mentally, emotionally, and physically. My body ached so badly that there were days I could hardly get through.

"You know when you watch a colony of ants? Constantly working, hauling more than their own body weight, fighting, and protecting their queen? That's what was happening inside me: crawling, hauling, protecting, fighting.

"Through Christine's work and this specific part of the process, I learned that there's a different kind of armor—an upgraded armor that is flexible, light, fluid, allowing things to flow in and out—instead of the one I had been wearing that kept everything I desired and longed for on the outside, and everything I was afraid of on the inside. I've found new confidence, open to receiving rather than shielding. A new journey of alignment in boldness and light, calming myself in the midst of chaos, creating new masterpieces of art again and celebrating the life that surrounds me, even in the smallest blade of grass, to the mountains set in the backdrop, while honoring God's work and His creation of me. I know now that the strength I have is not just my own, nor did it ever have to be."

It Takes Practice

I often run retreats for men and women. While at the retreat, participants are immersed in the unknown, but there is safety because the setting is consciously curated, and because a trained facilitator has inspected and prepared the space, blessed it, and prayed over it. Clients are surrounded by others on a similar path, and there is space for them to be heard, process what's happening, and take the time and space to respond. This helps people stay in a place of safety, openness, anticipation, excitement, and curiosity. They know that although the exercises and challenges may be uncomfortable, they are held tightly in a safe container.

The challenging ongoing work of integration begins when they go back home into their "real" lives and are now faced with a picture of what they created in their past but are witnessing in present time. (Everything we experience today, we actually created over the past days, months, and years. It takes time for the physical to catch up to the mental and emotional, so we must remember this!)

This feeling of disconnection between their new world and their old world often happens to clients who are just beginning this work or those who don't have ongoing support to help them integrate the work. One woman, Jessie, shared that when she walked through her front door after getting home from our retreat, she wanted to tense up and recoil. "I felt like a deer in headlights," she told me later. "I could practically feel my armor locking back into place as I stepped back into that familiar environment. The old program was coming at me hard!" How could she have done all that work only to circle back to the same place she'd started? Had she traveled back in time?

The visceral reaction is real. When you're in the unknown, or on an adventure, it's easy to try on a new version of you—a version without armor. The real test comes when we are called back home, back to work, back to relationships, to repair and rebuild. This is why it's so important to have a support network of others who are on a similar journey or who are on the other side of what we're facing. This can be done through therapy, coaching, community, or wisdom circles.

Our bodies store massive amounts of information deep in our tissues, organs, water, and cells, not to mention our psyche. Just imagine how long it took for all those pains and past experiences to stack up! It took years, decades, perhaps even lifetimes to accumulate this armor. It makes sense that it might take a little practice to take it off.

I remember the moment that I knew that Jessie had finally embodied the work we did at the event and through our coaching. When fighting with her partner, it had been her tendency to shut down and go cold, sometimes even giving him the silent treatment for days. However, this time, she gave voice to her feelings, and asked for what she needed. This led to a game-changing conversation with her partner that totally shifted the foundation of their relationship. Clear communication is now her new normal.

It takes time to integrate this work and normalize it, but what I often see for my clients is that, within weeks or months, things look radically different. Within a year, the person is often unrecognizable; they have fully embraced a new identity with a whole new set of operating systems, and their external world has reorganized itself to match them.

We are always evolving. The good news is, it does not take as long to release the past as it took to create it. You can collapse the timelines moving forward when you shift your allegiance, begin fighting for the things that truly matter, and begin to create the life you truly desire.

CREATION HAPPENS IN ORDER

In order for you to drop your armor with pure intention and discipline, it's important for you to understand how the creation process works, and in what order it occurs. There is a sequence to how things are created or manifested into existence.

Everything is first created in the spiritual realm. Then, it moves through thought, then speech—and then, finally, into the physical realm, where it becomes real.

When you look at the Biblical story of God creating the heavens and the earth and everything in it, you can see just how powerful and consistent the process of creation is.

First, "the earth was formless and void or a waste and emptiness and darkness was upon the face of the deep." When God said those famous words—"Let there be light!"—light came. Then, God called into being a separation between the sky and water. The next day, He brought forth dry land and created all kinds of abundant vegetation. Then came the stars, sun, and moon, which were useful in distinguishing time and the seasons. Next came the birds in the sky and the creatures in the sea, which were soon followed by all manner of "livestock, crawling things, and wild animals of the earth according to their kinds."

Finally, only after everything else was created, did God create man "in His own image."

Let's dig a little deeper.

In the beginning there was nothing—no-thing—but Spirit, the Word, and the void. Infinite consciousness, and infinite possibility. Long before we begin any project, enlist any dream, or experience any experience, there is the *potential* of it, which exists in the spiritual realm.

From there, we see that the Spirit of God hovering over the nothingness decides to speak. At this moment, He commands, "Let there be light," and light appears. So, first there is the void. Then, there is a thought, often coupled with a conscious or unconscious desire to experience something. Then, words are spoken, and finally the physical manifests. There is always a thought before there is a spoken word. Thought exceeds even light in speed. While light travels at the rate of 186,000 miles per second, thoughts travel in no time at all.

Spirit. Thought. Spoken Word. Creation.

So, what does this mean for our own process? Long before I started my fitness studio, I had a vision floating around in the back of my mind. Call it a dream, call it an idea, call it a wish or desire. It existed in the void. It was not physically real, and it certainly did not feel tangible. I didn't even tell anyone about it for years, but it was always there. Then, one day, I began to tune in to the real potential of having this space. I gave myself permission to feel the excitement and potential of it. The desire and longing to see it come to pass grew within me. It did not take long before I began to share openly with my voice about this dream. Once it was out there, the resources began to form quickly around me to support the physical manifestation of my first location. (What's extra fascinating is that, seven years after opening my original location, I purchased a new location that looked almost exactly like the original vision I'd held in my mind for years.) Once I began to observe creation patterns more and more, and began to tap into my God-given desires by giving them more thought and speaking life over them, things began to transform at a surprising rate.

All things that we have and experience today were, in some way, shape, or form, created over time and through space—the good, the bad, and everything in between. And, just as we bring things into our lives, we can also remove them. When we do so intentionally and consciously, things begin to reorganize and move fast.

This brings us right back to that protective armor we've been dragging around. Just because it's on you now doesn't mean it has to *stay* on you. Just because you've become accustomed to it doesn't mean you can't exist without it.

It's time, Warrior, to get rid of the weight. It will only slow you down on the journey ahead.

HOW TO DROP THE ARMOR

Many people like to use the term "letting go." Honestly, I find that hard to wrap my head around. The concept of letting something go when I am already freaking out is terrifying, and only adds to my armor of self-protection and self-judgment. Instead, think about "dropping" or "putting down" your armor for a time, knowing that if you truly want to come back to it, it will be waiting for you. My experience is that, for most of us, this approach is much easier. (And, I don't know about you, but I have rarely, if ever, gone back to things I put down once I was free of them.)

If you're ready to drop that armor, it's helpful to start with a guided visualization experience. The body repeats what it remembers, and we also know that our body experiences in two ways: actually being in a situation, and imagining a situation. This is why movies are so incredibly effective at taking us on a visceral ride, and why we often leave invigorated or moved in ways we can't explain.

For me, guided visualizations are a powerful way to move things and bring things to the surface. We don't need to go in and analyze all the details of what something is or why it's happening. We don't need to go down a long rabbit hole and relive the memories. This process simply gives you space to remove the weight from your body and put it down.

During a meditation or visualization, you may find that memories or events pop into your mind. You may experience tears or strong emotions. You may or may not know *exactly* what it is that you are putting down. There is no right or wrong here. The exercise is simply an experience, and you can unpack it later, over time—or not.

Most people notice that their bodies immediately feel lighter after this visualization. This is the key to moving forward. *Put down the weight.* Put down the past. Put down what no longer serves you and walk forward, embracing the adventure within.

Read through the following visualization, and then actually do the exercise as soon as possible. (You can also access the full guided audio version at www.dropthearmorbook.com.) Close your eyes, and let your imagination take you where it may. I like to stand up so I feel this in my entire body, but you can also lie down or sit on a meditation cushion. I encourage you to do this more than once. Make this part of your daily morning practice, or use it anytime you feel like you have consciously or unconsciously put your old armor back on.

Guided Visualization

Find a comfortable position, and take five slow deep breaths, breathing in for four to six counts through your nose, and exhaling slowly a minimum of four to six counts through your nose with your tongue on the roof of your mouth. Take a gentle pause at the top of each inhale and exhale as you consciously connect your inhale to your breath, your heart—the Spirit. On the exhale, just release the need to be anywhere else at this moment.

Bring your full attention to this time and this space. Bring all of your energy, focus, and intention to this loving experience and the road ahead.

Meditate for a moment on this question, without judgment: "What got me here that is no longer going to get me there?"

Gently let yourself know, "I'm going to take this armor off now. This armor is blocking out the very thing I desire to allow in, and keeping in the things I long to let out. This is not the armor that I will be called to use moving forward."

Take another deep breath in through your nose, dropping into your body. Soften your feet, your ankles, your knees. As you exhale, relax even more.

Now, imagine that you are walking down a path in nature. It is lush, green, and a little bit rugged under your feet. As you walk forward, you feel a tingling in your body; it's something pulling you forward, calling you by your name. You can hear God calling you, and you feel your heart swelling with desire, curiosity, and longing to experience something more.

You notice that, as you walk down the path, a curtain of greenery closes behind you. The path of your past is closing. That is no longer the way you will travel. You are leaving the past behind and stepping into a new future.

The path starts to widen, and you feel that you're coming to the edge of a garden. As the path closes behind you, there's nowhere to go but forward. Yet, you can't step forward. There is something required of you before you are allowed into the garden—where you will receive your assignment, your direction, your guidance, where you will be able to see more clearly the vision God has for you.

What's required is that you take off the armor you've been wearing for the old world, the old survival game, the old ways of being and striving and operating that no longer serve you.

You're standing on the edge of the garden. Before you

cross over, you're going to take off this armor.

Feel the weight of the armor you've been putting on every day. It's heavy. It's thick. You might feel the weight on your shoulders or tightening in your chest. It may even feel like it's trying to pull you back, back down the dark path, but you're not going that way.

You're going to drop your armor and move forward.

Start with the heaviest piece, the armor plate on your back. Feel that pressure on your shoulders, the burdens you've been carrying. Visualize reaching behind your back, unbuckling this armor, and placing it down at your feet. You no longer need it. It's no longer required. You do not ever have to put that on again.

As you do this, you hear these words:

"Come to me, all you who are weary and burdened, and I will give you rest. Take my yoke upon you and learn from me, for I am gentle and humble in heart, and you will find rest for your souls. For my yoke is easy, and my burden is light."

Take a deep breath in, and feel how light your back and shoulders are now. You are not here to be looking over your shoulder. You are here to follow and be led by God—by the Holy Spirit. You are here to remember who you are and move forward with conviction, fully supported. There is a lengthening as you feel a string lift the crown of your head toward the sky. You become instantly taller.

Then, move to the front of your body. With two hands, gently lift the armor plate off your chest and place it on the ground. With it, release all of the tension and the tightness in and around your chest, all of the hardness in front of your heart, anywhere that you have been holding onto resentment, anger, pain, betrayal, or fears of abandonment or rejection. In this moment, feel it all fall to the ground. And as it hits the grass, it instantly dissolves into a million light particles. You instantly feel lighter and hear these words:

"Moving forward, you will have a soft, open heart and a strong back."

Without that armor on your back and chest, observe how light it feels to be open through the front and the back. It's almost as if a portal to your heart has opened up. It may even feel like rays of sun are pouring into this place that was dark and heavy for so long.

Next, we are going to take off your helmet.

Your helmet is the incessant noise you are constantly tapped into to keep yourself distracted from what's going on inside you. The incessant noise, never-ending advice, judgments, and to-do lists only create more confusion and block out your ability to see with your spiritual eyes and hear the voice of God leading you.

So, take that heavy helmet off. Let it fall to the ground and dissolve into a million particles. As you do, feel the space opening up in front of you, beside you, behind you, above you. Your mind is clear. Your head is lighter, renewed.

Now, take off the cuff around your neck—the thick band constricting your voice, your ability to fully express yourself. Where you are going requires your full, authentic expression. Your voice is a gift bestowed upon you to share with the world. Take off the cuff. As you do so, let out a deep breath or whatever sound wants to arise. Drop the cuff to the ground, and immediately feel space and ease around your throat and neck.

Lighter mind, clear eyes, clear ears, open throat, open heart, and strong back. It feels so good.

Now step out of the heavy weights and chains around your hips, thighs, and feet. It's time to drop whatever fears, thoughts, doubts, or worries you have entertained about moving forward or about leaving something behind. If you are constantly weighed down with this armor around your legs and feet, you will forever be trudging, sinking, and forcing. Choose now to take a step of faith into the next season of your life. Right now, lift one leg and take a step forward.

You are standing barefoot on the grass. You are lighter, free. You can breathe deeply and see more clearly. There is a new spaciousness around you.

Scan your body and tune in. Is there anywhere else that feels heavy and thick? Take the armor off there, too. Check your hands. Are you holding tightly to ideas, attachments, or anything else that will get in your way? Open your hands, relax your fingers, and let those things fall to the ground. With open hands you can move forward and receive the resources, support, and love that you need for this new venture. Wiggle your fingers and feel the lightness in your hands as if you are holding feathers in an open palm.

Last, but not least, step out of your old skin. Where you are going, you will be completely restored. You will have a completely new identity—not one shaped by the world, your past, or other people, but by God. So right now, imagine that you are unzipping this outer identity skin.

As you leave that skin behind, turn your gaze to the pile around your feet. Notice how much dead weight you were carrying. It is no longer yours to carry. That is no longer your story. You're ready for a new journey.

Look out into the gorgeous garden and feel the invitation to walk forward and explore what God has in store for you. You are light, free, and curious with eyes of wonder.

Hear these words: *"For this journey, we pack light. We take only what's essential, and let God provide the rest."*

Take a deep breath and just be in this moment. Let it linger. You can pause here, or you can spend some time traveling around the garden.

Then, when you're ready, begin to come back into your

body, leaving your armor where it fell. Wiggle your fingers and toes. Take a deep breath, feeling the new lightness in your body and spirit.

***

You have just completed the first essential phase of your journey. Thank you for trusting in this process. Moving forward, choose to only pack what's light and essential because you are already equipped with everything you need for this journey. That is part of leaning into trust—and it is absolutely part of creating something new and radically different than the past.

As you move about your day, stay grounded and anchored in this lightness you found in the visualization. If, at any point in time, you are triggered and feel like you have put your armor back on, take a moment to consciously feel the weight in your body, and then drop the armor again. The more you understand what it feels like when the armor is gone, the more you'll be able to tune in, refine, drop, adjust, and move forward moment by moment.

This is a practice, dear Warrior. As with all things, mastery takes constancy, repetition, and time. Give yourself that gift.

WARRIOR INITIATION

Once you have completed the visualization, grab your journal and write down any thoughts, visuals, or awareness that came up for you.

Here are some prompts to help you. Feel free to expand them as you see fit.

- Go through each of the four types of armor—physical, emotional, mental, spiritual—and think about how it felt to drop that armor. Did you notice a shift? Where is there still work to do?

- What was *in* that armor that you dropped?

- What are you committed to putting down as you move forward?

- What are you committed to embracing/leaning into?

- Where are you being called now that you are lighter, freer, clearer?

- How will you engage differently as you move throughout your day?

CHAPTER SEVEN

Unlock Your Heart

"To forgive is to set a prisoner free and discover that the prisoner was you."

— **LEWIS B. SMEADES**

*O*n the eve of my eighth birthday, my family had just moved to Raleigh, North Carolina, from Italy. It was a weird time—settling into a new country and trying to fit in with the culture and language. Since we were new to the neighborhood, I didn't have any friends yet, but my mother planned a birthday party for me and invited some of the children in the neighborhood. She always worked hard to create beautiful moments for us.

In the morning, I jumped out of bed and ran into the family room where I found a lovely porcelain doll with blazing auburn hair. She was perfectly dressed and came with her very own rocking chair. Around her were piles of balloons and a sign that read, "Happy Birthday!" Anticipation was in the air. I was excited—thrilled to play with my doll, meet new friends, and eat ice cream.

What happened that day was anything but thrilling.

The time came for the party to start, and the time went. I waited and waited for my new friends to arrive, but as time went on, only one girl showed up. I kept waiting and hoping that more would arrive. But it was just the two of us. I was so embarrassed. My little girl's heart shattered into a million pieces. That day, I felt the sting and wounding of rejection. The words speaking into me, "No one likes you. No one cares about you." Those words cut deep, and stayed with me for decades. I still feel them sometimes.

From that day forth there was both a deep fear and huge expectation around my birthday. *Will I be remembered? Will I be special? Will anyone even care?*

Later, as I began to organize events, that wound haunted me. Each time I planned an event—a sleepover, a holiday party, my wedding, a new product launch in my business—my entire nervous system would be hijacked by a combination of fear and dread. *What if nobody shows up?* I so badly wanted to have a new experience and simultaneously wanted to avoid the shame and pain of reliving that humiliation and rejection. And, because I was hauling around that baggage, it became a self-fulfilling prophecy: I would overextend myself in the planning stages, going *way* over the top so that people would come, only to sabotage the whole thing by forgetting to send the invites in time or waiting until the last minute to do key things. The event would be a total flop, or I would cancel it, thus reaffirming my story from that birthday so long ago.

See? I was right to be worried. No one cares. No one ever shows up for me. I have nothing to offer.

Sometimes wounds pierce so deep that we experience a brokenness of our innermost being. There is a shattering at the core of our identity, and that broken part of us remains locked up at the age when the event took place. Psychologists often refer to this as *arrested development*— when a child, preteen, or adolescent is subject to an experience of trauma, grief, or neglect that they are unable to resolve, make sense of, or overcome. As a result, part of them becomes stuck at the age when they first experienced the wounding.

Arrested development creates chaos, defensiveness, and chronic breakdowns. When someone suffers from this, it is difficult for them to switch in and out of different roles in life and self-reflect because they are still stuck in a childhood or teenage state of mind. When something triggers that state of mind, they instantly feel like the age they were when the original event happened—and act accordingly.

Perhaps you've been in a relationship with someone who acts like a toddler in an adult body any time they are challenged or don't get their way. Or maybe you've been the one living in that space, throwing tantrums, blaming, attacking, or getting defensive, and feeling incapable of self-reflection, self-discipline, or self-control. If this sounds familiar, know that you or the person in question are reliving the original wounding; your body and mind are doing everything in their power to not feel the pain. Is it any wonder that it's hard to have a peaceful conversation or take responsibility for things in that state?

Additionally, a person who is easily offended is also easily manipulated and controlled. Think about it: when someone is offended, instantly their life force is dedicated to defending, attacking, justifying, debating—to arguing rather than creating. It's a complete waste of precious time, energy, and resources, a costly distraction that pulls us off course from our vision and plunges us into a pool of toxicity. Before we know it, we are no longer treading water, but sinking.

Like our armor, our wounds only serve us when we are fighting for the wrong things.

Wounds leave a mark on our hearts, an imprint in our nervous system, and a story in our psyche that will be retold over and over again until we choose to heal them. The wounding in our hearts and souls can continue to oppress us, depress us, divide us, sabotage our progress, and disconnect us from God, each other, and the abundant life we are destined for—or, we can choose to rewrite the stories of the past, open our hearts, and move forward in a different way. We choose to take that story and use it to heal, restore, empower, and support others who are struggling in the same ways we once were. We can be conduits that bring healing. This is what happens when we drop the armor and step onto our new path as Warriors of the Heart.

THE GATEWAY TO THE SOUL

There are three very distinct and clear realms of the human being: body, soul, and spirit. Each one of these facets of our being is unique in its design and purpose.

Our physical body is obvious. It's the bone, tissue, muscles, cells, and all the other matter we are carrying around each day. The body is a miraculous, self-healing, and highly responsive vessel we get to call home for our time on Earth. However, we are so much more than the physical. Most of us are highly aware of our physical bodies, yet may be completely disconnected from our soul and spirit.

In his book, *Moving Mountains*, John Eldredge does a beautiful job of capturing the difference between soul and spirit.

> *"Your spirit is the life breath of God within you, giving life to both body and soul. It is the LIFE FORCE of God within you. Your soul is composed of a number of capacities, including heart, mind, and will. Your spirit is the sunshine. Your soul is the stained-glass window it shines through."*

In other words, each of us has been made alive through the Spirit of God breathing into our own spirit. The spirit is what breathes life into us. It is the part of us that is one with God. Our soul is the vast mystery and beauty of who we are created to be beyond the physical: our unique personality, mind, emotions, and will. Will we fully express ourselves and what we are called to do in this lifetime? Or will we repress and hide ourselves because of our past? I often say that the ultimate battle (between light and darkness, good and evil) is for our souls. The enemy wants to separate our soul and our spirit from God, where we belong. The battleground is the mind, for whomever takes our thoughts captive takes our hearts captive—and this means our minds, hearts, and will have now turned themselves over. Will we be ruled by love or fear?

In previous chapters, I recommended that you pack light for our journey—that you take only what is essential and allow God to supply the rest. This is where we take an inventory of what we are still carrying. Maybe you've successfully dropped your armor, but the past is still there, reminding you of your failures. How can you leave it behind in a loving and gracious way?

Personally, I am not a fan of simply cutting people or things out of our lives without doing any inner work. In my experience, this gives us the illusion that we have moved on without the true freedom of surrendering our burdens.

To move ahead and stop fighting the same battles day in and day out, we need to open the clenched, tight parts of us that we've been holding onto for dear life. In this chapter, we will address how to reconnect with and find wholeness, healing, and integrity in our heart and spirit.

Wholeness comes from unlocking our heart first, tending to its wounds, and restoring it as a sacred place that opens the door to everything we are created for and could ever need. Your heart is the access point where the Spirit of God meets you, reminds you who you are, and fills you with a wellspring of new life. What's *in* that incredible heart of yours?

I invite you to bring your warrior spirit into this unknown place and explore.

This part of the journey for any Warrior works in tandem with the previous step, Dropping the Armor. From this moment on, know that this journey is *not a linear process.* Instead, it is a gorgeous (and often messy) multidimensional undertaking that will challenge your logical mind and bring you into greater presence and awareness. Sometimes, you will be tempted to overanalyze, defend, and hold onto control; when this happens, I urge you to slow down, breathe, soften the tension in your body, lean back, and get curious again.

WHY ARE OUR HEARTS CLOSED?

We have all been wounded.

As I write this, I have my sword positioned on the wall behind me. A sword has the qualities of being solid and strong, yet flexible and balanced. The blade can maintain its shape and edge under impact and pressure. It's also flexible in the sense that it will also bend under resistance, but not break in half. The perfect sword is also balanced so it's easy to pick up and use. To me, the sword is a symbol of the piercing power of my words, but also the power of God and His Word to speak life and truth back into any situation. It is there as a reminder that I have the power to wound others, and also the power to heal through the precision of my words and actions. I can use it to cut down or build up. More, God's Word slices through untruths and reveals the true nature of love and freedom.

As we've discussed, wounds come in many forms from many places: the loss of a father or mother, rejection by our first love, friends who suddenly turned on us, the absence of someone when we needed and longed for them most. Perhaps they came from physical or emotional abuse, or a moment when, after putting ourselves out there courageously, we were mocked or laughed at. Wounds can feel like betrayal, shame, guilt, contempt, violation, judgment, or neglect. They can be big or small. They can result from many wounds over time, or from one event, one conversation, or one look that triggered a huge reverberation throughout our lives. They can feel like being stabbed with swords, like being shot in the heart by arrows, or like bleeding to death from a thousand scratches.

As children, we experience so many of these moments of wounding, only to repeat them as we go through life. What we've experienced becomes our lens of reality, the filter through which we love, parent, fight, and make decisions. It begins to distort our thinking and view of the world. As a result, everyone around us is also exposed to and affected by our wounding. Our children catch it; they start to copy it, and often repeat the same "mistakes" we made. We then say, "It runs in the family," and resign ourselves to repeating the family history. Alcoholism, drug use, sexual abuse, cheating, rage, avoidance, fear, and anxiety all have roots, and those unaddressed and unhealed roots keep these wounds alive and moving through our lineage. If we don't address them, these become the legacy we leave behind, rather than the health, joy, peace, wealth, and blessings we are called to pass on. If we want to break the generational fears, patterns, ways of thinking—and yes, the curses—and stop passing the baton, we need to get to work on healing our own wounds and restoring inner order.

LOVINGLY MOVING FORWARD

When we are finally willing to face our pain, see it through different eyes, find the root cause, heal it, and say yes to a new life, the doors to true freedom and growth open for us. As we learn to go within our heart space and walk with God, He is able to bring this "brokenness" and wounding to the surface. We will talk later in detail about the process I used myself to restore my heart and come back to my God-given identity—but for now, know that the key is to choose to move forward *lovingly*.

This—the *loving* part—was the part that was always missing for me in the past. I was a master at cutting cords—at cutting people off or out of my life. It was easy to jump ship when something wasn't going according to plan. The problem was that, when something hurt or wasn't working out for me the way I wanted or needed it to, I would often leave it behind in a horrible way. I would let things build and build until they turned into volcanic eruptions of chaos, justifying my desire to run away. I could not lovingly walk away from things. There always had to be a fight, drama, and stress involved. Can you relate? I burned many bridges this way without realizing it. I hit a point where I realized I didn't truly have any close friends to call my inner circle—friends who I truly trusted and could come back to. My ex-husband and I, nearly seven years after our divorce, were still at odds. I had told myself for years, "I'm over it. I'm good. I'm on to the next thing." But I wasn't over it at all. I had let those things go in a harsh way, and—as you will hear me repeat many times—*how* we do something always creates more of the same. Like a boomerang, those same scenarios just keep showing up again. I tried to move on, but never fully emptied myself of the anger, resentment, and bitterness that was still inside me. I cut cords in anger or by rushing to the next thing. I was fearful of staying in the pain for too long or feeling the hurt. I moved on, distracted, full of everything that was never going to get me where I longed to go.

Learning to release the past in a loving way changed everything for me. It was a pivotal moment in which my heart finally unlocked, emptied, and began to soften. Later, this would be crucial to my ability to receive the love, mission, vision, and joy that God had waiting for me all along.

So many people tell me they are not able to receive the love they crave, the help they need, the resources they are seeking, because they are empty. "No," I tell them. "You are not empty. The truth is, *you are too full.*" You are so full that there is no room for anything new. You are so full of resentment toward your ex that there is no room in your heart to fully love your current partner. You are so full of fear that there is no room for faithful forward action. You are so full of ideas about how "all men" are, or how "all women" will treat you, that you have no room to see the amazing person standing right in front of you. You are so full of past failures that you are unwilling to see how much you've gained in the process.

We are not empty. We just *feel* empty because we are full of dense, poisonous thoughts and emotions instead of those which give life and nurture us. Have you ever eaten a whole bag of potato chips only to feel hungry again? You are starving for real nourishment—and this is no different.

So, are you ready to empty yourself so you can be filled with that which nourishes your body, spirit, and soul?

It begins with getting intimate, my love.

Our biology craves touch and connection. Our hearts long to be fully seen and held. And yet, so many of us will do almost anything to avoid the nakedness and deep vulnerability that comes with being fully seen, and therefore fully loved.

Intimacy = Into-me-see.

It's time to see what's inside you—to unlock that powerful and magnetic heart of yours so you can attract what is aligned and repel what is not for you.

But before we go there, I want to familiarize you with the two states that rob us of experiencing intimacy. These states instantly lock our armor back on without us even realizing it!

The first state is your past—whether you're living in it or traveling to it. This can look like wallowing in regret and nostalgia or dreaming about the "good old days." This behavior leaves you comparing today to yesterday, which puts you in a place of lack and fear. Repeatedly time-traveling to the past also brings up all the resentments, fears, bitterness, and disappointments associated with your past. When we go backward, we begin to feel heavy and dense. The weight comes on, and we feel sluggish, unable to move forward.

The second state is the future. When you travel too often into the future, you are unable to enjoy and find contentment in the present. This is the world of "what-if." *What if it doesn't work out? What if I don't make it? What if I can't control it? What if I run out of time, money, or energy? What if he/she doesn't love me enough to stick around? What if* … Here we find ourselves riddled with anxiety, uncertainty, stress, and worry. These feelings keep us frozen in fear.

Most of us have a favorite state we like to hang out in. Some of us ping-pong wildly between the past and future, which feels like a roller coaster ride. The goal is to find your center and normalize being in the present moment, and time-travel only with the intention to heal or create. If you can be where your feet are planted, it is easier to look back with fondness and appreciation and look ahead with excitement and curiosity.

There are three steps to the process of becoming present. I have found these extremely helpful in supporting myself and my clients to unlock our hearts and restore those wounded places. These steps are:

- Radical acceptance
- Forgiveness
- Inner standing

After each of these are explained, you'll find helpful journaling questions to consider as you move through each step.

Step 1: Radical Acceptance

Radical acceptance paves the way to forgiveness by bringing us into compassion, humility, peace, and rest.

Many of us like to jump right to forgiveness or forgetting, cutting the cords and burning the bridges, but there's a critical step that must happen first. Forgiveness and release cannot occur without *radical acceptance.*

"Radical acceptance" is the ability to accept things that are beyond our direct control, without the need to judge them, analyze them, or try to make sense of them. Radical acceptance embraces the idea that suffering does not come directly from our pain or past experiences, but rather from our attachment to the stories we have made about that pain, and our attachment to needing to understand the reasoning behind it. This keeps us cycling in the suffering loop. Non-attachment then becomes a key to overcoming the suffering we have been putting ourselves through. While grief, fear, anger, and disappointment are normal emotions, we suffer far more when we lack acceptance of the situation.

In psychological terms, "acceptance" is a person's ability to be in an uncomfortable, negative, or painful situation without attempting to change or escape it. Acceptance can be found when we release everything that is outside of our direct control and go inward. This also means noticing our triggers. We can quickly tell if something still has a hold on us by how quickly our body reacts. Our thoughts race, our heartbeat increases, our energy shifts, and our entire body is flooded with chemicals screaming *freeze, fight, flee, fawn!*

I used to struggle with acceptance because it felt like by "accepting" what I had gone through I was giving up, failing, or somehow weak. I made others "earn" my forgiveness, then fooled myself into thinking I had forgiven them when in fact I was still holding onto the scores of the past and wishing things had gone differently. Rather than accepting what had unfolded, I held a whip over myself and others, ready to crack it at any sign of noncompliance. I hoped and wished for people to be who they were not, rather than loving and accepting them for who they were.

We will never be able to break free from our past and move into a creative place while we are still full of dissatisfaction. In other words, we cannot design a life we want if we are always fixated on what's wrong! Lack of acceptance blocks the flow of blessings and abundance in our lives. The truth is, you will never be able to accept someone else if you can't accept and love yourself exactly where you are—and that means accepting all your poor decisions and messes as well as your talents and successes. I was often dissatisfied with where I was, and constantly felt the pressure of being behind. I constantly felt as if I should be further ahead, doing more, being more. In turn, I was dissatisfied with others who weren't keeping up or weren't where I needed them to be.

Below are some telltale signs that you are lacking in acceptance. Please note this is not an exclusive list, but rather some common examples I have come across in myself as well as my clients and students.

Thoughts	Feelings	Actions
I can't deal with this	Helpless, hopeless, victimized	Blaming others for your circumstances
This isn't fair	Frustrated, angry, feeling stuck and unable to move forward	Holding grudges and reminding people of past mistakes
Why is this happening to me?	Angry at the world	Lashing out
This isn't right	Judged all the time	Constantly defending yourself while judging others
They should have/ shouldn't have	Frustrated with yourself and others	Giving up on projects or new habits easily
I wish they didn't ...	Regret, sadness, grief	Not taking action to move forward
It's their fault I am ...	Resentful	Withholding love or shutting down

Acceptance turns the game around. It allows us to find rest and move forward. I believe all things happen for a reason, whether we understand them or not, and that God eventually uses all things for good. With acceptance, we can acknowledge that an event happened (or is about to happen) without all the drama.

The picture of Jesus in the Garden of Gethsemane provides such a powerful view of this. He knew full well that he had been betrayed by one of his closest disciples, Judah. He knew he had been sold out and was going to be crucified the next day. His time had come, and that what was about to take place was part of a greater plan for the salvation of humanity. Even in the midst of his most difficult and trying time, Jesus went to the Father with his distress and cried out to Him. Not only did he trust God with his fears, sadness, and requests, but he also trusted the perfect plan God had for his future.

The Serenity Prayer, originally written by Reinhold Niebuhr, and later adopted and popularized by Alcoholics Anonymous, is a beautiful reflection of this.

> *God, grant me the serenity*
> *to accept the things I cannot change,*
> *the courage to change the things I can,*
> *and the wisdom to know the difference.*
> *Living one day at a time,*
> *enjoying one moment at a time;*
> *accepting hardship as a pathway to peace;*
> *taking, as Jesus did,*
> *this sinful world as it is,*
> *not as I would have it;*
> *trusting that You will make all things right*
> *if I surrender to Your will;*
> *so that I may be reasonably happy in this life*
> *and supremely happy with You forever in the next.*
> *Amen.*

We cannot change the past. We cannot change the raw information of what happened, but we can change the meaning, judgment, and emotional charge around it. We can change the story we tell ourselves about it, and the meaning we continue to give it. We can rewrite the story in our nervous system, body, and heart. This does not mean we are giving up; rather, we are moving forward in hope and faith. We do this by asking God to grant us the strength and calmness of mind to accept the things we cannot change or control.

As a Warrior, you probably want to fight your battles alone, and you will keep fighting until you are completely worn out. But some battles are not meant for us to fight alone. And some battlegrounds or circumstances, especially the ones that shattered us, require divine intervention and divine re-orchestration. I believe we don't possess the power through our flesh, ego, or willpower alone to do this. Instead, when we come up to the walls of our own limitations, our Creator steps in to provide us with what we need. Then, we must consistently empty ourselves to receive more.

One final thing to note is that God is a God of process. Like a loving father, He is not interested in how something makes us feel at this moment. Rather, He is interested in the outcome: how it refines us, how it builds us, how it expands our capacity to love and serve others in renewed ways, how it ignites our gifts and calls us to build something beautiful from the ashes of our past. He is building up our character.

Here are two verses that have been helpful reminders for me:

- *"Create in me a clean heart, O God; and renew a right spirit within me."* (Psalm 51:10, KJV)

- *"I can do all this through Him who gives me strength."* (Philippians 4:14, NIV)

Acceptance is not a one-and-done. It's a daily practice of releasing and allowing. However, as you master this practice, you will find that its effects ripple far beyond you. Acceptance gives us the freedom to disagree on our ideas and still choose to love one another as human beings. It accepts that we live in a broken world, with heartbroken people who end up making poor choices. It gives us the ability to access compassion and the freedom to rebuild something beautiful from the ashes of our past.

Step 2: Forgiveness

I have often heard clients say, in a defensive and irritated manner, "But I *did* forgive them!" However, their tone and body language conveyed anything *but* forgiveness.

True forgiveness is a gift. It is bestowed, not earned. If you look at the word itself, "for-give" literally means "to give ahead of time." Once I was able to fully acknowledge my own flawed humanness and forgive myself for all the mistakes I made, I began to see others through the same lens.

Forgiveness requires us to make a conscious decision to release our resentments, desires, and thoughts of revenge toward others. It also invites us to acknowledge and feel the full range of emotions, from grief and anger for the pain we endured to kindness and compassion.

We are human. We are imperfect, flawed, and messy. We are capable of the most beautiful and loving things, as well as the most hurtful and uncalled-for. When hurt, we hurt others. We can continue to judge and throw blame, or we can extend grace and love.

Choosing to forgive does not make the behavior right or discount the events. It just releases us from the chains of anger, regret, shame, and blame, and opens a path to move forward. True Warriors of the Heart extend mercy even—or perhaps especially—when it does not seem deserved. That's what sets them apart from those warriors who are still stuck in proving their power and position.

Forgiveness is the medicine so many of us have been seeking. It cleanses the mind, purifies the body, and renews the spirit, and there is no peace without it. It restores lost time, uncovers old identities, and paves the way to new life. Most of all, it opens the door to the greatest gift available to all humankind: unconditional love.

We all want to feel whole again in our heart, mind, body, and spirit. This wholeness is available from our Father, God, through Jesus, who met us here on this earth, walked among us, and sacrificed his own life so that we could be free and blameless. As is written in Mark 11:24-25: "Therefore I tell you, whatever you ask for in prayer, believe that you have received it, and it will be yours. And whenever you stand praying, *forgive*, if you have anything against anyone, so that your Father also who is in heaven may forgive you your trespasses."

As I began to lean into opening my heart through prayer and meditation, I was given this exercise by God. It is so simple and powerful, and it kept coming up in my mind. Later, as I revisited the Word of God, I found verse upon verse that supported and reaffirmed this process of freedom from the past. What I love is that God showed it to me first, then brought me back to His Word to affirm it, just in case there was any doubt in my mind. His words will never contradict His direction. Whether you begin there, or go there after you begin, you will find that He speaks to us and moves us in a multitude of ways, and that His words will always confirm the whispers He places in our hearts. As we learn to walk with God, we also will learn to recognize His voice and presence. He brings things to the surface when it's time to lovingly work through them, and He will meet us there.

Sometimes, He takes our hands and walks us through a memory, leading us out the other side gently. For example, I was called to revisit the memory of the day we lost our family home. I was seventeen years old, preparing for my upcoming graduation and my new academic journey at Florida State University. However, as I've shared, our home was foreclosed mere weeks before my graduation. My mother, brother, and I were forced to significantly downsize our lifestyle, move into an apartment, and totally change our future plans. Just like that, the future I thought I was going to have and my idea of family life (as unstable as it was) came crashing down. I would not go on to attend FSU. I would no longer have a family home or a family unit. That day was the day my father left us, his family, for good. When I opened my heart and let

God in, what was once a story of deep loss, embarrassment, and anger toward a father who left us became a story of my Spiritual Father laying a new path before me, preparing me to trust Him as I moved through life. In my meditation, He showed me all the ways that He, my Spiritual Father, had been there for me, preparing me for my future calling. The old story made me believe I had a father who didn't care, and that I would lose everything again and again—but the new story showed me a very different reality.

Sometimes, He simply sits with us and holds us as we watch our experiences from a distance. While we watch, He whispers a new story in our ears. This happened for me when I revisited the night when my father attempted suicide. With God's arms around me, I felt, for the first time ever, what it felt like to be safe and unconditionally loved amid external chaos. The love that poured into me rewrote the whole scene, and I began to feel the wound soften and heal over.

Other times there is simply a feeling of His presence infusing the entire scene. The entire chamber of our heart may be filled with a light or energy that we can't describe. As we invite Him into the dark places, the broken places, He makes us whole again. The young, frozen parts of ourselves begin to feel safe in the arms of our Spiritual Father, and something moves and stirs within us. Things are reorganized, restructured, and restored in our past, present, and future, and we see a light guiding our way forward.

Dear Warrior, we are designed to be free agents, not captives! Let us break free of the chains of the past now. We repeat what we experience, so the more you experience *this* moment, the more your new story will come alive and take the place of your old one.

Forgiveness is a decision; therefore, it happens instantly. We extend it and we receive it in this moment. Here and now, it is done, and we claim inner healing knowing we have received it and extended forgiveness to ourselves and others.

Feeling forgiveness fully in our hearts may take some time, so remember that feeling and doing are not the same thing. Just as you may not feel super fit after your first workout, or even after the first month, there is so much happening beneath the surface of your skin. The same is true with this practice. The integration and maturing of your mind and heart will happen over time. Be kind and patient with yourself and others in the process. The work works if you keep showing up.

Forgiveness Prayer Practice

Take a few moments to tune into your breath. Settle into a quiet space of prayer and connect to the Spirit of God, which is the Holy Spirit. Invite the Heart of God to come in and assist you with this process. This is the time for relationship and union.

God will never force Himself on you. You are created in His image, in perfect love, with free will. He awaits your permission to come into your heart and heal you; He wants to be in agreement, in union, with you, not to barge in and take over. Know that you are in full control of what you invite and allow.

Take a breath, and let's begin.

- Feel the loving arms of God, the Father, King of Kings in His perfect heart, holding you securely and tightly. Notice Him looking at you through loving eyes even in the moments you messed up, and showing you grace, mercy, compassion, and understanding.

- Invite Him into the place of your wounding. Was there a specific time and place where this happened? Go there. Take a breath and invite Him into the space where that wound lives in your heart and body. For me, this means inviting Jesus, through whom all things are restored, to walk into this place with me.

- Thank Him for forgiving you in your darkest moments and ask that He work in you and through you to forgive others as you have been forgiven. Forgive yourself, and ask for forgiveness from those you have hurt (knowingly or unknowingly).

- Infuse the healing power and love of God into this entire scene. Fill every corner of your heart as you pour love back into the time and space of the wounding. Notice how the scene and story begin to change shape.

- At this moment, renounce any lies you took on as truth. Break any and all agreements with the old messages, lies, and stories.

- Rewrite the story as you see it now. What do you see and hear from this new place? What is the truth you will remember going forward? What no longer has a hold on you?

Take a few more deep breaths. Sink in and let your entire body, soul, and spirit remember this moment.

Step 3: Wisdom and Understanding

How many times have you heard yourself say something like:

- "I need you to understand what I am saying!"

- "I need them to understand why I did this, what I was thinking!"

- "I need to understand why on earth they did that!"

- Or, even just, "I don't understand."

Why were you seeking that understanding? Did you ever get it—and if you did, what did it actually provide you in the end?

FORGIVENESS LETTERS

You can uncover where forgiveness is needed through writing "forgiveness letters" that focus on whatever is stirring inside you right now. Simply write a letter to the person (or people) who is coming up in your mind and heart right now.

I have found it incredibly powerful to write the first letter to myself. From there, the rest come easier. These can be to people who hurt you, or people you hurt. Write everything that is inside you until you feel empty. Then, you can choose to burn the letters or share them with the person they're addressed to. However, remember that the point is not to get a response from anyone, but rather to practice emptying yourself, releasing yourself from the internal prison you had created. This is such a powerful practice to move forward, experience freedom, and make room to receive what has been waiting for you all along.

My guess is that it gave you some illusion of control or temporary ease from discomfort, but it didn't erase your anger, disappointment, or unease about the situation.

Too many of us feel like we need to comprehend the particulars before we give ourselves permission to move on. Such efforts are a waste of our time and resources and often perpetuate our suffering (as outlined above in the section on radical acceptance). You don't need to understand why someone did what they did, said what they said, or thought what they thought. In fact, you don't need to understand *any* of it.

Instead, redirect your energy, focus, and intention toward the recognition of what truly matters. I call this *inner standing*. It goes with self-reflection: the ability to see within ourselves, and to see ourselves in others. Good, bad, ugly, or glorious, we possess the potential to unleash it all.

Inner standing comes from a place of humbling our ego and allowing compassion, acceptance, and unconditional love to take over our minds and hearts. When we embrace God-centered wisdom instead of ego-driven knowledge, we are no longer directed by the propaganda, lies, and deceptions that have been implanted in our psyche. We are no longer on a hunt for validation and setting the score right. We know that all is perfect, and everything that transpires ultimately moves us toward learning and expansion. Inner standing gives us a new set of eyes. When we see through our fixed, physical eyes, we can only see a sliver of what's going on. On the other hand, when we see from the top down, with our spiritual eyes and heavenly view, we can take in the full landscape of a situation. Our spiritual eyes also offer us access to a new emotion: a heart of compassion. While empathy allows us to feel what others feel, compassion allows us to mobilize the feeling in a positive way—to *act* differently and *respond* differently. This is how we begin to break generational patterns of wounding.

When we are no longer willing to repeat the same old story and pass it on, we break free from the past and rewrite the storyline for ourselves, our children, and our children's children, as well as those we lead, teach, and interact with. By activating the gifts of self-reflection, awareness, acceptance, and forgiveness, we receive the healing available to us and pass it on. Most of all, we develop the ability to identify and embody unconditional love.

THE REFINER'S FIRE

In the fall of 2018, I was attending a coaching certification conference with colleagues who were trained in creating breakthrough experiences.

One evening, we gathered around the fire pit, and one of the men in the group facilitated a visualization exercise for us. As I dropped into this meditative space, I found myself asking God to give me a glimpse of the relationship and *the one* He had for me. I didn't know when, or if, this relationship was ever going to be a reality (since, as I've shared, my relationships historically tended to be fraught with drama). But I asked anyway.

At that moment, I saw myself standing in the woods. Sensing a presence behind me, I turned around ... and I saw him. He was tall and muscular with dark hair. I could make out the contours of his face and eyes, but not the details. There was an energy about his presence. A sense of safety and warmth swept over me. At that moment, he wrapped his arms around me, and I allowed myself to receive his embrace. This felt like home. We just stood there, holding each other, breathing each other in. And then, I looked up and saw him smiling down at me—again, no details, but a feeling and a knowing. There he was. There I was. There we were. In perfect time, in perfect order: a divine appointment.

I opened my eyes and looked into the crackling flames of the campfire. I felt the cool breeze of a fall evening settling in around me, and thought, "That was sweet, whatever that was."

And that was that.

A few weeks passed, then a month. I began to revisit that feeling. I was ready to begin the journey of inner work I knew I had to face to have any chance of experiencing a safe embrace like that—an embrace that melted me into a sacred space of oneness. There were conversations to have, and old residues and relationships to clean up. I needed to learn to gently care for and pour love into my heart to ensure that my armor did not come back, and I knew I could not rush this process.

And so, I got to work on unlocking the power of my beautiful heart, lovingly releasing the past and emptying myself so I could receive the support I needed to move forward. It was during this time that I first experienced many of the ideas and practices I've shared in this chapter.

This process is not easy, and it isn't instantaneous. In fact, I found myself in discomfort much of the time. However, don't be tempted to skip the preliminary details and preparations and jump forward to the reward. Rare is the case where we are already equipped to handle the good things we are seeking in our lives. We can't get and maintain the good parts without the work. We can't get the body without the training. We can't get to financial prosperity without learning to manage and invest our money wisely. We can't experience intimacy, acceptance, and connection while remaining unwilling to get honest and vulnerable with ourselves and others.

Most of us have not yet cultivated the strength, stamina, or faith to sustainably show up for the things our hearts long for. If we get them too soon, we only end up making a hot mess of it. In order to get to the rich, juicy, delicious part, we have got to go through seasons of wilderness and darkness. Most of us will sabotage or quit our mission before we get there because we don't want to sit in discomfort with our aloneness. However, as the saying goes, "God doesn't call the equipped, He equips the called." If you are willing to walk the path, you will be given what you need to survive it.

I love and resonate deeply with the element of fire. Fire can be destructive, but it also offers inviting, lifesaving warmth and necessary purification. Throughout scripture, fire represents the presence of God. Moses encountered God at the burning bush; later, God appeared in a pillar of fire to lead His people in the wilderness (see Exodus 3:2; 13:21). In the New Testament, the gift of the Holy Spirit comes to the apostles as flames of fire (see Acts 2:3).

A refiner uses fire to heat metal until it is molten, but the fire does not destroy the metal. Rather, the molten state allows the impurities within the metal to separate and come to the surface so that the refiner can remove them. A refiner's fire makes the metal better and stronger, bringing out its full value. It literally brings the treasure out of the dross and into physical existence.

Similarly, the Fire of God does not consume or destroy us, but instead refines and renews us. In our darkest moments, we discover and come face to face with the Heart of God. As we get to see and know His heart, we discover our own heart—our fierce and loving heart that has been humbled and redirected. A Warrior of the Heart loves fiercely and leads courageously, equipped with strength, grace, compassion, kindness, faith, acceptance, steadfastness, understanding, and a heart that chooses love as the standard.

WARRIOR INITIATION

- What happened in the past that you are still holding onto, unwilling to accept, judging, or feeling like a victim to? What are you still hoping and wishing would have gone differently? Is there a different story you can begin to tell yourself about this event? Can you begin to see what gifts, strengths, and talents were placed in you that this event unlocked and ignited?

- What parts of yourself are you still not willing to accept?

- Who needs your forgiveness now? Who have you been withholding forgiveness from?

- Do you see a parallel between your ability to accept others and your ability to accept the same things within yourself?

- What is a situation in your life right now that requires inner standing (wisdom) rather than reasoning?

- What stories are you able to rewrite and see through new eyes?

- What does it mean to you to connect to the Heart of God?

CHAPTER EIGHT

Remember Who You Are

"It's not who you think you are that holds you back. It's who you think you are not."

— **DENIS WAITLEY**

My mother was from a relatively small town in Italy. She grew up in a time and place where social status and formal education were considered symbols of a person's worth and value. From as far back as I can recall, I remember the strong cultural importance placed on people's influence, education status, and occupation. It was as if there was always a comparison between who *they* were and who *we* were.

Much fuss was made about so-and-so being a doctor, an engineer, or a professor—and even more fuss was made about how we should behave around those people, dress around them, and speak around them. Whenever we would visit such people or have them in our home, I was constantly reminded how *important* they were and how I needed to "be on my best behavior."

Now, there's nothing wrong with caring for your physical appearance or being respectful of others; respect is essential to relationships. The problem was that I learned to do these things to seek approval, please my mother, and not feel inferior to others. I can still feel the flood of shame and irritation that would come over me at times as a child. It created a ton of confusion. Intuitively, I knew this didn't make sense; something was off. The fact that someone was a doctor or a lawyer didn't make them "better" than us.

But I went along with it. Why? Because I was told to.

I was *told*. That's how it was. *That's what "good" children do. That's what it looks like to be polite and respectful.*

And so it happens that ideas, fears, and insecurities that are not our own—not from within us, or from God our Creator, but from generations of flawed humans before us—are handed down from one generation to the next.

In Italy, there were no phys-ed classes in elementary school. Everything was focused on academics, and I had little to no exposure to sports other than playing in the garden or taking ballet lessons. So, it was natural to feel like a fish out of water when, upon moving to the States, I was required to spend an hour a day picking (or getting picked for) teams, running, and competing at different sports. Needless to say, I did not enjoy this process at all.

Then came middle school. There I was, one of the last people to get picked for the kickball team ... again. Then, some random kid told me I sucked at sports, which dug the dagger in deeper. That day, a part of me made a decision that I was not an athlete—that, in fact, I did not have an athletic bone in my body.

In one day, I acquired a wound that would affect my identity. I let some boy—a boy who was insecure in his own right, and who resorted to bullying others to make himself feel more important—tell me who I was, rather than trusting what I knew inside. I believed his lie: *You suck at running. You are not good enough to make the team. Don't even try!* For the next two years, I avoided all sports. I refused to get dressed for gym class. I avoided any activity that involved running of any sort. I refused to try out for anything where there was a chance of failure.

The truth? I was really, *really* good at sports. Talented, in fact.

I finally decided to put myself out there. I went for soccer tryouts, partly because my dad was a soccer fan and I wanted to impress him. Also, I had some friends who were into soccer and I was feeling the pressure to fit in. Something beautiful happened at those tryouts and in the upcoming season. To my surprise, a gift showed up I never knew was in me. I realized, "Dang! I *am* pretty good at this sports thing." Little did I know I would soon become one of the most naturally athletic people I know. I went on to become a lover of sports—an avid skier, an amazing runner who consistently won races, a world class triathlete competing at two world championships, and eventually a coach helping others to do the same. I was a lover of all things to do with fitness and challenging my body.

The lesson here is that I believed a lie that was *totally opposed to who I am at my core,* and to the gifts God gave me. It was an assault on my natural talent, my passions, and the skill sets that opened doors to entrepreneurship and wealth for me.

I trust you get the gist.

What changed is that I gave myself permission to do it differently. To gain wisdom and follow where I was led. As I pushed back on the lies and leaned into more of what I knew deep inside, I rediscovered what I knew all along but had been ignoring.

Today, most of my clients are experts and leaders in their fields who hire me to help them break free of the rigid boxes they've locked themselves into—to dissolve the doubt and confusion that has been looming over them around their identity, value, worth, and purpose. A huge part of that work is breaking free of this one-dimensional identity they have constructed and helping them identify the lies they believed and internalized about themselves. Only then can we discover who they are at their core, beyond the titles, the degrees, the relationship status, the bank balance, or the toys in their garage.

The more lies we believe about who we are, the further we get from who we are created to be and the reason we are here, in this body, at this time.

Everything we believe about ourselves has been planted in our minds through our experiences, interactions, and conversations. Even before our creation, God planted seeds inside us to help us remember who we are. Our soul is uniquely designed. Our spirit is one with His Spirit. After our birth, the people and environments around us either watered those seeds of truth and life or strangled them with seeds of doubt, confusion, shame, and so forth. Sometimes those seeds were planted with good intentions, but they were poor seeds that produced bad fruit.

So, what seeds were planted inside you that have influenced your identity? Which seeds have you watered and fertilized, and which have you allowed to lie dormant?

We can quickly find the answer to this question by looking at the scenarios we have manifested over and over in our lifetime. Our current reality is a direct product of the seeds we have nurtured—and there is no seed more dangerous to life and to our divine purpose than *doubting and distorting our God-given identity and value.*

It's time to ditch all the lies about who you are, who you are not, and who you need to become in order to be happy, fulfilled, wealthy, and wise. Instead, it's time to remember who you actually are, and to accept and love all that you are—your soul, your spirit, your heart, your uniqueness.

The Greek word for spirit is *pneuma*, which means "connected with breath" or "breath of life." It has also been defined as "connected to God." Your spirit is the heavenly, spiritual part of you that is in union with God. Your spirit is always postured toward God. The joy, presence, peace, wisdom, knowledge, and grace of God can only be experienced through His Spirit, and in our spirit. This explains the scriptures, teachings, and philosophy of having "God within us" and our ability to do all things through Christ who is alive inside us. It is the spirit that gives and senses peace, true love, and the everlasting. When our spirit becomes disconnected from God, there is an inner restlessness that can't be explained, only experienced. The peace has gone.

The Greek word for soul is *psyche*, which encompasses the mind, will, emotions, desires, and unique expression of a human being. Our soul is essentially our unique personality—the "blueprint" of our humanity. It is witnessed and expressed through our personal preferences, the choices we make, the things we bring into the world, what lights us up, and what shuts us down. Moreover, it is our unique life force which can be directed by our will, by external forces, or by God. This is why we often hear terms such as "selling your soul," and hear misaligned activities described as "soul-sucking."

When your soul is not fully expressed and connected to the Source of life, it feels like you are dying a slow death inside. The ultimate battle you will fight in this life is *the battle for your soul.* What you give your heart and soul to is what you ultimately entwine your spirit with. Our spirits are designed to be in union with God, however many of us have sold our souls to the lies we were told and the ideas we were taught to value. This results in us closing down our hearts so we can no longer fully access the Spirit within. When we do that, spiritual peace and access to unconditional love become impossible.

I know this place well. I spent years feeling like my soul needed a bath. I had disconnected from God, from my creative life force, and from the ability to give and receive real love. My heart became hardened, angry, unforgiving—until I came back home and remembered who I was, and who I was not.

It's hard for us to understand the magnitude of this soul homecoming until we have experienced it. This journey is an experiential and relational one; we cannot think our way through it.

HAVE YOU FORGOTTEN WHO YOU ARE?

There is a reason we are attacked at the very core of our being, nonstop, from a young age. There is an entity, a spiritual enemy, that is against God—against everything that God created, everything that is life-giving, and everything that was ordained to multiply and prosper in its natural state. That force wants you to forget who you are and where you come from—for if you are disconnected from your spirit, your very essence, you are disconnected from the Source of life and from love itself.

Love sustains life. Love nourishes life. Love multiplies life. God, at His essence, is love, and love is the foundation of the whole universe.

When we forget who we are, we step out of love—and where there is an absence of love, there is darkness and despair. Instead of drinking from the life-giving well, we remain thirsty and starved, chasing empty promises that never provide what we truly need. We believe that if we look a certain way, do a certain thing, earn a certain status, that we will gain what was promised.

These false promises are shiny, subtle, alluring, and enchanting.

They seem like the real deal, but they never come from the Source of life. They come from copycats. *"Beware of the false prophets, [teachers] who come to you dressed as sheep [appearing gentle and innocent], but inwardly are ravenous wolves."* (Matthew 7:15-16, AMP)

The ultimate copycat, of course, is Lucifer, who separated from God.

The primary function of angels was to glorify God and interface between God and the people. Lucifer, one of the most magnificent of these angels, was described by Ezekiel as, "the model of perfection, full of wisdom and exquisite in beauty." (Ezekiel 28:12, NLT) He held a high-ranking position and had great power and influence, but that was not enough for him. He became so impressed with his own beauty that he started to desire the honor and glory that was given to God. Because of his pride, he separated from God—and fell from heaven, taking a third of the angels with him.

Not all powers in the universe have an agenda to sustain love, life, and creation. Even the new "love and light" movement can lead to pride, self-glorification, and self-worship. You will know when you are separated from God when you are battling for selfish gain and your spirit is not at rest. The very things we seek in our disconnection are the things God has already given us, through Him.

The spiritual realm is vast, deep, and wide, and we are more than just physical beings. The spiritual part of us is *eternal* while the physical is fleeting, yet because we are in a physical world, most of our focus around identity is rooted in the physical nature of ourselves rather than the spiritual and soul level.

So, if we are going to remember who we are at our core, we must open our eyes to the fact that not everything we witness, believe, and are told is truth. Not everything is Love with a capital L. So, it's time to start paying attention. The more you remember who you are—and who you are not and were never created to be—the more you will experience the truth of you, and the fullness of life for which you were created.

This is not the time for judgment. Your heart has been opened, and emptied, and filled again; we are done with judgment. Now, we are simply exploring and bringing to the surface what needs to either rise and exit, or rise and be confirmed.

We will begin by clarifying and redefining who and what we *are not*, as well as *where we do not come from* so we can eliminate the old lies from our frame of reference once and for all. Then, we will rediscover where we *do* come from, and what God our Creator has to say about who we are.

WHO ARE YOU *NOT*?

The world has taught us to define ourselves by what we do, what we have, what we accomplish, and our relationship status.

Think about it. When you go to a party or are first introduced to someone, the question is almost immediate: "What do you do?" It's so ingrained in us. We come home and tell each other what we "did" today. We focus on all the things we "did right" and "did wrong," and the never-ending list of things we still "need to do."

I admit, I still catch myself in this loop more often than I'd like. In fact, at a recent women's wealth conference I attended, I found myself asking people, "What's your name?" and then, immediately, "So, what do you do? What business are you in?" It's crazy how much of our focus is around work and busyness. Perhaps these are just formalities we have fallen into over time—societal norms that don't seem like a big deal at face value. However, when we lift the veil, we see the problem with this identity game: we think that what someone does will reveal to us who they are.

So, what were the identities you were told you were—that you needed to assume, needed to be?

The best way to tell if you're dealing with your true nature or an assumed identity is to notice whether it's conditional. Identities will usually be framed something like this:

- "If you want to [insert goal here], you need to be [insert quality here]."

My false identities go something like this:

- If you want to be an expert, be well-paid, and have clients pouring in, you need to become the most qualified expert in your space with professional pedigree.

- If you want to win, you need to be the strongest/ fittest/most successful person in the game.

- If you want people to like you, you need to be the shiniest and loudest object in the room.

Yours are probably similar. Many of our identities were assumed to help us survive and succeed. But they also block us from accessing our true identity as a Warrior of the Heart.

Other identities were forged in response to who we believed we had to be in order to be loved and accepted.

One of the most powerful questions I heard Tony Robbins ask people at his live events was, "Whose love did you crave the most growing up, and who did you need to be in order to gain their love/ approval/connection?"

As we discussed in Chapter Seven, we are wired for love, connection, and intimacy by design. It is part of our core identity to love, to be loved, and to connect with others. However, our life experiences often prompt us to change who we are at our core or compromise a part of ourselves in order to gain the love and connection we crave so deeply.

An identity developed around connection can sometimes be framed like this:

- "In order to be loved or belong, I have to be [insert quality here]."

In practice, this can show up as people-pleasing—being "the easy one," "the peacemaker," or "the caretaker." Many people receive a lot of connection and approval from identities and behaviors like these. However, this kind of love is conditional. Only when we remove the masks and identities can we receive true love and authentic connection.

Can You Spot the Lies?

Can you spot the lies that fed and established your false identities?

Here are some of the most common lies I have come into contact with in myself and my clients. As you read each one of them, really let them sink in. Ask yourself, "Is this really true? Is this the ultimate truth of who I am and all I am created for?"

- *Lie #1: I am what I have.* My identity is determined by my stuff and how much I have gained.

- *Lie #2: I am what I do.* My identity is determined by a job title, achievement, position on a team, or occupation.

- *Lie #3: I am my relationships.* My identity is solely determined by my relationship status: mother, fiancé, wife, husband, best friend, etc.

- *Lie #4: I am the labels others have put on me.* My identity is one of an illness or diagnosis, or being the _____ one in the family.

- *Lie #5: I am who others see me as.* My identity is determined and dependent on others' opinions, judgments, and moods.

- *Lie #6: I am my past.* My identity was shaped by my parents, my family, my traumas, and/or the circumstances in which I was raised.

- *Lie #7: I am my behavior.* My identity is the sum total of my habits, choices, and behaviors.

- *Lie #8: I am a God/Goddess.* I am the sole entity responsible for my life and outcomes.

It's dangerous to build your house on a foundation of sand. And each of the core identities listed above is like sand, always shifting and changing shape. These things change constantly with external conditions and other people's feelings, sometimes without any reason or plan, and can fall apart at any moment. If we have built our whole sense of self on the foundation of these factors, when the thing that makes us who we are crumbles or exits our lives, we crumble right along with it. We become lost and completely forget who we are.

Lie #1: I Am What I Have

As I've shared, we lost our primary home when I was seventeen. So, when I began rebuilding my life and was able to get my own place, purchase my own cars, make my own money, put the kids in private school, and begin to see assets accumulate, money got a hold of me. The big house, the massive landscaping jobs, the copious amount of stuff we were surrounded by started to become a weight. Before I realized it, I was waking up with anxiety around "losing" my things. The fear started to seep in. My identity had gotten hijacked! I had to come to the realization that I am not the building, I am not the stuff, I am not the amount of money in my savings or retirement accounts. I am so much more than that.

When everything in your life begins to revolve around one "I am," it's time for a personal reality check.

I often work with clients whose parents were relentless about grades and school or sports performance. They were only seen and acknowledged when they brought home the perfect grades, achievements, and trophies. There were so many expectations to live up to, and so many opportunities to be lavished with attention or crushed and called out for missing the mark (sometimes literally). Later in life, the trophies become status symbols: exotic cars, bigger houses, lake homes, airplanes, etc. But what happens when our stuff disappears? Who are we then?

Lie #2: I Am What I Do

I am a natural athlete. However, once I decided to embrace that part of myself, I attached an "athlete" identity to it. I couldn't rest until I scored a certain number of goals. Trained for a certain number of hours. Won the race. Won another race. Crushed the competition every time, even in a simple game of tennis with family. I not only ate a certain way to fuel my performance, but I also made everyone else feel bad for not doing so.

Later in my life, my "athlete" identity morphed into the "self-made business owner" identity. But the inner message was the same: *if you want to be worthy, you need to be the best.*

It felt great to tell people I was a business owner, entrepreneur, and the ultimate boss of my own reality. For a while, it was fun and enticing. I felt like the sky was the limit ... until that identity got such a hold of me that I could not separate myself from it to see the other layers of myself.

I became obsessed with the business owner within, and would only feel satisfied (for a brief moment) when I was making money, growing the business, serving clients, or "expanding" in some way. In that season of my life, I was also the sole provider for my family, so the pressure to produce was huge. But I was not connected to trust, and I placed a lot of my self-worth on the success of my "doing." The minute things didn't go my way, I felt like I was a failure as a person—which was, of course, a huge lie.

Lie #3: I Am My Relationships

How many times have you heard the saying, "You are the sum of the five people you spend the most time with"?

Many of us create our identity based on who is in our orbit. We think that if we marry the right person, work for the right person (or company), hang out with the right friends, or have the right connections, it says something to others about who we are. If our kids think we are the coolest parent on the block, we feel valuable and needed. If our spouse respects us and shows affection toward us, we feel worthy and lovable. If we are part of the club, our friends are well known and invite us to events, we must be worthy of special privileges. If we know certain people, we must be someone worth knowing.

It's very hard to have a genuine connection with someone when you're worried about what their true self says about you—or whether a glimpse of *your* true self will drive them away. As a result, relationships in which identity is at stake tend to be exhausting to keep up, transactional in nature, lonely, and unfulfilling. It's hard to build trust when every move we make is done in an attempt to support someone's self-worth.

If our identity comes from our current relationship status, it can also be a devastating blow when that relationship changes. Close friends turn on one another or lose touch. Children eventually grow up and move out. Loved ones pass away. Some of us have lost children in this lifetime. I have seen people completely lose themselves after divorce or a loss of a child, never to be the same. I have also seen people who realized they were more than that one role, taking those moments of loss and turning them into powerful stories that created change for the world, building businesses and foundations from the ashes.

Lie #4: I Am the Labels Others Have Put on Me

How much of your life has been dominated by labels—names you were called, qualities others assigned to you, certain diagnoses, or anything others told you about yourself that caused you to feel different or separate?

Some people limit themselves for their whole lives because they have become entangled and enmeshed with a label. That bully's comment about how I was "bad at sports" stuck with me for years. My clients who were told they were "sick," "stupid," "stubborn," or "too much" have internalized those definitions of themselves and made decisions accordingly.

Any label slapped onto us by siblings, parents, teachers, or even well-meaning friends can hold us back. In many families, one child is labeled as "the smart one," while another is "the athletic one" or "the artsy one" or "the black sheep." In school, there might be "the loud-mouth," "the teacher's pet," "the jock," "the class clown," or "the popular one."

A label is simply a description that our human mind conjures up to help us make sense of information so we can categorize it. *The Merriam-Webster Dictionary* defines the word "label" this way: "to assign to a category, especially inaccurately or restrictively." Isn't that interesting? Inaccurately, restrictively—and, may I also suggest, *incompletely*. No label could possibly contain the full picture of you.

Then, there are the limitations we take on based on diagnoses, both physical and mental. This is not to say that many people don't legitimately deal with various illnesses and conditions, or that symptoms and challenges are not present, and I am by no means discounting mental illness, physical illnesses, or anything of the sort. However, accepting that we are having an experience and telling ourselves that we "are" our experience are very different things.

When we are given a diagnosis, it might explain a lot about our current circumstances. However, when the lines become blurred, we can easily lose ourselves inside those labels. For example, a diagnosis of a learning disability can quickly become, "I can't learn. I'm stupid. I'm incapable. I'm forever frustrated." A diagnosis of depression or anxiety can quickly have people shifting from "I feel depressed" to "I *am* depressed," or from "I feel anxious" to "I *am* anxious." Over time, these "I AM" statements grow deep roots and become self-fulfilling prophecies.

I would like to suggest that the very labels that we have put on ourselves, or that were put on us by others, are often indicative of misinterpreted and misunderstood *gifts*. That, in fact, the areas where we are most gifted are also often the areas where we struggle to channel energy in the most focused and powerful ways.

For example, I know many entrepreneurial and creative people, including myself, who have either been diagnosed with or labeled ADD or ADHD. Our inability to focus in the way traditional institutions have deemed appropriate has been seen as troublesome for others. Often, the solution has been pharmaceutical drugs. What I have realized in my own life, as a parent of children with these diagnoses, and as a coach to many students, is that many of us simply need a different structure for our focus to flow. Humans are not designed to fit into boxes. We are designed uniquely, but across our evolution we've created factory-like systems in an effort to standardize things. Ultimately, this works against us.

Labels and descriptions do have their place, though. They can help us make sense of some of the confusion and upset of being human. Giving something a name can help us make sense of what we're experiencing in our mind and body. A personality test can help us see our true gifts more clearly and learn how to work with them in a productive way instead of judging ourselves. At the end of the day, it's all information; it's what we choose to do with it that matters. It can provide great insight for us to take ownership and set ourselves up for better healing and success. However, labels stop being helpful when they begin to indicate that there is something "wrong" with us.

Where have labels helped you in your own life, and where have they held you back?

As you examine this, remember that, at any time, you can decide that you are not the labels. Rather, the labels are inaccurate, restrictive, and/or incomplete explanations of certain attributes you demonstrate. While they may be a part of the picture, they most certainly are not the whole picture.

Lie #5: I Am Who Others See Me As

This is related to labels, but not the same. This lie has more to do with letting your behavior create your identity, and with the false identities you create in order to be loved.

For example, it's easy to believe that if others see you as beautiful, you are beautiful. After all, as they say, "Beauty is in the eye of the beholder." But what about kindness? Helpfulness? Strength? Intellect?

If your identity exists in the eye of the beholder, you are also subject to that beholder's feelings, mood swings, and identity struggles. We often see others through the same lens we see ourselves through. Are you still kind if the recipient of your kindness doesn't acknowledge your efforts? Are you still giving even if someone doesn't say "thank you"? Are you still strong if others don't ask you for help?

Of course, we all want to be acknowledged for our best qualities. But if your whole identity can be influenced by how other flawed humans respond to you, you will never feel like you're on solid ground.

Lie #6: I Am My Past

It's easy to get wrapped up in the pains and stories of our past, especially when there was abuse or trauma. As we've learned, traumas create lasting imprints in our nervous systems, psyches, and souls. But we must separate the *memories* and *experiences* we went through from our true self and inner being.

You are not what happened to you. You are not what someone else did to you. You are not what your parents did or didn't do. You are not the result of anyone else's poor or great decisions. You may have experienced many of these things, for there are real life consequences of choices, but again, *we are not the decision.*

I know this distortion of identity intimately. I experienced so much embarrassment around my father's choices. I allowed his shame and anger to become my own. In a determined effort to *never* repeat his mistakes, I ironically ended up embodying many of the same traits that robbed him of the joy and fulfillment he was created for: perfectionism, "never-enoughness," and lack of trust among them. I am forever thankful that I woke up in time—that my breakdown moments shook me loose from this, and that I was able to choose to walk the path of deep inner healing.

Even if you don't have a traumatic or challenging past, it's likely that you have assumed at least a few of the collective identities of your ancestors and/or past generations. Maybe you came from a long line of doctors, engineers, or professors, and there was an expectation that you would follow the same path, even though it wasn't your true calling. When you look in the mirror, do you see someone who is living a split life, trying to be who they are "supposed" to be rather than who they were created to be (and secretly dream of being)?

Conversely, are you trying to run away from a family identity? For example, perhaps you grew up in poverty and experienced great loss as a child. After years of scraping by to make ends meet, you swore, no matter what, that you would never, ever go back there again. In an attempt to break free of poverty and scarcity, you enslaved yourself to the fear of loss. Now, while your outer world reflects riches, when you look in the mirror you still see a "poor kid" trying to prove his worth.

If you're not sure whether your identity is being defined by your past, here are a few questions that may reveal where there are still ties to be dissolved:

- *Are you still trying to hide it?* Are you unwilling to share your stories, talk about what happened, or accept that certain events actually took place?

- *Are you avoiding anything that reminds you of your past?* There is a fine line between having new standards of what we will allow into our lives and outright avoiding things because we are afraid to face what comes up when we confront them.

- *Are you shutting down?* Are you numbing yourself to cut off the potential pain?

- *Are you picking fights about anything that activates a wound?*

- *Are you easily offended and/or do you feel constantly judged?*

- *Are you unapproachable or threatening to others?* When our inner child/past self is feeling threatened, we can become the aggressor in an attempt to protect ourselves, even if the person in front of us is not a threat.

- *Are you always trying to control your environment?* Are you trying to keep things neat, tidy, and under wraps so no one sees how close you are to freaking out?

If any of these are true for you, don't judge yourself. Just take your new awareness into the next part of this chapter so you can begin to work with it.

Lie #7: *I Am My Behavior*

We are human. It is 100 percent guaranteed that we will make mistakes. We make poor decisions from time to time. We get overwhelmed and forget important things, like our anniversary or our spouse's birthday (yikes!). We lose our temper and yell at the people we love most. We get exhausted and give in to yet another night of mindless television so we can escape reality. We can easily fall off-track, get distracted, and get out of order if we are not anchored to solid ground and consistently checking in with who we truly are and where we want to go.

Regardless of what your behaviors are, however ...

You are not your actions.

That is not to say that our actions and choices—both conscious and unconscious—don't reflect our character and our beliefs about ourselves.

They do. They also reflect what we believe we can handle, what we believe we are capable of, and what we think we are worthy of.

Most of all, they reflect what we believe about God—who He is, what He is capable of, what He thinks about us, and what He will and will not do for us and the world.

Classic signs that you have gotten your identity mixed up with your actions include:

- Constantly beating yourself up about "who you are" or what you did.
- Calling yourself and others names and attacking character.
- Blaming yourself for "screwing up."
- Blaming others for how they made you feel or how they ruined things for you.
- Withholding forgiveness from yourself and others.

This is a heavy place to live. We are not designed to carry the burdens and mistakes of our past. That is what the gift of forgiveness is for. The gift of salvation is truly the gift to be freed from the "sins" of our past.

On a side note: I, and many of us, have a lot of trauma around the word "sin" and how it has been used to control and coerce people throughout history. However, when we dig deeper into the Hebrew definition of "sin," we find that the word for sin, *chet/chata*, simply means "to miss the mark, to fall short." When we act out and behave in a way that has us missing the mark for what God intends for us, we fall short of receiving *all* He intends for us. We miss out on the love, abundance, and the gifts available to us—not because we are being punished, but because we are aiming at the wrong target.

This shift in thinking has been instrumental for me in coming back on target in my life. I know without a doubt that, when I miss the mark,

I fall short of the full potential of the moment. Maybe I missed out on an intimate moment with my husband, a joyful experience with my kids, or a great opportunity in my business, all because I was aiming to do things my own way. Not because I was being punished. Not because I was doing something "bad." Simply because I wasn't fully present and aiming correctly—because I was living in the future, trying to rush and race against time, or reliving the past.

If you look back at your past decisions, you will notice that the decisions that feel like "poor" ones are those that led you further from peace and freedom. Because you were aiming for the wrong things—instant gratification, superficial needs, worldly security, ego fulfillment, etc.—your choices fell short of your true potential and God's design for you.

When you are aiming toward God and His love, there is an internal sense of peace and order. There is calm, even in the storms. When I began to get my aim right and put my focus back on the things that were true for me, everything good in my life began to multiply and increase. As I received the forgiveness that was always granted to me through Jesus Christ, and extended myself more and more forgiveness, I was able to access new levels of compassion, empathy, and grace for others as well—to forgive them for missing the mark, because they are also human.

I believe this is what it means to walk in righteousness. It's not piety, superiority, or religious dogma. It's to walk the right path, from the right place in your heart, with your focus on the right things.

Lie #8: I Am a God/Goddess

We have already covered this extensively in this book, but it bears repeating: you are not the sole entity in charge of your life and destiny. As humans, we are not Gods or Goddesses with a capital "G."

There are a lot of teachers today trying to convince us we are sovereign creators. I went down this route for a season. Many things manifested in my life that I set out to accomplish. But at some point, I lost touch with the fact that we plan our course, but God ordains our steps. I began to think that I was the ultimate source and creator of my reality. I took on an identity as the Creator. And while some of that was true, it was an incomplete truth.

Constantly trying to be the sole creator of your reality is exhausting and unsustainable. Constantly trying to manifest and hold the highest mental/emotional/physical state possible *through your own will* means you will be in constant battle with your deepest longings, fears, desires, and needs.

So many people—my past self included—are unwilling or terrified to admit when they are struggling, sad, grieving, or simply in need of help because they are afraid to "manifest" something bad into their world. This can quickly become a sort of toxic positivity, where one is only willing to accept the positive aspects of life and unwilling to love and accept the rest. This idea teaches that if something bad happens to someone, they *must* have brought it on themselves through consequence or karma. In such a worldview, there is no room for compassion, grace, deep nurturing, or service. There is only judgment.

What is in us needs to be seen, felt, honored, laid down, and surrendered. It needs to be processed and moved. We are designed to need God and be reflections of His love and presence in the world, not to be gods ourselves. We are designed to be filled with the Spirit of God, not to be full of ourselves. We are incomplete and imperfect on purpose; we are made complete in union with the Spirit, and become whole again when we allow the empty, lost, weak, scared, lacking parts of us to be filled by the Source of all.

WHO ARE YOU AT YOUR CORE?

We have already determined that most, if not all, of us have bought into lies about who we are. After reading the previous section, you probably have a more concrete idea of who you are not.

But if you are not what you have, what do you, who you're with, what happened to you, or how others see you ... well, then, who are you?

Given what we now know, it only makes sense to go directly to the Source—the One who created you, and all of us—and ask, "God, who do *you* say I am?"

Who God Says We Are

For most of my early life, I saw the Bible as a book full of suffocating rules and outdated stories that were simply not relevant to me. Truthfully, I never spent much time in the "Good Book" on my own; mostly, I just picked up what I heard through the occasional church service and random scripture that popped up on my news feed. Mostly, I treated it like a fortune cookie, keeping the things I liked and throwing out the rest.

Until, one day, God's Word clearly called me back. His words whispered for me to put aside everything I thought I knew about what was written and instead begin to receive His words at a deeper level—not through a third party, but through my own heart and the prompting of the Holy Spirit. I came alive in ways I had never experienced before. The entire way I looked at myself changed, as well as my ability to receive and give love.

Suddenly, I was able to take on a new identity—one based on a series of truths rather than a pile of lies. I learned that:

- *Truth #1*: I am created in His image.
- *Truth #2:* I am created in love, by love, to be a vessel of love.
- *Truth #3:* I am created on purpose, for a divine purpose.
- *Truth #4*: I am chosen and beloved by the One who knows everything about me.

- *Truth #5:* I belong, for I am His child.

- *Truth #6:* I am worthy, for I am His heir.

- *Truth #7:* I am multidimensional and uniquely designed on purpose.

- *Truth #8:* I am gifted and talented.

- And, most of all ...

- *Truth #9:* I am human!

Our Spiritual Father has already established our identity in His Word. It's unfortunate that so many have never experienced or received His words firsthand, because there is quite a love story to be revealed if we are willing to hear from Him with our minds and hearts open to truly receive.

Truth #1: I Am Created in His Image

Once I received this as truth, it completely changed the way I look at myself and others.

As a mother, I already know what it's like to look into the eyes of your child and see both a reflection of yourself and someone who is beautiful and unique in their own way. My children are created in an image of me. They are not me, but they possess many of the innermost parts of me. In them, I am carried into the world, and my legacy continues. They sometimes can also be mirrors of me—of the seeds I have planted inside them. It brings me so much joy to know that the same desires, passions, and joys that make my children light up are the ones I share with them.

Before, when I would look in the mirror, I would see a catalogue of faults and a few things I was proud of. Now, I look for the parts of me that are created in His image. I look for the loving parts, the beautiful parts, the forgiving parts, the just parts, the merciful, wonderful, miraculous parts. It's an entirely different view.

We have been trained to focus on the wrong images, and therefore have formed distorted images of ourselves. But what if you could fall in love with yourself again?

Seeing yourself through God's Word requires that you choose to see the beauty inside yourself. It also requires that you get to know Him differently—not as everyone else has told you He is, but in an intimate, personal way. In any new relationship, you relish the other person. You want to get to know all the parts of them. You see them in a new light. This is the light in which I invite you to see God, and yourself, again.

Truth #2: I Am Created in Love, By Love, to Be a Vessel of Love

God is perfect love.

He does not only love; He is the very essence of Love.

Love is a state of being. You and I were created from love, through love, by love, in loving formation. Can you even begin to wrap your head around that much affection? We were created as vessels that would allow the essence of Love to move in us and through us into others. We are literally here to infuse our families, our businesses, and this planet with pure love.

The original design of co-creation begins with an act of love and sacred union between a man and woman—a couple who came together in perfect design to plant a new seed, nurture it, and hold it safely until it was fully formed and ready to be birthed into this world. Regardless of what happened with your physical parents or how you physically came into this world, the very fact that you are alive is an act of love. There is no other reason than that.

Truth #3: I Am Created on Purpose, for a Divine Purpose

You are not an accident. God does not create accidents. You are here intentionally, and your soul was given physical life for a purpose.

Again, I come back to being a mother. As I look at my children, I can see their gifts, their talents, their unique abilities, their desires, and their passions. I see all the challenges they are being taken through and I know that all of these have come together to shape their *unique calling and purpose*. I can see it at work in them, and can see a vision for their future.

If you are a parent, why do you believe your children are alive? Can you see a vision for their future, or are you limited by your own past? If you, a human, can see a vision, gifting, and future for your own physical children, how much more do you think the divine, perfect love that created you has in store for you? Sees in you? Desires for you?

I pray that you will choose to live purposefully wherever you have been planted. For where you are today is preparing you for what's coming tomorrow. How well you serve, lead, and love right now will determine what you experience in the days to come. So, be intentional, and live on purpose!

Truth #4: I Am Chosen and Beloved By the One Who Knows Everything About Me

For decades, I struggled in relationships because I wanted to be the "chosen one" to the men in my life, the chosen one in leadership positions, the favorite guest at parties, and the chosen one amongst my friends. This kept me disconnected from the fact that I was *already* chosen. The perfect relationship already existed for me. The perfect role, the perfect job for where I was. The perfect situations to form me and shape me.

The love of my life, my husband, showed up once I finally owned and remembered the fact that *I am already chosen. I am* the right one already. As I often say now, "You will find the one when you realize you *are* the one." You will find the right partner, the right position, the right calling, the right inner circle when you are willing to believe you are already the chosen one for this position.

Truth #5: I Belong, for I Am His Child

So many of us have been cast aside, abandoned, and rejected by our earthly fathers, mothers, and families. The wound of abandonment and rejection ran deep in my family. My father was abandoned by his earthly father when he was just a few years old. Later, he felt the sting of his mother choosing other men over him. Was it truly a surprise that he would later abandon his own children? I experienced what it was like to lack the closeness, protection, and presence of my father as he abandoned himself to alcoholism and work. In my first marriage, my in-laws routinely threatened to disown their children.

Physical families may hurt you, cast you out, reject you, shame you, or try to control you. Even if they have good intentions, they will almost certainly judge you. But there is a family and a home beyond the physical world that is very real and very much alive, waiting for us to come home—and no, I don't mean after we die.

As humans, we are created by God. He is our Creator, and He also yearns to be our chosen Father. He longs for us to place our trust in Him, rather than trust only what the world offers us. He desires us to come back home to His protection and provision and under the covering of His blessing. He is a father; He has always been a father. We were and are designed to live in union with Him and walk in union with Him. Humans can reject Him, but he will never reject us.

Now, we are invited to come back home. He has made the way for us. Through Jesus Christ, He created the bridge between the world and the heavens. We have the opportunity to bridge heaven and earth right here, right now. The way through is called "the narrow gate" for a reason. Many will be offered the way, but few will choose it; many will continue to place faith, trust, and identity in the empty and temporary promises of our world and the approval of their physical parents. But there is so much more.

Once I began to remember my true Father, and placed my trust in Him, all my physical relationships changed form. They were healed, restored, and transformed. So, let me ask you: can you learn how to be a son again? Can you learn how to be a daughter who is deeply loved, deeply cherished, provided for, and protected?

In God's family, there is room for all. Love never runs dry. There is always enough love, affection, and space for all. You can come as you are, without needing to prove your worth or do anything special to earn your place. It is really that simple. It's a choice—an invitation for Him to come back into your heart, and for you to receive His love.

And then, it is done.

Truth #6: I Am Worthy, for I Am His Heir

If God is truly a God of all, then we are children of the One who has access to all things. If Christ is King, and we are His beloved, then we are also His heirs.

I believe that God wants to pour blessings upon His children, but His children have been programmed with teachings of poverty, shame, and unworthiness. This is garbage. It needs to be thrown out, plucked from our minds completely. This subcurrent of distorted thinking is an enemy tactic to keep us separated, striving, and struggling rather than connected, receiving, serving, and blessing others from a place of overflow.

The key is to get our hearts right. We are always worthy of love, but many of us don't receive it because our hearts are fixed on the wrong things and closed off from the right ones. We are always worthy of receiving support, but we block it because we try to do everything ourselves, demand perfection, and are critical of others. Knowing you are worthy of love is different from expecting to be waited on hand and foot and demanding things go your way like an entitled and ungrateful child. If you enter into a relationship with God with the right heart posture, you will cultivate the ability to receive help, guidance, or gifts without it being distorted by ego.

Also, be wary of feeling like you need to "earn" the right to your inheritance. For example, my mother is an amazing giver. She gives and gives from a place of love. However, she has had a hard time learning to receive anything for herself that was not essential or practical. For someone to lavish gifts on her and "spoil" her feels overwhelming to her—and, from the perspective of someone trying to do the lavishing, it's frustrating. I know that, growing up, her family "got by." They had what they needed, but not much more.

May I suggest that we are created to have more than "just enough"?

I am happy to report that finally, in her mid-seventies, my mom is learning to say yes to gifts, experiences, rest, and ultimately, more love! It's been so rewarding on my end to observe her lighting up with joy as she gives herself permission to experience more of life, be served by others, and enjoy beautiful material things.

We are created to live from a place of overflow so that we may give freely of our gifts, time, energy, money, and resources. I don't believe we are designed to empty ourselves nonstop and then keep giving from empty wells. I believe we are designed to be deep wells that are constantly fed, nourished, and refilled, so that we may give to others knowing that everything is always provided to us—and so that, if there are dreams and visions placed in our hearts, we can proceed knowing that the one who placed them there will also provide the ability to fund them!

I invite you, right now, to remember that you are *already worthy*. You are already chosen. You are already an heir. You are more than enough through Christ. The question, knowing this, is: can you operate from this moment forward from a place of humility, gratitude, appreciation, patience, trust, and joy?

Truth #7: I am Multidimensional and Uniquely Designed On Purpose

There are many parts of us. Learning to love all of ourselves is what makes us feel whole. Not only the "good" parts, but also the rough parts that point us back to places of fear, wounding, or brokenness that still need tending to.

There is a child inside you, and also a wild man/woman, a conqueror, a warrior, a lover, a king/queen, a sage, and so many more. As we have discussed, you have a physical body, an emotional body, and a mental body (which make up your soul), and a spiritual body. However, some of us are so focused on one dimension of ourselves that we forget about the others! I encourage you to get to know all of you—to light up, connect with, care for, and nourish your physical, mental, emotional, and spiritual bodies daily—because there is no one like you in this world, nor will there ever be.

Lisa Bevere, one of my favorite authors, explains it this way: "You are uniquely loved because you were uniquely made. You are without rival!"

Psalm 139 reminds us that we are "intricately and wonderfully made." You are an original design, and all the parts of you get to belong in this design.

The world we live in has many of us competing to look the same, think the same, and act the same. It's no wonder this leaves many of us grappling with our identity! We are literally fighting our authentic design. We are not designed to be clones and replicas. You were not made out of a factory lineup, and you are not designed to be a machine. You are an original, organic, wonderfully created individual who holds unique coding, unique DNA, unique talents, unique gifting, a unique calling, and a unique relationship with your Creator. Once we stop fighting our original design and truly embrace it, the need to compare and compete evaporates, and instead we can drop into a place of full acceptance and expression of ourselves across our multidimensional wholeness of body, soul, and spirit.

If you aren't sure how to access your full multidimensionality and uniqueness, ask God to reveal it to you. You may be awed at what you learn.

Truth #8: I am Gifted and Talented

What are you naturally good at? What comes easier to you than to others? What lights you up and energizes you? When we are exposed or experience certain things, we expand, and life grows richer and more meaningful. We have renewed perspective and an immediate sense of wanting to share this moment or experience with others.

Our passions fuel us with life. They are there on purpose. They might not, at first, seem to relate to any one area of your life. However, as we mature, we realize that often our "calling"—our most fulfilling life's work—exists where our gifts, talents, passions, and expertise overlap.

We see wildly talented and gifted people all around us every day. We celebrate and pay attention to the natural abilities of athletes, musicians, artists, innovators, speakers, teachers, builders, and other creatives. The thing is, we often neglect to acknowledge the talents within ourselves, especially if they lie in areas other than those upon which the world has placed a high value.

Certain things just come naturally to us. We will be drawn to these things more than others, and will demonstrate aptitude and instinct for them. We don't have to "earn" our gifts and talents, but we do need to recognize them, develop them, and put them to use. They are our gifts to the world.

Your talents are supported and enhanced by your spiritual gifts, which are bestowed according to Grace. Like your talents, you don't need to earn or qualify for them. In fact, you likely use them naturally in your daily life without even knowing it. However, once you recognize them, you can learn to channel them effectively, enhance them to support your connection with God, and use them for good.

For example, many Warriors are also highly sensitive and intuitive. Sometimes, under the label of "empath," they take in and process all the energy in the room. While this is a gift, it can also feel like a curse when this gift is not anchored in a solid identity. When we are young and spiritually immature, our gifts can easily be abused, misused, or go to extremes. For example, empaths who lack boundaries are wide open all the time, leaving them depleted, exhausted, and taking on everyone else's burdens. Once they become aware of this gift, however, they can begin to use it selectively and channel it to support their natural talents and passions to create a full, dynamic expression of their purpose.

Similarly, the gifts of wisdom, discernment, prophesy, vision/ insight, generosity, kindness, charisma/energia (energy), servitude, teaching/encouragement, faith, and healing can either support Warriors in fulfilling their God-given purpose, or work against them by feeding into false identities. For example, gifts like wisdom, discernment, and insight can backfire for Warriors who haven't embraced their true identities as children and heirs of God, because their logic will always be twisted in the direction of their own unworthiness.

I often coach clients on discovering their gifts and talents, harnessing them, and channeling them on fertile ground. Often, we try to be like someone else because we want what they have and are trying to get it the way they got it. This never works well. We are designed uniquely, and what's meant for us becomes fruitful once we learn to apply our talents and gifts in the right areas of life.

So, consider what comes easily and naturally to you. Perhaps it's artistic expression, writing, speaking, or mathematics. Maybe it's organization, developing processes, or teaching others. What do you do that naturally brings others and things to life? What attracts people and opportunities to you? What is it about you that is magnetic? These are your areas of talent and gifting!

Whatever your talents and gifts are, pick them up and run with them! You have been given these things for a reason, and that reason is so much bigger than you or anything you can wrap your head around. Put them to work. Multiply them. Don't hide or misuse them out of fear. These talents and gifts, when used well, will make you feel more like yourself—the beautiful, multidimensional, unique being your Creator, God, designed you to be. As all the external influences fall away, your intimacy with God will increase, and your talents and gifts will shine through.

Truth #9: I am Human!

Who can possibly bear the burden, weight, and responsibility of playing God? I certainly know I cannot. I tried that for years and was riddled with anxiousness. The moment that stopped was the moment I decided to fully remember that *I am human*. This has allowed me to extend compassion, grace, and love where once there was criticism and judgment. The identity of "humanity" I once thought made me less than has made me so much more.

Your humanity and its inherent flaws do not negate the truths of your God-given identity. In fact, it is only possible to embrace the truth of who you are created to be when you accept that you are human. As a human, you can be filled by the Spirit of the One who heals, who restores, who forgives, who cleanses and renews us daily. As a warrior of the world, you have likely been trying to do this on your own, as your own source; nothing is more exhausting. However, as Warriors of the Heart in union with our Creator, we are made whole; we become fully human, and open ourselves to receive all the gifts of that identity.

***

I also suggest you read "A Father's Love Letter," a compilation of Bible verses formatted as a love letter from the Heavenly Father to you. This letter influenced my heart and relationship with the Father deeply. Read it and keep it accessible anytime you find yourself seeking clarity on your identity. You can find a link to this incredibly-moving piece at www.dropthearmorbook.com.

CHANGING SEASONS

My dear friend, Miguel Sanchez, once said to me:

> *Enjoy the view from where you are today. Enjoy the sunrise and the sunset. Take it all in.*

But don't fall so in love with the view you become afraid to get up and move when God calls you.

God is steadfast and unchanging. He is always the same. He is always on time.

And He is always moving. Always calling us into the next place.

Enjoy the view from where you are, my sister, but don't love the view so much you become fixated by it and forget who you are.

Those words spoke such life into me.

Because we are deep wells and multidimensional beings, there are infinite layers to us; these are exposed as we navigate through different challenges, growth curves, and milestones in life. These layers peel away old versions of us and reveal new ones. Each new season prepares us, forges us, and calls us forward to meet the next. In each season, we remember more of who we are, stop hiding, and show up in new ways.

We are refined through this process of seasoning. Like clay on a wheel, we keep being shaped and formed into new vessels. We are forever remembering more of the one we were created to be, forever restoring what has been broken, renewing, and re-birthing the new. For a while, we will play certain roles, hold certain positions, and be in certain relationships. For a season, there will be things that interest us, and we may become students for a time or a lifetime.

Remember, seasons come and go. They change. We, like all creation, are cyclical in nature and will experience each season differently. Just as each season brings with it new promises and new horizons, it also requires that something old fall away. There are times of planting, when things seem to be showing life again after a long period of darkness. There are times of high energy and flourishing. There are times to harvest and prepare the soil for what will come next. There are also times of death, stillness, and going within. Life becomes more beautiful and meaningful when we learn to honor the seasons in our life and know that, no matter what season we are in, it is all part of God's design for us.

WARRIOR INITIATION

- What false identities have you been clinging to in your life?

- What lies have you believed about who you are and what you need to do, be, or prove?

- What would it feel like to see yourself the way God sees you?

- What part of your God-given identity can you reclaim right now? Which are you resisting?

- How would you describe your current season of life and how does this affect your current perception of your identity?

CHAPTER NINE

Know Your Enemy

"If you know the enemy and know yourself, you need not fear the result of a hundred battles. If you know yourself but not the enemy, for every victory gained you will also suffer a defeat. If you know neither the enemy nor yourself, you will succumb in every battle."

— SUN TZU, *THE ART OF WAR*

A battle always has two sides, two opposing forces. When you're on one side of the trenches, the force on the other side is your opposition. Your antagonist. Your enemy.

As we explored earlier in this book, as Warriors, most of us have been fighting our whole lives—against others, against conventions, against expectations, and most especially against ourselves. We are always battling, and when one battle ends, we find another to jump into.

Societally, we are also conditioned to fight. We battle cancer, PTSD, and anxiety. We fight epidemics, pandemics, oppression, and tyranny. Just like in our personal lives, everything is a fight. It's a language we are comfortable with.

Now that we have shifted our allegiance, dropped our armor, opened our hearts, and connected with our true identity, the idea of "battling" our way through life in a never-ending cycle may hold less appeal. We have seen, clearly, how fighting the wrong battles for the wrong things can sap our strength, rob us of our life force, and make it harder to enjoy the life that we were ultimately created for.

We are moving forward as a new type of Warrior, awakened from the spell, with eyes wide open, paying a different kind of attention as to what's at hand. We clearly know where we are headed and where we are not. At this point in your initiation, I trust you are taking the bait less and less, fighting fewer of the wrong battles over the wrong things. I trust you are starting to see the true nature of the battle, and what is truly at stake.

At the root of all battles, in the world and within yourself, is an opponent who:

1. Is a force that exists in opposition to life and love in its purest form.

2. Is a thief of what God has planned for you—a thief of all the blessings you are designed to receive, and everything you are created to multiply in your life and the lives of others.

3. Loves to distort what God created and use it against us.

As is written in the Book of John, *"The thief cometh not, but for to steal, and to kill, and to destroy: I am come that they might have life, and that they might have it more abundantly."* (John 10:10, KJV)

Biblically, we know this opponent as Satan, the fallen angel once known as Lucifer, the "morning star" who became overrun with jealousy and pride. He later became known as Satan, the Hebrew word for "adversary" or "superhuman adversary" of God (*hasatan*). His mission is to capture souls and take over all that God created for His own—to destroy life and everything beautiful that comes from it.

You may have experienced many different definitions of the enemy or darkness throughout your own lifetime. It matters less what you call the enemy, and more importantly that you hone your ability to recognize him and how his evil fallen angels operate in all their guises.

The next step on the path of the Warrior of the Heart is to become acutely aware of the enemy's battle tactics and strategies. We need to understand the bait being dangled so we can walk past enchanting temptations and disregard the slight-of-hand. We must avoid getting caught up in the wrong battles so we can keep ourselves clear to focus on things that multiply life rather than take it away.

THE TACTICS

Before we examine the enemy's tactics, I want to point out one very important truth. Many of the enemy's tactics present as behaviors or external forces through people or circumstances, but they are all rooted in *emotions fueled by thoughts.*

Emotions are given to us on purpose, for a purpose. We are designed to feel the entire range of human emotion fully and deeply—from immense love and ecstasy to deepest pain and despair. Emotions serve as beautiful, God-given GPS signals to show us when we are disconnected or unplugged from our innermost being, from God Himself, and from the fruits of our blessing. They are there to redirect our minds, hearts, and bodies to reconcile and restore any brokenness, wounding, and faulty belief systems so we may be made whole again and reclaim our identity as God's children and heirs.

My purpose in this discussion is not to diminish emotions or make them wrong in any way. Rather, it's my intention to help you open your eyes to see how your emotions are bringing you more life or keeping you in captivity. I am a highly emotional and sensitive being, and I consider it a great gift to experience the depth of my life experience through emotion. Grief is essential to healing and moving on to new seasons of life. Anger is essential to stop injustice and abuse and move us into courageous action. We are not here to remain apathetic and numbed out. Emotions are fuel for our inner fire. However, that flame should move us into right action, not toward self-destruction.

The enemy distorts and tries to use against us what God created *for* good. Emotions are human, and we have them on purpose. But when they are used against us, they no longer serve the purpose of helping and guiding us.

Take fear, for example. Fear has a purpose. It's there to alert us when something in the atmosphere is off, when there is a predator in our midst. It's a survival mechanism. Think of the ocean. It is beautiful, majestic, powerful, and unpredictable. It can hold us as we float or swallow us with one tidal wave. A healthy fear of the ocean reminds me who and what is actually in control. I can enjoy the ocean. I can swim in it, float on top of it, and navigate it on a boat. I can observe its wonder and beauty. But I cannot make the ocean obey me. I cannot control it. The ocean does what the ocean does.

To "fear" the Lord, as often described in the Bible, is also healthy. Fear is a necessary ingredient to the reverence, awe, and appreciation we *must* feel for the wonder and power of something so much greater than us—our Creator, and also creation itself. God's Creation has the potential to give life, and at the same time take life away.

On the flip side, there are unhealthy fears. These fears can engulf us if we are not careful. When this happens, the fear that was created to be used as an instrument *for us* becomes a weapon used *against* us. We fear losing false identities. We fear change. We fear others' opinions of us. We fear experiencing our own emotions! We fear God's retribution and punishment instead of inviting the discipline, direction, and love of a Father who knows us better than we know ourselves (see Psalm 139). We become consumed with irrational thoughts or obsessive tendencies. We become paralyzed and unable to move forward. We become angry and lose control.

The battle shifts when we become consumed by or devoured by our emotions. Instead of focusing on our true enemy, we begin to battle ourselves through our thoughts and unchecked emotions. It is easy to become engulfed—or, as I like to say, hijacked—by the thoughts that feed our emotions. When we fall into that trap, we allow ourselves to be taken over by anger, shame, guilt, or fear. Then, suddenly, we aren't the Warrior anymore. Instead, *we* become the enemy, attacking ourselves and everything in our path. Too often, that "thing" in our path is the very person we would give the world for: our wife, husband, child, friend, or loved one.

Emotions are often referred to as "energy in motion." All energy has a *source*. That source can be God allowing us to experience something for a moment or a season so we may grow in character or redirect ourselves toward a greater purpose and divine calling. After all, contrast provides great clarity; before we know the right way to go, we often choose many wrong paths. On the other hand, the energy can come from the enemy, with the intention to keep us locked in a loop of suffering and distraction, unable to access our true Warrior power.

I've experienced this many times after I've made a bold declaration to double down on the calling God was putting in my heart. For example, once I committed my work to the Lord and devoted myself to supporting men and women to restore the health of their relationships, I hit a season where it felt like there was one thing after another coming at me. It was all there to distract me, derail me, and discourage me from pressing on. It was also there to refine my ability to activate my inner Warrior in a new way—to fiercely protect the territory of my mind and energy by setting clear boundaries and not fighting battles that were not mine. This is the enemy's ultimate goal: to keep us fighting the wrong fights, well away from the *real* battlefield.

The battle is for the soul, but the battleground is in the *mind*.

In the next section, we'll dive into the enemy's playbook and look at some of the tactics that have been used against us in the past, and which may be used against us in the future. These tactics are:

- Deception

- Doubt

- Disconnection

- Division

- Distraction

- Disorientation

- Disembodiment

- Discouragement

This is by no means an exhaustive list. In addition, no one tactic stands alone. Many of these are intertwined, with one leading into the other so that, before you know it, you're entangled in a mess that feels so dense, heavy, and impenetrable that you don't know how to break free. Once we have awareness of what tactics the enemy is using against us, we can deploy the associated antidote to protect ourselves, diffuse the battle, and move forward.

Ready? Let's go.

Deception

It's easy for the enemy to use a carefully selected piece of information which tells only a sliver of the story. Then it can distort or invert the truth. That is how deceit works: by blending lies with enough truth that they feel not only plausible, but probable. How many times have we seen a clip of something and made gross assumptions about the rest of the message? This happens all day, every day—especially today, with information coming at us on a second-by-second basis. For someone to take the time and space to get to the root and direct source of something is rare. Most things we see and hear are pieces of truth.

Let me ask you: if something's 98 percent true and 2 percent lie, is it still truth? If your kids tell you 98 percent of the story but omit a crucial 2 percent, are they still telling you the truth? If your partner has an emotional relationship with someone else but has not physically engaged in intercourse, is it a lie if they tell you they are "just friends"? If your best friend tells you most of the story, but not the parts that make them look bad, does that still mean they trust you?

When we hide things, we distort the end result, manipulating information and others' emotions to gain a specific outcome. Like the shiny apple that is rotten to the core on the inside, there's something just ... *off* about it. Yet, because it looks solid, sounds probable, and we can't put our finger on what's wrong, we believe it, and act accordingly.

This is why it's so critical that we remain connected to our heart, our body's wisdom (including our gut instinct), and most importantly, the Holy Spirit, the giver of wisdom and understanding, also known as the "mighty counselor." We must train ourselves to connect and attune to the different ways God speaks to us. This way, we can recognize when we are being deceived.

Information is easy to manipulate. Have you ever been in an argument with your spouse where you both had the same exact information, yet you were in complete disagreement about what actually happened? "This is what happened! You said that! No, I did not say that! That's what I heard!" Well, which one is it? Who is right? I get this when I am coaching couples all the time, especially when there is a battle going on over control of a situation or the need to be right. Both versions are true on some level to each person based on their perception of reality, where they are sitting, their past stories, and so forth. But are they *fully* true?

On a collective level, numbers are some of the easiest data to distort and manipulate. How many people do you personally know who get paid to "make the numbers look good"? How many statistics have you seen take different forms based on the point the media or researchers were trying to drive home? We saw this clearly during the pandemic of 2020. The numbers and information keep changing depending on the agenda of the news outlet or individual sharing them. To this date, the numbers are *still* shape-shifting to match whatever the discourse is.

The main thing to remember here is that there are many small-t truths, meaning the truth as individuals see it with their physical eyes. It may very well be their "truth," but it is not universal, capital-T Truth. It is not God's Truth.

At the end of the day, deception is just another attempt to control outcomes through manipulating people's behaviors or emotions. It's a way for someone or something else to distract us, sap our energy, and control us for their own personal gain. This needless pursuit of power, using whatever is at hand to control others and attain what is desired, is part of the fallen human condition.

Be careful of getting sucked into distortions of truth—especially those "98 percent" games—and be *very* careful when you engage in conversations about what is right or wrong. When we enter into these games mindlessly, we are baited, and we end up taking on the same energy as the enemy that is coming at us. We can become fearful or anxious, which draws us into the battle and soon has us fighting back with the same weapons of deception and misdirection that were used against us. When we fight fire with fire, we only amplify the fire and deplete our life force. Think about this.

Often, deception comes from a well-intended source, not a person who truly means you harm. They simply have not filtered their information or cultivated the skill of discernment. Let's be clear: that person is *not* the enemy. The enemy is *using* that person's words or actions to bait you. Therefore, you need to differentiate between the person and the thing trying to get at you. Too often, we make our loved ones, friends, and colleagues our enemies rather than acknowledging that they, too, are caught up in the game of deception. All of us, at some point, have allowed our mental and emotional bodies to be infiltrated by fear, anger, judgment, and so on. In those moments, we did not practice self-discipline or self-awareness. We did not pause to ask the right questions or process our emotions in a healthy way. Instead, we spewed whatever vitriol was coming through us onto whoever and whatever was in our vicinity.

In the end, though, the deception itself is not what matters. The information we are handed is almost always irrelevant. What matters is the *filter* we run that information through and what *meaning* we give it.

So how do we combat the enemy that is deception?

The Antidote: Discernment

We must develop the skill of discernment and cultivate a spirit of discernment in all things. Some of us are more naturally gifted in this area than others, but we all have access to discernment if we are willing to train ourselves. Putting all our trust in mankind is never a good idea. Humans fall to temptation. We miss the mark. We get caught up in situations, people, and things. We get broadsided by the messages, events, and tides of the world— that's part of our humanness! However, knowing this, we must slow down, tune in, connect to the Holy Spirit, discern, and then move accordingly.

We'll explore discernment as a practice and skill set in more detail in Chapter Thirteen. For now, think of it as the antidote to deception, one that we can begin to employ by waking up, slowing down, and asking better questions. When we are in deep connection to the Spirit of God, we discover truths hidden to those still serving the wrong masters.

Doubt

It's only fitting that doubt should come on the heels of deception. If you feel you are inadequate, unloved, unworthy, useless, or incapable, you did not get those ideas from the Holy Spirit.

Once we receive and take in distorted information, it plants seeds of doubt. If we absorb the information and give it energy by ruminating on it, we will begin to question our gifts, mission, desires, and even our identity. We will start second-guessing our decisions, resulting in less clarity and more confusion. Perhaps we will even begin to believe there's something wrong with us. So many feelings of unworthiness— that we are undeserving of love, peace, joy or abundance—come from doubt rather than any valid information or tangible proof.

When we begin to step into our potential and gifts, the enemy will often hurl doubts at us like flaming darts. Sometimes, it may feel as if we can't shut down the voices inside our heads, and that we are being attacked at every level. I've experienced this multiple times. Today, I am getting better and better at discerning those tactics and cutting them off sooner rather than later.

Below are just some of the angles from which the enemy employs this tactic:

Doubting Your Dreams, Desires, and Visions

- "This is ridiculous!"

- "This will never work. What are you thinking?"

- "This is way too much for someone like you. How will you ever accomplish this?"

- "This is for other people, not you."

- "There is no way you can handle this."

- "You will fail at this just like you always do."

- "You don't have the means to make this happen."

Doubting Your Talents and Natural Gifting

- "This? Ha! Nobody cares about this!"

- "You need way more than that in order to succeed."

- "You're not good enough."

- "Your competition is so much stronger, fitter, better, more powerful, and better positioned to win than you are. Just give up now."

- "Your gift is useless in this equation."

- "Nobody needs what you have to offer them."

Doubting Your Ability to Follow Through

- "You don't have what it takes."

- "You never finish anything."

- "It's too late. You are too far behind."

- "You can't make this happen."

- "You don't know how to do this."

Doubting Your Character

- "Who do you think you are, anyway?"

- "You are such a fool! Such an idiot!"

- "You are so lazy!"

- "It's your fault this happened. You should be ashamed of yourself."

- "You'll never amount to anything."

Do any of these sentiments sound familiar?

The last thing the enemy wants is for you to embody the fullness of your potential. His plan is to derail you at all costs, to rob you of your inheritance and God-given assignment on this earth. And there is no better way to get under your skin and into your innermost heart than doubt. Why? Because the enemy tactic of doubt goes *straight to the core of our identity*.

What we believe about ourselves is foundational to everything we initiate. What you identify with, and who you identify as, determines the entire course of your life. Every action you take, every thought you entertain, every word you speak, and everything you respond to and run from are intricately directed by your perceived identity. Identity also determines your self-worth and what you believe that we are capable of and meant for. This is why it's so important to do the identity work we outlined in Chapter Eight. Who but a child and heir of God could be truly worthy, deserving, and capable of an abundant and prosperous life without constant strife and hardship? If we keep trying to do it on our own, some of those doubts I listed above may actually be true. But Jesus tells us, *"With man this is impossible, but with God all things are possible."* (Matthew 19:26, NIV) This is great news for those of us who are choosing to give our hearts back to God. We are equipped because He equips us. We are safe because He provides safety and direction, establishing our steps along the way. We are worthy because He is worthy, and He is alive in us. We are finishers because He is faithful to finish a good work in us if we remain obedient. We are more than enough when we walk hand in hand with Him.

The seeds of doubt are not our own, but we are the ones receiving them and giving them attention, energy, and focus. They can only take root if we let them. Where focus goes, energy grows—and if that energy gets big enough and strong enough, it begins to take on a life of its own and form a stronghold in our minds. Before we know it, there is a thick wall of resistance between us and what we desire, or between us and the work we have been given to do.

The Antidote: Faith

The antidote for doubt, of course, is faith.

Jesus reminds us of this in Matthew 17:20-21, where he states, *"For truly I tell you, if you have faith the size of a mustard seed, you will say to this mountain, 'Move from here to there,' and it will move; and nothing will be impossible for you."*

We *can* combat the enemy tactic of doubt by remembering our true identity and using it as a shield and sword against the negative voices inside. We remember who our Creator, God, says we are, and choose to believe His promises over and above our doubts. When doubt tries to play on our imaginative mind, creating imaginary failures and obstacles, we can choose to activate faith, speak words of truth and life over our situation, and direct the power of our heart (emotions) and mind (imagination) toward the promises of God.

Make a list of all the times in your life when you faced doubt but chose to remain faithful and take action accordingly. What did you do? What outcomes resulted from you activating faith?

Now, recall a time when you allowed doubt to be the dominant force. What did you do or not do? What outcome did you experience?

It is powerful to witness the contrast between the forces of doubt and faith in our lives. In what areas of your current life could you exercise more faith and entertain less doubt?

You are created for great work and for great things. The road has been prepared for you. Do not entertain the voice of doubt for one second longer! *"For we are His workmanship, created in Christ Jesus for good works, which God prepared beforehand so that we would walk in them."* (Ephesians 2:10, NASB)

Disconnection

If we are created in love, by love, and for the pure expression of love, doesn't it only make sense then that the ultimate tactic to disrupt love is disconnection? It literally means to unplug us!

We are hardwired and soft-wired for connection in every sense of the word. We literally can't thrive or function without it. Isolation is the worst kind of torture; it closes our hearts and weakens our bodies. That's why so many of us stay in the wrong relationships or compromise our values just to be accepted by a community. Pull the plug from the Source of Love, and we won't be able to feel or experience love, let alone share it with others.

This level of isolation is exactly where the enemy desires. It wants us thinking thoughts like:

- "I am separate from myself."

- "I am separate from God."

- "I am separate from others."

- "I am unloved."

- "I am unlovable."

The enemy has a master plan to tear families apart, tear marriages apart, tear our souls and dreams apart—all so it can pull us away from the intimacy and connection that is accessed through our hearts, and sap our determination to go on when life presents us with obstacles.

One of the first places disconnection occurs is through the trauma and conditioning of our early childhood years. When we feel that first sense of abandonment, the first pangs of rejection, or that first humiliation, stories get embedded in our psyche and our nervous systems. In those moments, part of us makes an agreement with the stories, and we begin to let them define us. These stories become our identities, and we are doomed to spend much of our lives repeating, reaffirming, and ingraining those stories and wounds of the past—right up until we shift our allegiance, drop the armor, open our hearts, and reclaim our true identities.

We know that trauma is real. The events that happened were real. The disconnection we experienced as a result is also very real for us. In moments or seasons of great stress or trauma, our bodies and minds responded in ways that helped us survive the situation. This is part of our body's incredible design. However, a disconnected heart and mind cannot experience unity, trust, and intimacy—which is precisely why the enemy wants this for us. This is why we are called to heal the past, change the story, and transform the outcomes from our history.

The pandemic of 2020 provided a case study for disconnection as a tool for destruction. While isolation and distancing measures were necessary for a time to keep everyone safe, no one can deny the negative ripple effects we all experienced during those two years. Lockdowns separated the elderly from their children and friends, separated families, separated people in the workplace, separated children in school. We are still recovering from horrible losses and broken hearts from this experience. Because so many life-giving connections were broken, we are experiencing an increase in anxiety disorders like PTSD and depression in adults—and, disturbingly, our youth too.

The Antidote: Reconnection

The antidote to disconnection is reconnection—to plug ourselves back into our Creator, the Giver of Life, and allow Him to move into our innermost being, restore our hearts, and bring us back into right relationship. Getting into healthy and safe relationship with God after a period of disconnection can feel daunting, especially if you have been isolated for some time. It will require you to activate the spirit of faith and adventure within you, embrace the unknown, and be willing to lean into your heart, soul, and spirit.

When we reach this stage of the Warrior journey, I often hear from clients, "I don't know how to connect. I don't know where to start."

The key is to release all expectations and go slowly. Practice getting curious and just being with yourself, and with God. Practice inviting God to come and sit with you, walk with you, hang out with you. Have a literal conversation or just sit without needing to do or accomplish anything other than being in connection.

On a human level, reach out to someone you haven't seen in a while and invite them for lunch or coffee—but do it differently. Start connecting with those you love at a heart level, not just an intellectual level. Ask them *how* they are doing, not *what* they've been doing. Ask them what they are excited about, what they dream about. Then, share what is on your heart. And remember, being you is more than enough. People are craving real, authentic relationships more than ever. The more you bring your authentic self to the table, the more you invite others to show up authentically—and that's the fabric great connections are made of!

Division

In a suspenseful movie scene, when someone hears a strange noise, one friend will inevitably say, "Let's split up." If you're anything like me, you'll yell at the screen, "Don't do it! Stay together!" You know that, as soon as they go off in different directions, they'll start getting picked off one by one.

For the enemy, the perfect byproduct of disconnection is division. It's an age-old tactic. As the saying goes, "Divide and conquer." If you can split your opponent's forces—or better yet, get them fighting amongst themselves—you will more easily maintain control and win the battle. When we waste our energy judging, blaming, justifying ourselves, or arguing over trivial matters, we cannot give our attention to the real issues at hand. *"Every kingdom divided against itself is laid waste; and any city or house divided against itself will not stand."* (Matthew 12:25, NASB)

The deceit at play here is that, oftentimes, these divisive tactics are the very things that we gather together around. Like a brood of teenagers stirring up gossip and drama, misery loves company. So do envy, fear, and criticism. One of the issues my executive clients often bring to the table is that their executive teams can't seem to get along. Instead of having transparent discussions, setting the North Star, clarifying values, and making decisions about how best to move the company forward for the benefit of the whole, these leaders are playing "referee," trying to appease all the different players. Sales teams are pitted against marketing teams. Engineering teams are pitted against operations teams. And Human Resources teams seem pitted against ... well, everyone. Often, inside these organizations, there is chaos, disorder, and confusion with everyone swimming in different directions and taking orders from misaligned leadership. The result is that projects get bogged down and delayed, sales grind to a halt, frustrations rise, and employees feel unappreciated and disrespected. The company becomes a divided household.

However, in these scenarios and many others, the problem being blamed for the division is rarely the problem at all. No single employee or team, however difficult, can cause that kind of strife. No single problem, no matter how large, can destroy a healthy company or family. No single political figure, no matter how polarizing, has the potential to destroy a nation. The real problem, of course, is that the culture has been infiltrated and turned on its head by division.

The first order of business, therefore, is to clean up the atmosphere and get people back on the same team. We are always stronger together.

So, in situations where you notice division, don't give into the temptation to avoid confrontation or choose a side right off the bat. Lean in where you are tempted to avoid. Collaborate where you are tempted to compete. Accept someone you are inclined to judge. Get curious rather than defensive. Because every time we match the energy coming at us, we amplify it. We can't reverse poisoning by drinking more poison. Instead, we need to lead with the energy we want to experience—the antidote to the poison we have just been fed.

Oh, but there is so much temptation to drink the poison. Don't do it. Bring the medicine of unification instead.

The Antidote: Unification

Recently, I was working with a newly separated couple who were working toward co-parenting together. They have three beautiful children together and are also business partners with equal shares in their company. On one hand, they both wanted to figure out a way to communicate with each other constructively and keep the well-being of their children at the forefront. On the other hand, they were so caught up in pointing fingers and calling out what the other person was doing wrong that, for months on end, their discussions rarely got to the real issues they were trying to address! They were each constantly broadsided with another perceived attack from the other. Attack. Defend. Get the last word in. Anticipate another attack. The game went on and on. I kept having to redirect their focus to the *main* thing they were trying to solve together. Their North Star was peace and happiness for everyone. If they wanted that outcome, they had to stop fighting and making each other the enemy.

I am happy to report that, at the time of this writing, they are finally able to put the past behind them and take ownership for their own parts of the breakdown. They are working toward a productive relationship dynamic together, not only as co-parents but also as business partners. It took a lot of acceptance, healing, forgiveness, and new rules of engagement for them to get to this place—but they have arrived.

The key to overcoming division is finding the North Star again—the guiding light everyone can see. Identify one area in your life where there has been strife and division. Get quiet and observe which enemy tactics are being used to divide the whole.

Next, identify one thing that everyone can agree on. What is the one thing that unifies you? What is the thing you both/all ultimately want and are fighting for? This is your North Star. Decide to focus on that one thing, your North Star, the next time you come into a space where division is happening. Recognize that there are many ways to get there.

Cut ties with gossip, finger pointing, and "refereeing." Refuse to engage when these things arise or when people are highly triggered. Take a moment to calm down and regroup, then invite others to rally together and work on the unifying factors. Try asking everyone in the room, "What is the one thing we are all working toward, even though our methods may differ?" If you want to really take this to another level, ask yourself, "How can we all contribute to the North Star, with each of us operating in our unique gifting for the benefit of the whole?"

To be clear: this is not an invitation to compromise your values or disregard your beliefs. Instead, this is an invitation to find common ground, to hold space for both yourself and others while keeping all eyes on the goal. Remember, everyone has their own small-t truth and perception of reality, and while others' actions may be out of alignment with our personal values (or even the values they themselves claim to hold), that doesn't mean we throw the person away. We can love the person and still have boundaries in place to create standards of behavior that benefit all.

Distraction

Imagine trying to drive a car while constantly looking out the side window. It would be impossible, right? But that is exactly what most people are doing every day.

When you're distracted, you're off course, and potentially putting yourself in serious danger. In the age of 24/7 news feeds and instant access to information, we easily get sucked into a vacuum, speeding mindlessly in the wrong direction. A few clicks on our phones and, just like that, we're caught up in a mindless trap, and our original objective feels a million miles away.

For me, social media is a huge distraction. I also used to get caught up in endless text and email conversations, responding to messages as soon as they popped up on my screen. All it took was a *ping!* and my nervous system would jump. Can you relate? How much of your time and energy is wasted each day on distractions? It's alarming when you sit down and do the math.

A distraction might also come in the form of something positive or something we really want, such as a shiny new project idea, a last-minute meeting, or an invitation to join a group or attend an event. All of these can feel exciting—but is the timing really appropriate?

Then, there are the things we feel obligated to do, like maintaining that "open door" policy that constantly takes us away from our work to help others, or cramming more PTA fundraising activities into the schedule.

Still other distractions take us out of our bodies and away from healthy choices. Does your body *really* desire mindless comfort food or that third coffee, or is it actually asking for nourishment, quiet, and rest?

Distractions are a constant fact of life. They happen to everyone, all the time. I have repeatedly battled several while writing this book, including taking on new projects before I was finished with the current ones, taking on work and clients who weren't the right fit, and generally trying to do more than was necessary or healthy at any given moment. When the writing process got hard, I looked for reasons why I couldn't do it—and, like magic, there they were.

It's necessary to field some distractions over the course of the day. However, with a bit of awareness, we can clearly see when we've crossed the line and have moved out of alignment and into the zone of friction. When a tire goes out of alignment on your car, you can no longer drive with ease. It gets rough and bumpy, and the steering wheel pulls right when you want to drive straight. It's a compounding stack of distractions—the bumpy ride, the slight pull, the increasing effort it takes to hold the steering wheel in alignment—right up until the whole thing breaks down and leaves you stuck on the side of the road.

The goal of this enemy tactic is to break our focus and flow and move us into the place of overwhelm, where nothing gets real traction or creates real impact. Flow state is that sacred space where you are suspended in time and things are just channeling through you. Everything falls into place, and you are firing on all cylinders. While it's not something that happens all the time, it is a state you can cultivate, and it's pure magic. In the high-performance coaching world, we teach that every time we move away from the task at hand, it takes a minimum of twenty to thirty minutes to really get refocused, and it takes even more time for tasks that require more creative power or high-level decision-making. If you get distracted and break flow, it's not the easiest thing to drop back into. This applies in all areas of your life; when you break flow in your relationships, your parenting, your work, or your rest, it will get harder and harder to drop back in.

Every distraction is a wrong exit on the way to your destination.

This does not mean you need to be rigid. The key is knowing what direction you are headed and what it feels like when the wheels of your body, soul, and spirit are in full alignment and working order. It also means getting crystal clear on what it feels like when you are *not* in alignment and your vessel is fighting you every step of the way. This awareness will help you discern what is a distraction and what is an opportunity.

The Antidote: Focus and Protect

Awareness is the first step to change. Once you have awareness, you can more confidently slam the door on distractions.

Here are two key practices that will help you reduce distractions and reclaim your flow.

First off, do a "brain dump" of every single unfinished project or task that is swirling around in your head—everything you are currently working on and everything you know you should be working on or want to start. We can do all things, but we can't do all things at the same time. Too often, we have multiple open projects on our burners and nothing is moving forward efficiently. This only feeds our discouragement and doubt!

We must determine how to focus on the right things at the right time. Once your master brain dump is complete, remind yourself that this is simply a holding tank for all your ideas, not a to-do list! Ask yourself, and more importantly, ask God, "What is the authorized work that will yield the greatest results here?" Decide what your main thing will be and give it the proper time and space on your calendar. Then, decide what your top priorities will be for this period and protect them fiercely! You can get to the other items eventually, but things move forward where there is order and focus.

Secondly, master the art of elimination. Choose a normal day and record everything you do. Every time you switch tasks, jot it down. The simplest way to do this is to have an hour-by-hour agenda; you can print one from your Google calendar or use a simple sheet of paper. Whatever your method, record it all: time spent scrolling social media, time arguing with your daughter, time answering emails, and so on. At the end of the day, look at your list and observe where you were in flow, and where you got distracted. Do the math. Add up how much time was wasted on unnecessary activities and interruptions. If you really want to shift the game, calculate energy expenditure as well as time. Percentage wise, how much do you think each distraction cost you energetically?

Be intentional, and flag the things you are committed to reducing or eliminating altogether. Warriors know how to protect what's most important. Begin by blocking your time and giving your authorized work a protected place on your calendar. This includes time for your spiritual life, health, and family. Fill in other items as needed, but remember to leave white space for unexpected emergencies or simply to catch your breath!

This practice has given me so much more freedom and clarity. I know exactly what I will be giving my time to at all times, and anything outside of that is an automatic "no."

Disorientation

Oh, this is a big one! While it goes hand in hand with distraction and disconnection, disorientation needs its own section because when we are confused and unclear, it's a sign that we are under attack by the enemy and need to pay attention!

Often, we don't realize we are distracted until we are completely at a loss about where we are, where we are going, and even who we are. This can show up as mental congestion, conflicting thoughts that fight against each other, or an inability to see possibilities or the potential for growth.

While disorientation is rampant everywhere, let's look at the fitness industry for a moment. When I owned my health studio, I saw people taking advice from one expert trainer after another, each with their own "signature method" that they promised would produce results. These poor clients bounced around like ping-pong balls between paleo, vegan, and keto diets, only to keep gaining weight and feeling sick. They would try fasting protocols, weight training, running programs, and a mortgage payment's worth of supplements, all to no avail. It was pure chaos, and at the end of the day, most of them were even more confused, discouraged, and exhausted than when they started. First, they'd been sold a bundle of lies about what an optimal healthy body should look like. Then, they were sold a bag of tricks that promised them they could achieve it. Sure, the latest protocol could offer short-term results. But like most things undertaken in a state of disorientation, those protocols weren't what was actually needed.

Do you know what most people were totally unwilling to do? Shut out the noise, go within, and listen to what their unique bodies needed. They didn't know how to listen to their own bodies and stop the comparison games for long enough to get real answers. They fell victim to the enemy tactic of disorientation and ended up wasting thousands of hours (and, in many cases, hundreds of thousands of dollars) on what amounted to distractions.

This is the game. The enemy gives us a little dose of what we are seeking so we keep chasing. That dangling carrot offers a little taste of power, a little taste of weight loss, a little taste of affection or connection or abundance ... and we want more. When we don't get it, we move on to the next thing, the next promise. The taste is enough to keep us wanting, but it never offers the fullness we are created for. This is disorientation at its finest, and it is a dangerous place to be. When everything outside of us is guiding us, those influences jerk us around like puppets on a string.

The Antidote: Clarity

Isaiah 30:21 says, "*And your ears shall hear a word behind you, saying, 'This is the way, walk in it,' when you turn to the right or when you turn to the left.*"

If confusion comes from being disconnected from our body, soul, and spirit, clarity is the antidote. True clarity comes from God and from deep within our innermost being. It can be accessed by connecting to that secret place where our spirit and the Holy Spirit are one within us. When we are attuned to the Truth within, we can still hear what's going on outside, but the voice of Truth, our North Star, is stronger and clearer than all the external noise. Only from this place of calm and clarity can we make decisions based on what we require, not what others are telling us to want or need. When we are off course, we can look back and see where we missed the mark, and take steps to correct our mistakes.

Years ago, I would regularly take clients out for runs on the magnificent network of wooded trails in our community. One day, several clients went out for a run just as the rain started to come down. Thinking they could outrun it, they carried on. Before long, I received a call. "We're lost! We can't find the trail and it's pouring out here!" I invited them to stop, look around, and tell me what landmarks they saw. I soon realized that they were less than 200 feet from the main road! They had literally been running in frantic circles just a few dozen steps from the very road they were looking for. This is how fast we can become disoriented when something unexpected comes our way. If those runners hadn't slowed down to assess their surroundings, they could have been out there for hours, and someone might have been seriously hurt.

So, Warrior, it's time to cut those puppet cords. Refuse to take the bait of false promises, tempting shortcuts, or "downpours" of distraction that lead you into a never-ending loop of confusion. This will require you to slow down, go within, and cultivate your faith so that, when God provides clarity, you are ready to move on it.

One of the fastest ways to break the disorientation is to interrupt the pace you are moving at. Here is a practice you can do daily for a week to help interrupt your habitual pattern.

Take twenty to thirty minutes and go for a slow walk. Set a pace that is markedly slower than your usual. As you walk, shift your breathing to your nose rather than your mouth. See if you can slow down your breathing pattern and match your steps to your breath. You might take three or four steps for each inhale, and then three to four steps to each exhale. Slow and steady.

Notice the speed of your thoughts, and invite your thoughts to slow down. Begin to look around you in slow motion. Engage all five of your senses: sight, sound, taste, feeling, and touch. This is a meditative walking practice designed to shift your vantage point. Don't be tempted to treat it as a workout. Once you find yourself fully present and connected internally, ask the Holy Spirit to speak into you.

To take it a step further, move beyond walking and take this practice to the dinner table or anywhere else where you find yourself disconnecting. Practice slow eating and engage all five senses. Practice the art of full presence. The more you become present where you are, the easier it will become to sort through the confusion and find clarity.

Disembodiment

Our bodies are sacred, miraculous, self-healing vessels. They allow us to interact with the world, and with one another. Our senses and nervous systems give us feedback as to what we are feeling, what fuels us, what is a full yes or a full no for us. When we are connected to our bodies as we are divinely designed to be, they can provide us with deep insight and information.

We are not meant to be ruled by the body, but to operate in connection and harmony with the body so that it can provide the balance to our soul and spirit as part of our whole, integrated being. When the body works *with* us and *for* us, we experience well-being on all levels.

In an unhealthy or "hijacked" nervous system state, such as feeling overwhelmed or under attack, we disassociate from our bodies. We disconnect. We begin mistrusting and fighting against our amazing vessel. We no longer feel safe inside our bodies. It becomes harder to sense what is right or wrong for us, what is life-giving, what is truth, what is deception, and what is truly nourishing. We lose the ability to sense the instinctual wisdom within.

Disembodiment arises in many ways. Here are just a few:

- Pushing the body repeatedly past its physical limits without proper rest and recovery. All push with no real recovery is a recipe for disaster.

- Taking medication to cover up symptoms like chronic headaches, inflammation, digestive issues, mental fatigue, or physical pain. These symptoms are often red flags for larger, underlying issues.

- Overeating, drinking, or consuming toxic food, drinks, or chemicals because we are busy, tired, or looking to numb ourselves or escape reality.

- Adhering to strict diets or protocols that starve the body of key nutrients.

- Living in the future state of worry or anxiety

- Living in the past state of regret, shame, and guilt.

- Prostituting or sacrificing the body, especially sexually, for the promises of security, power, money, love, or recognition.

- Punishing the body for not doing what we want it to do (i.e., not working hard enough, not losing weight fast enough, not staying energized enough, etc.)

- Ignoring the body's signals to slow down or stop altogether.

- Always being plugged into artificial tech/noise and inorganic materials in our environment. Lack of exposure to nature and stillness.

- Rejecting parts of the body due to shame, abuse, or neglect. This could be a result of any physical, verbal, or mental/emotional trauma or abuse that was present and has not been healed/processed.

- Going through deep loss or pain and not taking the time and space to properly grieve. Bypassing key phases of physical and emotional healing.

So, Warrior, are you honoring the temple, or defiling it?

1 Corinthians 6:19 (NIV) tells us, *"Do you not know that your bodies are temples of the Holy Spirit, who is in you, whom you have received from God? You are not your own; you were bought at a price. Therefore honor God with your bodies."* We are designed in these bodies, with these bodies, on purpose. The body is the vessel through which we get to experience this incredible life, with all its feelings, sensations, challenges, and adventures. It's the vessel that takes us into new places and spaces. It's the vessel that allows us to interact with others and carry out the mission and assignments we have been given. The vessel to make love in, worship in, sweat in. But we've been programmed to compete

and keep up and pretend, so we spend most of our time in our heads, in the future, in the past, or in someone else's business, and we forget where we physically are.

Your body is sacred. It's the container that your life force funnels through. Your physical and sexual energy are potent, powerful and created by God for you to multiply and prosper. When these energies are harnessed and channeled appropriately you will experience bliss, but when given to the wrong things they will rob you of the intimacy you desire and multiply your confusion, hardship, and disconnection.

Your sexual energy, and the act of giving it to someone or something, instantly unifies you and meshes you with the other. It's possible that you felt that hold and power if you have ever slept with the wrong person, stayed in the wrong relationship to get superficial needs met, used pornography, or entertained emotional affairs. It's entanglement, and it's a dangerous game that will sweep you out of your body faster than anything else.

In addition to how we use our individual sexual energy, there is also an attack underway on our original sexual identity: man and woman, male and female. This is very close to my heart as I have navigated many personal attacks on my identity as a woman. In my quest to fight every battle, meet every enemy, and never show weakness, I rejected the *unique design* of a woman, and instead tried to force myself to operate like a man. As a result, my body suffered.

God created man and woman. He created male and female. Our sexual design is intentional and unique. We are created with very different bodies beautifully designed to fit together and complement each other in all the ways; physical, mental, and emotional. When we deny our unique differences, we turn away from creation itself.

After twenty-plus years of working with both male and female bodies, I can tell you that a biologically male body and a biologically female body will respond very differently to life changes, various types of exercise, common stressors, and the seasons and cycles of life. I did not train men and women the same because their bodies responded differently.

I've also come to learn, both through my own experience and from speaking with hundreds of women clients and colleagues, that we are not designed to produce results in the same ways as men, either. The feminine body that tries to keep up with a masculine way of producing will end up burned out, exhausted, and completely disconnected from her unique ability to multiply and create in a nourishing way. She will likely struggle in having and holding healthy intimate relationships, and she will most often resent her work. A woman's body is designed to be a vessel of creation. Her body operates on cycles, rhythms, and seasons, and her energy levels vary accordingly. She is not designed to be a production factory 24/7. That is completely unnatural.

I use the analogy of birth. There is a time to get pregnant (the planting of seeds), a time for gestation (a time of deep rest and nourishment), a time to prepare for the birth of new life (the nesting/preparation phase), a time for pushing (go time!), a time for nurturing, a time for releasing—and then it repeats. When we remember this, we will naturally feel more connected to our bodies and more able to hold our connection to God and our divine purpose.

As I have watched women heal their relationships with their bodies and reclaim their lost femininity, I have seen them gifted with a renewed desire and passion for life, an increase in nurturing energy, new creative visions, and even new businesses that are a full yes for them. I have seen them thrive in their bodies where they were once stuck in chronic pain. I have seen them relax, learn to laugh, and be cherished again. I have seen them excited to support the men in their lives instead of criticizing them. They are finding balance and harmony again.

The Antidote: Honor the Vessel

As we come back into our bodies and into our hearts, we come back home. Our job as Warriors is to live fully embodied and become fierce protectors of our physical vessels. "Fully embodied" means to be whole in body, soul, and spirit, fully present and representing the very essence that we are. Whatever occupies this vessel will take over our hearts and therefore take charge of our destiny. What if, instead of rejecting our bodies and trying to change them, we learned to work *with* them, to re-integrate the disintegrated parts?

The enemy loves to attack creation itself—in particular, our vessels of life. If the temple of our body is defiled and destroyed, it can no longer host the presence of God, the Holy Spirit. In this absence, there is a deep void that must be filled with something. Before long, heaviness, darkness, chaos, strife, and sickness will begin to seep in. *"The thief comes only to steal and kill and destroy. I came that they may have life, and have it abundantly."* (John 10:10, NASB)

If our vessel isn't working well, we become unable to fulfill our calling, unable to fully show up for the people and relationships in our lives. We may find ourselves tired, mentally congested, confused, and perhaps even immobilized by pain. It's no wonder that disembodiment is a key tactic of the enemy.

Go and play for an afternoon by yourself without any technology, sedatives, or outside influence. Head to the woods, to the lake, to the park, or wherever you feel inspired to go. Give yourself an hour of complete free time where you don't have to do or produce anything but can just *be* in your body. Walk barefoot in the grass, then run, dance, or jump on things. Literally play. Notice what it feels like in your body to move without needing a reason to or some kind of structured program. Lay in the sunshine and notice what it feels like on your skin to soak up the rays. Smell the flowers, literally.

Notice how you feel in your body. Are you rigid? Are you anxious? Notice what feelings are coming up and where they live inside your body. Where is there tension? Where is there inflexibility? Where is there hesitation for fear of being judged or watched? Notice how your body responds to these thoughts and emotions, and as you notice them, ask them, "What are you trying to communicate to me right now?" Then listen to what your tense muscles, your heartbeat, your belly, and your whole body want to say to you. As you listen, you are engaging in a new relationship with your body.

Discouragement

Dealing with one enemy tactic on its own generally will not throw us completely off our game. But when they begin to stack on top of each other, life can start to feel heavier and heavier, and it can become harder to get out from underneath it all. Suddenly, it's like there's an elephant standing on our chest. The pressure is too great, and we feel unable to access the joy, inspiration, desire, or love we once felt. Instead, we are filled with disappointment, despair, and cynicism. Hope fades away, and we begin to question whether we will ever overcome this battle.

Dis-courage literally means "to be out of heart," so to be discouraged means to have lost confidence in or enthusiasm for something—to have lost heart for it. When we become disconnected from our innermost feelings, we reach a point where we have no more faith or belief, where we are at the end of our rope and can't see a way out. At this point, we have allowed fear to take over and consume us.

It begins with a little worry here or there, a little arrow to the heart when things don't work out or we don't get the answers we were hoping for. Then, we start noticing all the things that are going wrong. Before we know it, our worries are spiraling, and problems are manifesting all around us. Our fears have officially become our reality, and we have piles of evidence to support why things will not work out in our favor or why we should just give up. Our heart begins to harden under the weight.

I have been in this place more times than I like to admit, and I speak to clients and prospects every day who have been sitting in a place of discouragement for months or even years.

It bears repeating: the battle is for your soul, but the battleground is in the mind. By the time we are discouraged, we have allowed the mind to ruminate on everything that isn't working. We have been penetrated by the enemy's tactics and have given ourselves over to them. We have not been fiercely protecting our atmosphere, internal environment, and energy; instead, we have allowed ourselves to have open gates.

The Antidote: Come Back to the Heart

The way back to courage and faith is *through* the heart. Discouragement is defeated by coming back to our heart and fiercely protecting access to it. We must get out of our heads, quiet the noise, and begin to cut off the supply that is feeding the fear, doubt, confusion, division, disembodiment, etc. When you cut off the supply of what feeds something, it can no longer grow. Even better, when you are no longer busy feeding these enemy tactics with your precious life force, you can redirect *all* that energy toward creating the new. If we are masters at growing and feeding problems, we can also become masters at feeding energy toward that which creates solutions and brings life.

Feed love, or feed fear. Those are the only two options. However, implementing the former requires radical awareness. When we are discouraged and at the end of our rope, the only thing we can do is get radically honest with ourselves, our hearts, and God, and come back into the place that is life-giving.

When you are in that dark place, please know that whatever you are feeling and whatever state you are in, the thoughts coming to you have been planted there. They are not of you, and they are not of God. Therefore, you, through God, have the power to recognize them, cut off their supply, and meet the enemy on a battleground of *your* choosing.

Action

When you notice yourself feeling discouraged and weighed down, it's time to empty yourself. You need to release in order to receive. This is a universal law. If you are full, nothing new or life-giving can enter in.

Here is a simple practice to clear out the heaviness inside:

In a journal, brain dump all the things that have been weighing you down. Imagine you are emptying a garbage can full of all the things inside you that feel discouraging, toxic, and heavy. There is power in bringing the hidden things to the surface and shedding light on them, and in doing this from a place of genuine love for ourselves and a desire to "clean house." Take five to ten minutes (or longer if you need it) to just empty everything inside you. Keep going until you begin to feel your heart lighten.

For years, I was terrified to openly admit in any way that fear, disconnection, doubt, or any other enemy tactics were going on inside me because I did not want to manifest them or feed them. Ironically, that was the fear, disconnection, and doubt talking! What is hidden, when brought into the light with the motive of love and healing, will be renewed!

As you write, notice if the tone of your words changes or you begin to process the information differently as light is shed on the page. Give each of these things over to God, and ask the Holy Spirit to speak truth and life back into each of these things for you. As you lay the heavy burdens at His feet, what are you left with? For me it's often a lighter spirit, a renewed mind, and the bandwidth to focus on the things He has for me rather than the things I cannot control.

Meditate on Matthew 11:28-30 daily: *"Come to me, all you who are weary and burdened, and I will give you rest. Take my yoke upon you and learn from me, for I am gentle and humble in heart, and you will find rest for your souls. For my yoke is easy and my burden is light."* Remember that the antidote is always here and available. We need to ditch the savior complex and stop trying to carry the weight. We were never designed to do it all, know it all, fix it all, or have it all together.

Do what you can do. Let Him do the rest.

THE ANTIDOTES

We all get tired of fighting the wrong battles. There are so many ways in which we lose our footing, and so many ways in which the enemy trips us up and keeps us from the calling and life we are created for.

The first step is to understand how the enemy moves and operates through specific tactics. The second step is to know that you have the power and the authority to shut the door on these tactics.

As we've explored:

- Deception is defeated by discernment.

- Doubt is defeated by faith.

- Disconnection is defeated by reconnection.

- Division is defeated by unification and collaboration.

- Distraction is defeated by focus.

- Disorientation is defeated by clarity.

- Disembodiment is defeated by embodiment.

- Discouragement is defeated by coming back to our heart.

At any point, you can start recognizing and building barriers against the enemy's tactics. At any point, you can choose to redirect your focus and your vital life force, cutting off the supply that feeds these negative things. There is such power in awareness, in our ability to consciously choose who and what to give our attention and heart to. This is not about focusing on the enemy, but rather about being aware that there *is* an enemy, so that you are equipped and positioned to cut through the noise.

Remember, God will never give you more than you can handle, but sometimes you have to get raw and real and ask for help. He will always provide the way out. Once we see the enemy's tactics clearly, we can do something about them—and that is the first step to becoming victors instead of victims.

WARRIOR INITIATION

Deception

- How has the enemy used the tactic of deception in your life?

- How do you know when something is a distortion of truth?

- What worldly "truths" are simply not sitting well with you these days?

- What criteria do you currently have in place as a guideline for discernment?

Doubt

- When you find yourself falling into the trap of doubt and fear, where are the ideas coming from? How do they present themselves in your life?

- If you had a deeper connection with God, yourself, and others, what would you be doing differently?

Disconnection

- Where is disconnection showing up in your life?

- How can you find big and small ways to reconnect to God and those you care about today?

Division

- Where is division showing up in your home, business, and community? How are you contributing to that division?

- How can you disagree with a position while holding true to your principles and respecting others who hold different beliefs?

Distraction

- What is distracting you the most on a daily basis?

- What would it look like if you reclaimed your time?

- What would the hard no's be?

- What is one simple shift you can make in an area of great distraction to protect your time, energy, and focus?

Disorientation

- Where do you find yourself getting easily disoriented, lost, or confused?

- What tends to pull you off course faster than anything else?

- What information, practices, or habits bring more complexity rather than clarity in your life?

- Where do you need to slow down more, pull back, and ask better questions?

Disembodiment

- Where do you find yourself mindlessly going through the motions, sedating, or escaping with alcohol, drugs, TV, social media, instant gratification, or mindless activities?

- Does it feel safe to be in your body?

- What parts of your body and original design (creation) have you been rejecting or fighting against?

- When you are most grounded, calm, and at peace, what are you doing?

Discouragement

- When was the last time you truly felt confident and full of heart?

- What were you doing then that you are no longer doing today?

- Can you recognize how the enemy tries to discourage you?

- What has this discouragement (lack of heart) cost you? What will it cost you if you keep allowing this for another five years? Ten?

CHAPTER TEN

Understand The Nature of the Battle

"For we do not wrestle against flesh and blood, but against principalities, against powers, against the rulers of the darkness of this age, against spiritual hosts of wickedness in the heavenly places."

— **EPHESIANS 6:12 (NKJV)**

*I*t's no surprise that, as I embarked upon the writing of this chapter, I started getting broadsided with everything and anything to keep me from moving forward. I hit a complete block, and it felt as if a force was quite literally pushing against me from every angle.

For the first couple of days, I chalked it up to hormones and my feminine cycle. I gave myself some grace and rested, reflected, and caught up on simple tasks. Immediately after, Hurricane Ian hit the East Coast and the entire atmosphere shifted as the pressure dropped, the temperature changed, and the sunlight was hidden behind heavy winds and rain that made me want to hibernate. Then, it was the weekend, full of kids, a noisy home, and fall cleanup. I felt unmotivated and frustrated with myself at the same time.

As the list of excuses and roadblocks kept piling up, I became increasingly sensitive to everything around me, and my frustration grew into a bigger and bigger mountain. All I felt like doing was sleeping, drinking coffee, and wandering around the house aimlessly all day, filling the time with distractions, then plopping down with a glass of wine at 6:00 p.m. to connect with my husband.

Isn't it interesting that this came right on the heels of our last chapter on enemy tactics? Truly, it wasn't a coincidence.

There are times and seasons when we are called to be still, go within, and just let things be. I flowed with this feeling for a while until I realized something about this was different. I just did not feel like myself at all! I was in a battle for my life force. The voices inside my head grew stronger and more dissatisfied, and my body tensed to match them. I knew there was an internal battle going on in my thoughts, and a spiritual conflict that was feeding it.

Then, it was Monday morning. With the kids back in school and my schedule empty, I planned for a fresh start. Then, it hit me again. Zero motivation. No energy. No desire to do anything except get outside in nature. To say the distractions were coming from every angle would be an understatement. I needed to get grounded and connect to myself, the earth, and the Holy Spirit. I had to shift my physical state and my entire being. I needed to plug into life force.

As I took a step back and let myself breathe, I chose to take a different vantage point. I began trying to understand this resistance and unrest instead of fighting, forcing, or pushing through. What was *actually* going on here?

It was a battle alright. A battle for my energy and focus. A battle for my life force, which could either multiply myself and others or feed the guilt, heaviness, and depressive spirit swirling in the atmosphere. A battle for my trust against the spirit of doubt hovering over me, questioning everything I was doing.

I knew I had to pivot. Telling myself, "Just focus and get it done!" wasn't working. So, I got curious and started asking questions like, "How can I infuse more life force into myself right now? When I am deeply connected to myself and the Spirit, and things begin to overflow out of me, what am I doing?"

The answers came. "When I am connected, I am moving, walking, and talking. I am drinking copious amounts of fresh water. I am letting go of expectations and playing with things differently. I am trusting the path, one step at a time."

Then, I asked, "What doors do I have open that are sucking the life out of me?" I prayed for the awareness of how I could close those doors and release the enemy's foothold in my mind, heart, and body. The temporary distractions of coffee, alcohol, and small tasks around the house were real. Rather than ignoring or fighting the urges, I had to recognize that they were there for a reason, and my job was to address that reason, and then redirect my life force.

So, I jumped on the spin bike to physically move all the heaviness and density that was stuck inside me. There were all kinds of emotions in there, and to be honest, I had a good cry for the first part of my ride, shedding tears of frustration, negative self-talk, anger, blaming, and whatever else was in there. I emptied myself and got back into my body again. As I rode on, my mind emptied, my body activated, the dense energy dissipating, I listened to music that filled me up. I prayed out loud, knowing that God is omnipresent—always here, always listening, always available to provide what I need. I talked to myself and got curious about what was coming up. I infused myself with kindness, affirming words, and reminders of who I am, where I come from, and what I am here to do. *"For God has not given us a spirit of fear and timidity, but of power, love, and self-discipline."* (2 Timothy 1:7, NLT)

My energy rose, and clarity came over me. *"Who says you need to sit down to write this book?"* whispered the gentle voice inside me. *"Get up. Start walking. Start talking and voice-record this. Be in the energy of pressing on, moving forward, understanding the nature of the battle—and do not be delayed any longer. Do not hesitate. Do not entertain distractions. Trust yourself to stay in your body, do it differently, and let the words flow out of you."*

Man, did it feel good to connect to that inner voice again. And so, I began recording the text for this chapter as I headed out on a three-mile walk after that thirty-minute spin session. By the time I finished my walk, the chapter was well underway, and I was no longer entertaining the voices of doubt, delay, and depression. I not only felt a sense of accomplishment, but I was moving in the right direction again with ease.

Here's the thing: once I had the awareness, I made a conscious decision. I did the thing my mind and body perhaps didn't want, but needed. I listened to the quiet inner voice and simply obeyed.

Often what we think we need to do isn't what we need at all. I had been trying to force myself to sit down and get to work for days, but no words were making their way onto the page; the only thing emerging was a mounting sense of disappointment and frustration. All that forcing just made the mountain bigger and the wall thicker. Instead of giving in to that fear, I slowed down. I got curious. I held space for myself, and then did what I needed to do to bring life back to me. From there, I was able to pivot my focus and energy. I walked back in the door with a smile on my face to meet my husband. And then, the sun and blue sky reappeared after nearly a week of gray, wet, and cold—right in the midst of this recalibration.

Coincidence? I think not.

We all want mastery, but a Warrior must always be training the foundations—always aware and ready for battle. When they do engage, they know exactly what their position is and how to achieve their desired outcome. Today, I consider myself a Warrior Queen. I am fighting to show people what is possible when they make the conscious decision to live the life they are created for. I am a Warrior of the Heart, no longer a warrior of the world. And I am forever in the practice.

The battle I described above may seem simple, barely consequential, and yet it was a huge revelation for me. My old patterns would have seen me activating my inner warrior to push through and fight the mountain, beating both it and myself up along the way. It would have been all force, willpower, and ego. On the other side, I may have gained some forward momentum, but it would have cost me even more energy in the end. This battle was fought differently. Instead of pushing against the mountain, I dissolved it by focusing on what I was being guided to do, infusing myself with life force, and connecting myself to the Source of clarity and energy. I didn't try to fight the load; I released the dead weight so I could move faster and more efficiently. I gave myself permission to stop doing what wasn't working, and instead do it altogether differently. In that moment, I moved from power rather than force.

PREPARING FOR THE BATTLE TO COME

We are in a time and season where collective transformation is happening on a rapid scale and on an accelerated timeline. The events of 2020 did a lot to accelerate this awakening, and I believe this is ultimately a good thing. I have never witnessed so many people seeking clarity and direction. In a time of uncertainty and instability, many vital questions were asked. People were, and still are, feeling the squeeze at home, at work, in their networks, in their industries, and in their communities and inner circles.

Many people are pivoting their entire lives, waking up to what matters most, and forging a new path forward. Many are coming home to God, remembering their original design as children of God, as souls designed for freedom. Many are coming together to become powerful co-creators of a new life.

Others are still lost in the darkness and chaos, anxiously waiting for things to return to what they consider "normal." I see many hanging their faith and dependence on systems designed to program them and keep them enslaved.

Humanity is at an intersection unlike any other we have experienced. Each and every one of us has the power and capacity to shift our internal game. Ultimately, leadership starts within—and, when we truly begin to lead ourselves and make *that* the new normal, the ripple effect is huge.

It is the duty and responsibility of those who are waking up—including you, dear Warrior—to understand the nature of the battle. So often, when we're frantically trying to put out fire after fire, we find we are the very ones holding the match! Once we realize this, we are officially in full choice. We can choose to continue to play the same games we've always played or be the ones who change the game going forward. Fire burns and destroys, but it also offers warmth and supports life, inviting others to gather in community.

In order to move forward as Warriors of the Heart who dissolve useless battles and fight for what actually matters, we must train ourselves daily. This is no different than any other training. We master things by repetition. There will be days when you get it right, and days when old wounds start bleeding out again—but the more you practice, the more awareness you cultivate, and the more self-discipline and discernment you bring to the table, this will become an embodied and natural approach.

This chapter will prepare you for the battles to come, offering the skills you'll need to engage and fight differently.

Here are the steps we'll be discussing:

1. Cultivate awareness
2. Shift the vantage point
3. Find the neutral place

CULTIVATE AWARENESS

The easiest place to interrupt a pattern is before it begins. The second easiest place to interrupt it is the minute you recognize it. The moment you become aware that you are in a battle is the *moment of power*. This is the moment you have full choice to either forge ahead mindlessly or stop, consider, and change your course of action.

One of the hardest things for warriors and high achievers to do is simply *stop*.

We are so conditioned to fix, win, and press forward at all costs that we will often slay everything in our path—consciously or unconsciously—in an attempt to get to the finish line. As we now know, this comes at a high cost.

When things are heated, either in the physical moment or if you're going through a season of intense pressure, it is critical to put down the sword. A Warrior of the Heart knows that not every battle is worthy of engagement.

As I look back on the many battles I have faced in my life and what has empowered me to show up differently for myself and others, I see that there are three key principles that have helped me slow down and transform the way I recognize battles before I respond:

1. The physical reality before me today is actually a manifestation of my past.

2. I am a multidimensional being in a multidimensional world, therefore I must take a holistic approach to all situations.

3. There are spiritual forces at play at all times, and the battle is ultimately for my life force.

These are foundational when it comes to what I choose to look at. So, when things get heated, I always make sure I have addressed each one before wading into the fray.

We have explored all of these principles individually in previous chapters. Now, we will learn how to put them to work in real time.

Principle 1: The Physical Reality Before Me Today is Actually a Manifestation of My Past

Our current reality—the thing we are experiencing right now—is a sum of our past thoughts, emotions, words, and actions. It is the manifestation of what we have tolerated, reacted to, normalized, and fed our life force to up until this moment. That's why our choices, here and now, are the keys to unlocking a new outcome. Everything in creation was created through the Word. God spoke, and so it was. We must become guardians of our words and actions, for they either create life or death, and will always multiply or diffuse what is at hand.

Choose carefully what intention you initiate from, for it will surely come back to you. This universal law, the law of the "seed," is written into the very fabric of creation. When you react to an issue with the same level of consciousness that created the issue, you are feeding it, and will continue to manifest that same past over and over again. This is the consequence of free will: we reap what we sow.

This is important because if we keep fighting and reacting to things at the physical level, we are actually reacting to the past, and therefore creating more of the very things we are trying to get rid of. This makes change slow and difficult. We have the power to move, shift, reorganize, and form new matter, but it requires us to look at things through the lens of creation. What are we here to consciously create? We must focus on the desired future state while operating in the present moment. That is literally what the word "transform" means—to "move beyond the current form so that things change shape."

Let's look at an example.

I often work with couples who are trying to rebuild trust and create a new relationship dynamic together. Often, these couples find themselves fighting about what is happening in real time—or worse, bringing things up from the past—rather than responding according to what they want to create in the future. These fights pierce old wounds that have not fully healed, and before you know it, both parties are bleeding out again and moving into damage control mode. It feels like there is never any forward momentum.

Take a simple thing like a missed phone call. The fact that their partner didn't pick up the phone reminds the person of a time in the past when they were neglected, even though the missed call in this moment could be due to something completely unrelated. That memory triggers a flood of emotions, including uncertainty, fear, and rejection. Immediately, the one who was hurt and is now triggered may shoot their partner an accusing text message—a reaction to the past. The partner who receives the offending message may then feel attacked and respond in a similar manner from the place of their own wounding, getting defensive, angry, and frustrated. Before you know it, a chain reaction of miscommunication, blaming, and frustration unfolds. The fight is on!

These partners are meeting the situation at hand with the same level of consciousness that created these patterns in the past. As a result, they will continue to feed and experience more of those feelings and gather more evidence to support their frustration that "nothing is changing, nothing is working." And, as long as nothing changes, they are correct.

When we take a step back from the knee-jerk reaction—which is rooted in our past experiences—we see a broader picture of the present moment. From this new level of consciousness, we can then choose to engage in a way that is congruent to the future we desire to create. Instead of jumping into every battle with our weapons out and our blood surging, we can choose how, when, and what we are engaging with, and where we engage.

This works in any situation—whether you want a transformation in your marriage, your team, your health, or anywhere else. Before you go into battle, pause and ask yourself the questions below. Better yet, ask the Holy Spirit to speak truth into you about what's actually going on. After all, He does have a heavenly perspective.

- "What exactly am I responding to right now?"
- "Is this a manifestation of the past or a representation of the future I desire?"
- "What level of consciousness did I create this from in the past?"
- "What level of consciousness do I want to bring to this now?"

Principle 2: I Am a Multidimensional Being in a Multidimensional World, Therefore I Must Take a Holistic Approach to All Situations

Our physical bodies are amazing vessels, both affecting and affected by the environment we live in. That environment includes light, sound, frequency, thoughts, emotions, conditions, and so on; it is both inside us and outside of us. Taking a holistic approach means that, in order to transform a situation in the physical realm, we can't just barge in, rearrange the external décor, and then expect things to be different on the inside. We need to make shifts in our internal environment, too—including our physiology, soul (thoughts and emotions), and spirit.

The world teaches us to force things in the physical, but we are so much more complex and intricate than that. We are part of everything, can absorb everything, and also have the power to select what we connect and open ourselves up to. So, if we want to win the battles in our lives, we must shift the atmosphere within and around us as a whole. We must change the heart of the matter.

If we only address changes in the physical, we end up feeling like we are putting on a play, pretending everything is as we want it but feeling incongruent on the inside. Environments that require us to put on masks are life-sucking to live and work in, and can quickly descend into tyranny and abuse. If we address things in the mental and physical environment but ignore the emotional and spiritual, we end up where most warriors exist: climbing the ladder, getting the medals, and winning the game, but never finding peace. Shiny on the outside, super dark and cold on the inside. I see a lot of this when working with corporate groups, executives, and high achievers. We've heard the cliche, "Don't judge a book by its cover," yet we still fall prey to that temptation.

If we miss the heart (emotional) component, we become disconnected from our humanness and find ourselves feeling like numbed out machines— empty, disconnected, questioning people's motives for wanting to be with us. Lastly, if we don't recognize the spiritual component, we are omitting God from the equation and missing out on the essence of life itself—His unconditional love, the blessing and promises He has for us, and most importantly, the salvation (freedom) and grace which we could never earn.

The next time you find yourself in the midst of a challenge, trigger, or battle, take a moment to step back and see the situation multidimensionally. Ask yourself:

- "What am I seeing in the physical?" Address the behavior or situation from a neutral stance. Look at the physical as an observer. What are the raw facts vs opinions?

- "What thoughts are being entertained and fueled?"

- "What old stories are being retold and replayed out?"

- "What emotions are being played here?"

- "What energy am I (we) giving to this?"

- "What does God want for me (us) in this situation?"

Then, get curious about the emotions and stories, rather than fighting or challenging them.

Principle 3: There Are Spiritual Forces At Play at All Times, and the Battle is Ultimately for My Life Force

Understanding the physical, mental, emotional, and spiritual in tandem will get you much further than focusing on one element alone. To fully be integrated with and connected to our true purpose, we have to go all the way to the root. Every single thing is first created in the spiritual with and through God, and that means all things have spiritual roots. The spiritual is the base upon which all other elements are supported; without it, lasting and sustainable change is not possible.

The awareness that God is alive and active within us, around us, and for us at all times—and that the enemy is always aiming to disrupt our connection to God—gives us a completely different foundation for our everyday battles. Not everything out there is love and light. Not everything is evil, either. Not everything we engage with is what we see at face value. Not everything is simply resistance, an accident, or a coincidence. Recognizing that there is much more at play than meets the eye allows us to get curious about what else is going on in any given situation.

Looking at life through a spiritual lens means remembering that the people and circumstances in our lives are not the enemy. Instead, we can see that there is a larger game being played on a multidimensional level. The true enemy, through the tactics discussed in the previous chapter, works to divide us. We are easy to manipulate when we are divided—and we are easily divided when we are offended and defensive. We change the game when we come together to fight the battles that really matter. We are no longer pawns being controlled by outside forces, but players consciously moving the pieces.

Perhaps you cognitively have grasped this concept in the past but have not felt the power and presence of the Holy Spirit. Now that you have rediscovered your true identity and seen yourself the way God sees you, you will be more easily able to step into this elevated perspective and see the spiritual nature of every encounter.

Although the spiritual realm is vast and wide, we have been given direct access to God at all times. There is no need to go through intermediaries to get answers. Invite the omnipresent Spirit of God to reveal exactly what is going on in the spiritual realm, and how you can be in right relationship to it.

SHIFT THE VANTAGE POINT

Conflict is a part of life. It's going to happen. But if what you're doing to heal and work through conflict isn't working, it's time to change how you're engaging—and before you can change how you engage, you need to change what you *see*.

The reason so many battles are recreated day in and day out is because we keep engaging from the ground level, positioning ourselves smack in the middle of the chaos, confusion, and entanglement. From there, we are ill-positioned to respond to anything except what is right in front of us.

Imagine that you are literally on a battlefield. Swords are clattering, explosions are going off, people are screaming. Your senses are heightened, your blood is pumping, and your body is reacting to everything defensively. Your vision narrows to what is immediately threatening you so you can take it down. Now, slowly pull yourself up and away from the battle. Put distance between yourself and the players down below. Keep pulling back until you see yourself standing high on a cliff overlooking the battlefield. I call this the "eagle's view" or the "heavenly view."

From here, you are no longer entangled in the messiness. It is quiet, serene even. Your mind clears. You get back in your body, calling your attention to the here and now. With this radical shift, you begin to see the bigger picture and all the players in a completely new way. You spot things you couldn't see before. New solutions arise, pockets open up, opportunities to move are now obvious. You can now see the greater forces at play and can voice clear commands rather than swinging blindly in the trenches.

At any moment when we are challenged—for example, when the conversation swerves into politics, we receive an email from an unhappy customer, or our partner makes a comment about last night—we can move into a heightened state of arousal. Depending on the context of the situation, our thinking brain gives quick feedback to our emotional brain, and we either perceive ourselves as being in a threatening environment or a safe environment. A threat stimulus (something that our brain perceives as a threat) triggers a fear response in our amygdala, which activates our fight-flight-freeze motor functions. Along with that, it triggers the release of stress hormones and revs up the sympathetic nervous system. Our heart rate goes up, pupils dilate, breathing becomes shallow and more rapid, and blood flows to the extremities in preparation to fight off the beast, run as fast as we can, or shut down. The reaction or response is unique to the individual, but the roots are often the same: something in the environment is perceived as a threat, and the body reacts accordingly.

We learn fear through our personal experiences and those of others, and we also learn it through stories and language passed down to us. The body remembers the experience of fear because all experiences and emotions are stored in the body. When a threat seems imminent, the body reacts to protect us based on what it learned from environments that caused us harm in the past.

Fear is a necessary emotion. The problem is not fear itself, which is designed to mobilize us so we can avoid danger, but rather when fear takes over and we become a hostage to it. Most of us will, thankfully, never need our threat stimulus to protect us on an actual battlefield, but that doesn't mean it won't turn on, even in situations as seemingly "safe" as a conversation that brings up conflicting viewpoints. If we have suffered abuse, injury, or other trauma, the response to *any* threat may be equivalent to the response to the greatest threats of our past, making our reactions seem extreme.

Awareness is key to shifting our perspective. Once we recognize that we are hot, bothered, fearful, anxious, attacking, defensive, or shutting down, we can de-escalate (or at least work with) our body's innate fear response. When we find ourselves in the middle of a heated debate, hyper-reactive to a comment, or simply in an environment that is triggering or hijacking us, it is our duty to disengage, find our center, and reorient ourselves. We have the power and authority to disengage! We must activate that power and pull back in order to access the heavenly view. Once we do that, we will feel more like ourselves, regain our strength, and be able to see clearly again. When we do this, the things that looked so threatening won't seem so scary anymore.

Imagine again looking down at the battle from the eagle's point of view. As you look over the lay of the land, imagine that all the people involved in the battle are simply characters or vessels, each operating from a different state or spirit. Now, put your hand over your heart. Imagine that your mind is dropping down into your heart space, and that the two are merging. Let your mind quiet down and allow your heart to speak up. Invite the Holy Spirit to give you eyes to see what's actually there. Then, ask yourself the following questions to clarify your new perspective and decide which actions will move you toward the future you truly desire:

- "If I was to give this battlefield a name, what would it be called?" People will often use words like chaos, drama, competition, control, and so on.

- "What is this battle really about?" Often, the battle is over control, safety, being seen or heard. We must recognize what the real fight is about. This is the only way we can address the real need.

- "What are the raw facts here—not my opinions or interpretations?" For example, "Fact: I did not receive a response to the last text message I sent. Opinion: This means my partner doesn't care what I have to say. Fact: Now we are yelling at each other."

- "What meaning did I give to this information?" Information is neutral until we give it meaning and energy. So, what is the meaning you're putting on this situation? For example, "I'm angry because when my partner didn't respond to that message I felt that he wasn't listening."

Once you can answer these questions honestly, with some distance from the situation itself, you are ready to move on to the next step.

FIND THE NEUTRAL PLACE

I can't recall the number of times I have heard a client say, "I *need* them to do X or say Y so that I can ..."

When we are fighting battles, we are often in a state of trying to convey our point to someone else, or force someone to do things our way. We want to ensure that we are being heard; we want to have the final word, or make sure they understand where we are coming from or what we think or believe. It's all about me, *me, ME*! Our inner three-year-old is desperately seeking to be seen, heard, pacified, and accommodated.

In each one of us, there is an inner child longing to be held, heard, and kept safe. It's healthy to care for children, to hold them and provide for them. We are dependent upon our mothers, fathers, and other caregivers for survival in the early stages of our lives—and, if we are not sustained and provided for, we die. Later in our development, we begin to realize that we are separate from Mom or Dad; that we, too, have a voice that needs to be seen and heard. This is how we begin to know ourselves. But if we get stuck at this stage through some sort of trauma or wounding from abandonment, rejection, or isolation, uncertainty settles into our being, only to be revisited throughout our lives until we reconcile these wounds.

Inside us, there is also an inner parent who can either hold space for this child, or one who has no time, energy, or tolerance for the child. The problem is that many of us have not fully developed our relationship with the inner parent that is loving, patient, gentle, and also directs us from a safe place. Many of us have only known an inner parenting relationship that is impatient, intolerant, angry, and disconnected from our inner child. This could stem from many things, including having parents who were not present, did not express or address emotions, or were unable to be kind or gentle with us. Many of the people I work with who struggle with feeling and understanding their emotions grew up in homes where their parents were physically present but emotionally unavailable, demanding, or gave affection based on performance.

Often, our relationship with God, our Spiritual Father, has a shocking resemblance to the relationship we held with our earthly fathers or mothers. This is especially true if we have not fully understood how to cultivate a real relationship with our Spiritual Father and recognized that our earthly parents were limited by their own abilities.

Many men I have worked with, including my own husband, never received a hug from their fathers or heard the words "I love you" from them. We are forever seeking the approval, attention, or affection of an inner father who was not available to us. In addition, some of us are forever trying to feel the warmth and nurturing energy that comes from the feminine or a mother figure. There is great safety and connection that stems from this place where we were originally fed (quite literally, if we were breastfed).

I share this because every human on this planet has a need and desire to be seen and held. When we lash out or focus exclusively on our own needs and point of view, we are missing a chance for connection and understanding—the building blocks of relationship and community. Too often, we find ourselves engaging in defensive arguments and rebuttals with our spouses, children, parents, or team members—fighting about the content while completely ignoring the context!

Finding the neutral place is key to engaging with yourself and others in a meaningful and constructive way. If we want to truly overcome the battles we are facing, then we've got to stop looking at the surface level and get under the hood. What is the root here—the context—that gives all this meaning to the content? What does this person or situation actually need? Once we get clear on this, we will have clarity on how to engage, if we engage at all. The original problem is rarely ever the root problem.

Content is irrelevant; context is key.

Once we create a safe space where everyone involved can be seen and discover what actually matters to them, the how-to part of the process generally reveals itself. Most likely, it will be a win-win. So, when you find yourself getting triggered by or reacting to a tense situation, stop for a moment and do an internal check-in. Holding space for yourself to find that inner standing.

Then, when you're ready, ask yourself:

- *"What is this battle actually for?"* You will notice that chaos is often a battle for direction or clarity, that competition is often a battle to be validated and seen in our uniqueness, that the battle for control is actually one for safety. When I can't find clarity, I have found it extremely helpful to ask the Holy Spirit to reveal to me the nature of the battle; the answer comes every time as a gentle whisper, a visual, or a word.

- *"Am I desperate to be heard and seen rather than seeking to understand?"* Acknowledge this part of yourself.

- *"How can I hold space for the other person? What do they want me to understand?"*

Often, this new perspective will be enough to diffuse the battle altogether.

The Golden Rule sums this up nicely: *"Do to others whatever you would like them to do to you. This is the essence of all that is taught in the law and the prophets."* (Matthew 7:12, NLT) At the end of the day, isn't that what we all want? To be seen, heard, loved, appreciated, and valued? The next time you are in the midst of a heated battle, consider what you want from the other side, and bring that to the table.

THE LAWS OF FORCE

I have always found physics and the sciences fascinating. Newtonian and quantum physics have done wonders to explain the practical side of what the Bible and spiritual leaders have been teaching us for millennia. I absolutely geek out on these subjects—not because I need science to give me evidence of truth, but because it affirms what we already know of the super-natural while allowing our brains to make sense of many intangibles we simply can't understand at face value.

It just so happens that Newton's laws offer us perspective on the nature of our daily battles as well.

Newton's First Law of Motion states: *"Every body continues in its state of rest, or of uniform motion in a straight line, unless it is compelled to change that state by forces impressed upon it."* Basically, what this means is that when nothing changes, nothing changes. Whatever the status quo happens to be is what it will remain until some outside force acts upon it. Moreover, if two forces coming at an object are the same, they cancel each other out so the object does not move. If, however, the applied forces are unbalanced, the object moves.

When something is "stuck" inside us or in our lives and there is no motion, that means there is either no "force" coming to move it, or there may be two opposite but equal forces (like fear and motivation) pressing on us at the same time.

When I have been down, depressed, exhausted, or frustrated, and just don't feel like moving, I know I have not applied enough "life force" to move me. The appropriate response, then, is not, "What is wrong with me? I never do anything I say I am going to do!" That would simply invite an opposing force of doubt, frustration, or anger to push me down even further. Instead, I ask, "How can I apply more life force?" Meaning, how can I apply more love, patience, kindness, light, joy, courage, faith, etc., to create movement where there has been none?

The first step may be to drink a glass of water, then walk outside barefoot on the wet grass and stand in the sunshine for fifteen minutes and let the force of that which is life-giving act upon my body and heart. Immediately, I will begin to feel a shift. Once I've done that, the key is to keep stacking life force in order to strengthen the motion toward creative energy rather than stuck or destructive energy.

We spend so much time beating ourselves up about what we are doing and not doing, when instead we could simply ask, "What force is at play here?" There are always forces at play. Forces that fuel life and forces that rob us of life.

Once we have an answer, we can apply Newton's Second Law, which states: "*The change of motion of an object is proportional to the force impressed; and is made in the direction of the straight line in which the force is impressed.*" In other words, force is only created as the result of an interaction. This is vitally important. If we stop interacting or engaging with the force(s) at play, the objects (meaning us) no longer *experience* the force. Note, this doesn't say the force ceases to exist, only that the object ceases to be affected by it. Isn't that interesting?

Many of us understand this cognitively but don't actually practice it. Think about the drama-fests happening at any given moment. There are forces of chaos, division, gossip, and turmoil at play all the time. But why press against them or get pulled in when we can simply diffuse by redirecting our life force elsewhere? Think about the petty disagreements we have with our teenage kids, parents, colleagues, or people on social media. There are no shortage of opportunities to engage, interact, and become entangled in other people's business and energy. We allow a "force" of pride, fear, or our need to be right to act upon us and influence our trajectory. This is all playing on our ego. If we want to save our energy for the battles that actually matter, we need to do a better job of selecting what forces we engage with.

There is much power in pulling our energy back, putting down our weapons, and taking a pause to reflect on things. This is an essential step if we want to move forward in a new light, shift the atmosphere in and around us, and transform the outcome. Note that stepping back does not mean people-pleasing or becoming conflict-avoidant. Those are just different means of engagement and are usually fueled by fear. Fear is a terrible counselor, and whatever we initiate in fear consciously or subconsciously will always come back and create more fear within us. Truly pulling back means changing your internal atmosphere so you don't suffer the lingering effects (forces) of resentment, frustration, anger, or bitterness.

We will unpack this more later, but for now, remember this: if you want to truly stop engaging with a force you're battling, you must call your energy, presence, and focus back into your space, body, and spirit. From there, you will be better positioned to respond—and, if necessary, to fight differently.

Once we stop engaging and get clear about the forces acting upon us, we can move on to Newton's Third Law: *"To every action, there is always opposed an equal reaction; or, the mutual actions of two bodies upon each other are always equal, and directed to contrary parts."*

For every action we take, there is a reaction. Even at a distance, there are gravitational, electrical, and magnetic forces at play. Whatever we send out—physically, mentally, emotionally, or spiritually—the "force" behind it acts upon our and others' reality. Also, whatever we send out will generate equal and opposite force, return to us *stronger* than what we originally sent out, and smack us in the face when we least expect it. The force gets stronger because one plus one does not equal one. The force returning to me is now the force that I sent out plus the force coming back. This verse sums it up perfectly, *"They sow the wind and reap the whirlwind."* (Hosea 8:7, NIV) Some call this the "Boomerang Effect."

The Boomerang Effect is fantastic if the "force" we are sending out into the world is one of love, excitement, curiosity, wonder, and acceptance. It's terrible if we are sending out a force of anger, resentment, bitterness, fear, or mistrust. Have you ever felt like there are storms hitting you one after the other? In many couples' coaching sessions, I hear some version of this same commentary: "My partner is like a tornado! He walks in the room and the storms come in with him. He doesn't even realize he's doing it, and then gets super frustrated when the storms keep coming at him. Does he not realize what he's putting out?" (To be clear, it's not always the man who's the tornado.)

We are all putting something into the atmosphere at all times. Let's put out more of what we want to see manifested! We can multiply the love that is our nature and God's nature through our actions. We can also neutralize the negative forces of other people and situations by providing an opposing, neutralizing force.

When I consider this approach, I immediately think of my mother, Anna. She has the kindest, gentlest heart of any human I have ever met. It doesn't matter who is in her sphere, she always seems to pour love into them.

For years she's worked as a cashier at a local natural foods store. She's now in her seventies, and she is a slow, methodical mover. You can imagine the frustration that some customers experience while they wait for her to get through their order! What's interesting, though, is that while she slowly scans the items, she is incredibly intentional about smiling, pouring loving words into her customers and asking about them and their families with genuine curiosity. It's as if she is pouring some magic potion into the air! You can see the customers' energies shift and their bodies relax as they begin to feel seen. She applies an opposing force to the stress of their day, and they are shifted right out of their angry or anxious state.

To this day, every time I run into people in Waterdown, they ask me how "Nonna" is doing—my mom, the petite grandma at the cash register, with whom they share their kids' pictures, their marriage updates, and their health problems, and from whom they receive a blessing when they rush in for their morning muffins. Her presence shifts the whole atmosphere to love and generates a force greater than what was present before.

That kind of love can *move* things.

Ceasing to engage and shifting our vantage point will stop our experience of the force, but not neutralize it. In cases like gossip or social media debates, it may be enough to simply redirect our energy and reclaim our life force. However, retreating and redirecting are not always the best strategies in intimate situations or challenges we need to face day in and day out (like dealing with an executive team or extended family). In these cases, we must disengage, identify the forces at play and the nature of the battle, and determine the best course of action. When we are called back to the battle, we need to bring the right weapons—the powerful neutralizing forces of love, emotional composure, and peace.

God has given us everything we need to be the change we want to see in the world. If we try to do it through our own will, ego, or flesh, we will fall short every time. Our pride will kick in, and our nature will be easily offended and quick to react. We need to do it through the super-natural equipping of the Holy Spirit that is alive in us, for it is His Spirit that gives us the strength, power, and wisdom to engage in worldly issues differently (see Romans 8). It requires us to set our personal agendas aside, humble ourselves, and allow His power to move through us.

CHOOSE TO ENGAGE DIFFERENTLY

When you truly understand the nature of the battle, meditate on the verses I have shared, and practice the methods I've presented in this chapter, you will begin to move from and lean on a completely different force as you engage in future battles. Instead of reacting to earthly things from a force (spirit) of anger, pride, fear, or control, you will respond from the Power of the Holy Spirit, which is a force greater than anything of this world. *"Greater is he that is in you than he that is in the world!"* (John 4:4, KJV) This is how we begin to mobilize the atmosphere.

You are a Warrior of the Heart, and with that comes the full power, authority, and potential of one who knows themselves to be a child and heir of God. Therefore, you *must* choose to engage differently from this moment on.

The word "choose" is key here. You are no longer a hostage to your old identity, nor to external forces. You have awareness, and with that comes great responsibility. More, you have the power, through the Holy Spirit, to see what is *needed* and bring that to the table. You are no longer reacting, but responding. You are acting in faith, not merely by sight. You are officially beginning to fight different!

In the next chapter, we are going to reveal your upgraded weapons. But before we dive in, take the time to work through the Warrior Initiation questions below.

WARRIOR INITIATION

- What battles are you fighting in your life right now?
- How and where have these battles been repeated in your life?

- With this new level of awareness, can you see what the battles are really for?

- What forces (spirits) are you actually battling against, and how have you engaged thus far?

- As you look at these battles from the "eagle's view" or "heavenly view," what looks different? How will you re-engage from this new vantage point?

- When faced with opposition in the future, what will you now bring to the table?

CHAPTER ELEVEN

Upgrade Your Weapons

"It used to be thought that the events that changed the world were things like big bombs, maniac politicians, huge earth-quakes, or vast population movements, but it has now been realized that this is a very old-fashioned view held by people totally out of touch with modern thought. The things that really change the world, according to Chaos theory, are the tiny things. A butterfly flaps its wings in the Amazonian jungle, and subsequently a storm ravages half of Europe."

– FROM *GOOD OMENS* BY NEIL GAIMAN AND TERRY PRATCHETT

*T*he world is vast, wide, and complex. As a result, we can often get caught up thinking that it requires vast, complex actions to mobilize things and completely reorganize the atmosphere.

In truth, it's in the small, subtle actions that the large things are created—that doors are opened, hearts are softened, and stories are written. We have all had an experience where we unexpectedly ran into someone, and a conversation ensued that created a ripple effect and changed the course of our lives forever. This is referred to as the "Butterfly Effect," and it's an element of chaos theory which posits that, "The phenomenon by which a small change at one place in a complex system can have large effects elsewhere."

When I was in the middle of my brutal divorce, I felt hopeless in so many ways. Discouraged and unable to see a way out of my dilemma, I agreed to have an impromptu coffee with a client of mine, Joanne, whom I was strength coaching at the time. She was training for her tenth or eleventh Ironman at the time, and was an incredible business owner and leader.

Funny, I thought I was there to support her. In fact, I was there for something quite different.

As we sat there sipping our coffee, I chose to be vulnerable with her. I was totally backed into a financial wall and was feeling a massive amount of pressure to do something fast to support my kids. At this point, I was convinced I would have to take a nine-to-five job and that my fitness coaching would always be a side hobby at best. As I sat there, I decided to share with her my dream of opening my own fitness studio. I shared from my heart, with no real expectation of anything coming out of it. She looked me square in the eyes and said, "Christine, you *have* to do this. Go after this. Give yourself one year to make it go. If it fails, after a year you can walk away knowing that you followed your heart and tried. But if you don't, you may always look back and regret this moment."

That one conversation, specifically that one moment inside that one conversation, changed the course of my future forever. It was in that moment of my vulnerable sharing that a doorway opened. Something within me shifted; what had once been just a crazy idea now truly became a possibility. Within days, I was driving through town looking for possible locations for PUSH!FIT ... and the rest, as they say, is history.

That one moment totally changed the nature of the battlefield for me. It redefined how I viewed myself, what I would focus on, and how I would operate moving forward. I went from being a woman whose identity was lost in the wake of a divorce to one who knew she was not only worthy but capable of supporting herself, supporting her children, and being able to follow her dreams.

But there's more to this than a simple moment of inspiration.

My friend showed up to our coffee date that day with *weapons* in her arsenal. With her words, she could have cut me down. She could have told me that I was stupid for putting my kids' futures on the line for my own wants, that I wasn't capable of building what I desired, or simply that the risk probably wasn't worth the reward. In my vulnerable state, I would have believed her—and everything about my life today would be different. Instead, she showed up with love. Encouragement. Faith in me and my God-given talents and abilities. With her Warrior heart, she helped me gain a new vantage point and changed the landscape of my battle.

Weapons are *instruments or tools* designed to create an outcome. Depending on the tool we select, and how we engage with that tool, we can completely change our experience of, interaction with, and outcomes around a situation or relationship.

Having the *right tools* at the *right time* for the *right outcome* makes everything easier, more enjoyable, and more successful. Have you ever tried to build something with the wrong tools? It is a long and painful exercise in frustration which usually breaks a few things along the way. In the end, we usually end up hoping the whole thing will stay intact and not collapse. I laugh when I think back on the times I've tried to do this in my own life. If I had just sourced the right tools, support, and instructions, I would have saved a lot of effort and aggravation!

I invite you to consider now what your toolbox or arsenal of weapons looks like when it comes to your relationships, your health, your confidence, your leadership, and your identity. Do you have access to the weapons that best support and protect you? How are they intentionally being selected and utilized?

Most of us don't even recognize the tools we have available to us. We don't know that we are already in possession of weapons that can mobilize the atmosphere for good or bad in a powerful way. And unfortunately, few of us have ever received proper instruction and wise advice on how to use them. Proverbs 22:6 (NKJV) says, *"Train up a child in the way he should go, and when he is old he will not depart from it."* Yet, most of our knowledge has come through hard lessons, heartbreaks, wins, losses, and general trial and error, not loving instruction. And so, we randomly continue to pick up the same weapons and tools used by our parents and society, and we keep using and abusing those tools in the same unintentional, mindless, and often destructive ways. Regardless of whether or not your parents trained you in the way of wisdom, we are all still childish in many ways. And, if you're anything like me, you had a rebellious streak and pushed back on anyone who tried to tell you how to do anything. Every time my well-meaning, God-fearing momma tried to impart wisdom on me, I fought back with a vengeance! In my book, she was out to lunch, irrelevant, and simply didn't understand me. I laugh and cry now at the foolishness of it all. Some of us *really* have to learn the hard way!

The good news is, we are born again. Our old ego-centered identity is dead, and we are given a new identity in Christ: a new "self-image" that reflects Him, and a renewed mind and heart that are focused on things above and not below. When we truly see ourselves as children of God, we eagerly and willingly lean into what the Father can teach us about the battles at hand. This includes looking at the weapons He has already put in our hands—the weapons we are either using for Kingdom purposes or misusing every single day.

The world deals in physical weapons: guns, ammo, swords, knives, greater numbers of men, etc. Heaven deals in spiritual weaponry: the things often unseen but experienced, the intangibles that move mountains. While entire books have been written on this subject alone, I want to dive into a few that have really shifted the game for me.

Some of the weapons at your disposal as a Warrior of the Heart are:

- The words you speak

- The responses you choose

- The presence you bring

- The laying of hands

- The pace you move at

- The timing you tune into

- The Word of God

- Prayers of faith and authority

In our lives, we have probably used these weapons to bring more love, compassion, and support to others. We have also probably used them to hurt others, force an outcome, get even, or win at all costs.

You can become a battle-ready Warrior of the Heart by upgrading your arsenal of weapons and learning how to use them differently. In this chapter, you will learn to *fight different*—to use your God-given weapons to fight the *right* battles, at the *right* time, for the *right* reasons—and also how to put them away when the fight at hand is not in service to God's plan for you and your future. At the end of the day, we are here to serve, reflect, and grow His Kingdom, not fight to the death over ego-driven empires that will be here today, gone tomorrow.

SPEAK DIFFERENT

Speak life, not death. *"Death and life are in the power of the tongue, And those who love it and indulge it will eat its fruit and bear the consequences of their words."* (Proverbs 18:21, AMP)

Meditate on that for a moment. We will *eat* the fruit of our words! That means that whatever comes out of our mouths we will also take in and digest. Yikes. Makes you want to think twice before you open your mouth, doesn't it?

Mark and I often speak on the topic of conscious language within our coaching circles, podcasts, and around the dinner table with family and friends. Heavenly language, or conscious language, sounds and feels different from worldly language. The lasting impacts of our words are undeniable. We have all felt the sting of a hurtful word or an attack on our character. Too often, simple words spoken years ago out of anger or ignorance can wound us for the rest of our lives, becoming the building blocks of generational curses, hurtful stories, and false identities.

Joyce Meyer wrote, "Words are containers for power. You choose what kind of power they carry." Let that sink in. Words are *containers* to carry power from one place to another—power that can bestow blessings or curses. Whoa.

I have a sword behind my desk—the same sword pictured on the cover of this book. The sword is there to remind me of the power of the Word, the power of my tongue, and to use this weapon wisely so that I may pour life into myself and others, never as a weapon to tear them down. I am constantly asking myself, "Am I regurgitating curses that were passed down, or am I cutting through those lies by speaking words of life and Truth into the atmosphere?"

In their jointly written book, *Words Can Change Your Brain*, Dr. Andrew Newberg, a neuroscientist at Thomas Jefferson University, and Mark Robert Waldman, a communications expert, state: "A single word has the power to influence the expression of genes that regulate physical and emotional stress." You read that correctly: *one single word.*

Furthermore, they assert that exercising positive thoughts can literally change one's reality. Likewise, negative words and thoughts can literally change the shape of things, in our internal and external environment. There are countless stories and studies on instances where disease or sickness was reversed through the power of thoughts and words. Miracles? Perhaps. Or maybe this is part of God's intelligent design.

We know, cognitively, that words matter. We have been *told* this. We have *read* about this over and over again in books, and heard it spoken at personal development conferences. But do we actually *understand* this in our integrated body?

The very act of being able to speak is a gift, in my opinion. With every word we speak, there is a responsibility. Like swords, words can protect and defend, or cut down the defenseless. They can keep us safe, or they can wound. They are a weapon in our hands—and how we use this weapon is up to us.

A lot of discussion takes place in the personal development space about how we speak to ourselves, and the words we use in our "I am" statements and affirmations. However, far less attention is paid to how we intentionally speak with others. Whether we direct our words at ourselves or others, we all need to practice using this weapon wisely. We must retrain ourselves on how we use words, what words we select, and how we choose to deliver them. This requires slowing down, checking in, and asking, "Is this really what I want to speak over this person/situation?"

It doesn't matter what words are coming at us in a situation. However, it matters greatly what words we choose to receive, and what words we choose to send back out—for what we send out either adds to the current atmosphere, multiplying the chaos, or shifts it completely. As we learned in Chapter Ten, as Warriors of the Heart, it is our responsibility to pick our battles and battlefields, and bring only that which we desire and are called to multiply.

In my earlier life and relationships, I would guess that a large percentage of our words, probably 75 percent of them or more, were spoken about what we didn't like about each other or the situation, what we didn't want, what we didn't see happening in the relationship or in the other person, or how the other person was letting us down. It's wild to reflect on how many of our words were spent on creating more of what we didn't want, rather than focusing on what was going right and moving in the right direction.

When we become aware of our words as weapons, we can consciously choose to position a clear intention behind every single word that comes out of our mouth. If we do not do this, we are like children bearing swords, slashing mindlessly at anything that comes into our sphere.

Weapons training, lesson number one: *take control of your tongue!* Slow down and think about what you want to say before it exits the portal of your mouth—because once it's out, you can't take it back. Consider whether your words will add life to the person before you or take it away, diffuse the situation or add more fuel to the fire, expand the conversation or contract it, build someone up or tear them down. Stop accusing others with statements like, "You did this!" or "You always ..." or "Why do you have to ...?" Instead, speak into how you feel, what you will and won't do, what you'd like to experience more of, and the outcome you ultimately desire.

Be the one who speaks differently. We are called to be in the world, but not reflective of this world. You are a Warrior, a child of God, heir to the Kingdom, and citizen of Heaven first and foremost. Speak words of life over yourself and those you come into contact with. Speak the Word of God over the lies of the enemy. Build yourself an arsenal of verses to declare out loud in challenging moments. Choose to respond to all things with heavenly language which reflects love, joy, peace, patience, kindness, gentleness, goodness, faithfulness, and self-control—the fruits of the Spirit—and watch your world change (see Galatians 5:22).

ACT DIFFERENT

Respond. Don't react.

As we discovered in Chapter Ten, every single action creates an equal and opposite reaction. Therefore, we must be discerning when we act, bringing to bear a full awareness of the actions (force) we choose, the intention (heart and mind) behind them, and how we choose to execute them. Every email, every text, every conversation, every meeting—truly, everything we do in our day is an act initiated with a motive.

If our motive is to defend, justify, coerce, manipulate, win the argument, or prove that we're right, then the same energy will come right back at us multiplied through the Boomerang Effect. Think about the last time you were in a disagreement with someone close to you and found yourself defending your position. The more you dug your heels in, the more they defended their own position, and the greater the oppositional force became between you.

There have been many times in my life where I was unconsciously, or even intentionally, manipulative in conversation. As long as I can remember, I have been fighting any possibility of being "controlled" by my partner—or by anything, for that matter. Because I was in so much *fear* of being controlled, I initiated many conversations and decisions from this root. This was, straight up, a spirit of manipulation and control at work in me and through me! As a result, more of that "control" force kept coming back at me: more things to feel anxious about, more uneasiness about things being "out of control," and more attempts by others to control and manipulate me.

Through my healing journey, I have shifted the root motive of the fight. I still refuse to be controlled by other humans, but now the root is grounded in steadfast love. My allegiance is to the Father, the King of Kings and Creator of all things, not to a spirit of fear or some bait being thrown in front of me to distract me. I refuse to allow a spirit of fear or manipulation to dictate my actions. I refuse to operate from neediness and lack. Instead, I choose to fight from a place of freedom and love.

Upgrading our weaponry in this area means not only selecting different actions, but also getting clear on the *intention/motive* behind the actions, as well as what spirit we embody as we engage in the actions. We can change an action but still be driven (motivated) by a spirit of fear. Or, we can choose to be driven by a Spirit of Love, and therefore the action will be different by default.

In the middle of an argument, it's easy to act out, raise our voice, slam a door, walk away, shut down, defend our position, ignore the other person, or stuff our emotions. All of these are actions we (consciously or unconsciously) select in the moment. Imagine what could happen if you gave yourself permission to slow down and check in before retaliating. Imagine what would change if you were more deliberate in selecting your actions. Imagine what it would look like if you became the master of your moves, fueled by love over fear—by moving forward rather than repeating the past.

It sounds easy, but as with most things, the real shifts happen through practice. A Warrior of the Heart knows that mastery is not gained overnight. It is developed intentionally, methodically, by focusing on the foundations and building on them one day at a time. So, in any moment of your day, *slow down*. Check in with yourself. Check your state, and see if it's in alignment with the right desired outcome. Check your motive, and see if your heart is coming from the right place. Is the Holy Spirit leading you, or are you hijacked by anger, fear, or pride? Ask the Holy Spirit to take over, then consciously select a faithful response. This is what it means to be obedient to the Spirit. If you find yourself unable to respond in a calm, healthy manner, step away until you can ground yourself and take action from a different state. Give yourself the gift of not creating more of a mess. Doing the right thing doesn't always feel good in the heat of the moment. Your ego will try and argue every step of the way. Do the thing you don't "want" to do but know is the right thing.

We do good not because we are doing it for others, but because we are doing it for God. We do it to honor Him because we are honorable leaders. We do it because leaders go first, especially when others are unwilling to move. We do good because, in doing so, we cast light in a dark place. It's amazing how much shifts and dissolves when opposition is met with kindness.

SHOW UP DIFFERENT

Presence is power. When you enter a space, with what *posture* do you enter it? Are you armored up, closed off, tense, rigid, and ready for a fight? Are you anxious or unsettled, ready to hide or run? Are you the tornado that just walked in the door? Are you the one that sets the tone in the atmosphere, and not always for the better? Do people walk on eggshells around you, or frantically run around behind you, cleaning up the mess you left in your wake?

I had a dear client whose nickname was "Hurricane" when we began working together. In the beginning, she thought it was funny—until she realized that so much of the drama happening in her atmosphere was of her own creation. Then, it wasn't so funny anymore.

Growing up, my father was the tornado. He had the power to bring the charisma and fun—or the confusion and rage. I never knew who he would be when he walked in the door. It was so unpredictable that, as the end of the day closed in, my entire body would become tense and anxious in anticipation for what was to come. It was awful to dread the moment of his arrival and still hold out hope that, this one time, he might be in a good mood.

Later in my life, as I struck out on my own and embraced my full Warrior spirit, I became the tornado. Even though I wasn't showing up drunk, I was in a frantic rush much of the time, anxious for everyone to move at my pace and respond to my every move and demand. I can only imagine how exhausting that must have been for my young children!

The ability to shift the energy and atmosphere of a room is both a gift and a weapon. And, like all weapons, we need to learn how to use it with intention, discernment, and skill. Today, when I walk into a room, jump on a call with a client, and engage with my children or family, I am hyper-vigilant about getting myself grounded and fully present before I step into the space. There is such beauty in the gift of presence when we learn to harness it and channel it differently.

Let's talk about body language and posture for a moment. Your body position and posture reflect your current state, and much of the time we are unaware of the state we are in. However, we are not fooling anyone! What's in us oozes out of us. Right now, do a quick check on your body positioning. It's such a simple and powerful indicator of what you will generate more of. If you are tense, rigid, and inflexible, you will likely notice that you receive that same rigidity back. If you are closed off, with your arms crossed or your shoulders curled in to protect your heart, you will likely hit resistance or be unable to receive feedback, ideas, suggestions, or even simple compliments! On the other hand, if you are standing tall, open, tapped into a gentle strength and confidence, you will draw opportunities, interest, and cooperation into your field.

A fun exercise I often give to couples is to sit in a chair, lean back a bit, and relax. Then, I ask them to have a conversation together *while remaining in that position*. It's hard to be angry and fight when your body position is set that way! It's much easier to be objective, curious, open, and receptive. Conversely, when you're on the edge of your chair, poised to jump up at any moment, it's much easier to fight and get defensive.

"Presence" is more than just physical presence. It encompasses your attention, focus and heart. When you enter a room, do you bring *all* of you in the room? Or are you dispersed, distracted, leaving parts of you all over the place; in past meetings, past conversations, past relationships, or fixated on tomorrow's unresolved problems? Are you paying attention to the others in the room, or are you glued to your phone or laptop, jumping at every notification? We've all been in a meeting or on a date where the person with us is physically present but absent in every other way: mentally distracted, emotionally unavailable. There is nothing enjoyable, attractive, or influential about that. This is one of my all-time biggest pet peeves. Wherever you are, *be there*. My children have come to know that if I am not fully present—meaning looking at them—they should not try to talk to me. I do my best not to multitask. Science has repeatedly proven it to be ineffective when it comes to productivity, and I'm terrible at it anyway. I've trained my kids that when they need my attention for something, we both get to be fully present for the conversation. That means I am not on the computer, on my phone, or doing any other task. It also means that they should knock on the door or send a text saying, "Are you free to talk?" We do not allow phones at the dinner table. I don't allow TVs in the bedrooms, and we no longer have one in our family room. We don't leave noise running in the background unless it's intentional music. All of this supports us in our desire to be present for one another and manage the atmosphere we are immersed in.

To upgrade your skill set, I suggest creating a "micro transition" practice. This means leaving a one to five-minute buffer between meetings, switching roles, or shifting from one task to another. Take those few minutes to simply pause, close the door on whatever you were doing or being before, and bring all of your awareness, energy, and focus to the role you are moving into and who/what you are showing up for.

I have recorded a guided recalibration practice to help you with this. You can download it at www.dropthearmorbook.com.

TOUCH DIFFERENT

Be the hand that heals.

Our skin is our largest sensory organ, carrying a cascade of information to our brains, spinal cords, and nervous systems. It is estimated that there are over *seven trillion nerves* running through our body, with our skin having over 200 feeling receptors per square centimeter! It is through our skin that we receive much of the pleasure we experience, and also how we experience physical pain. The benefits of skin-to-skin contact are many, including the increased production and release of oxytocin. Therapeutic techniques like reflexology, massage, acupressure, and many other modalities have well-documented life-altering and life-affirming benefits. It's no surprise that touch has a profound effect on us.

It was through the laying of hands, as well as the spoken word, that Jesus performed many of his miraculous works. Healing the lame, the blind, the plagued, the bleeding—it was often done through touch. The scriptures are bountiful on this subject; in the Word of God, the laying of hands and healing are interwoven. *"While the sun was setting, all those who had any who were sick with various diseases brought them to Him; and laying His hands on each one of them, He was healing them."* (Luke 4:40, NASB)

Through the power of our touch, we have the power to heal, to dissolve, to restore, to create safety, and to bring forth relaxation and release. Imagine the safe, strong hand of your father holding your hands as a small child, the warm gentle cuddles of your mother as she hugged away your tears, or the kind embrace of a friend. Imagine the electric rush of that first kiss or the closeness of that slow dance, or the first time you held your newborn child, skin on skin. In each case, touch has a marked effect on our nervous system, transmitting an emotional feeling as well as a physical one.

Touch is a powerful vehicle for bestowing blessings, love, and approval. In the Word of God and throughout our lives, we have witnessed blessings being passed on through the power of touch. In Matthew 19, parents brought their children to Jesus to have Him place His hands on them, pray for them, and bless them. "Let the children come to Me," He said. Think about how often you have wanted to impart a blessing over your own children. As you draw them close, the power of your words is amplified by your touch. It is physically felt and transferred!

It is heartbreaking that so many people have never felt the incredible power of nourishing, life-giving touch. It's part of our biological design, and we are meant to desire it. We flourish with the right touch, given in generous amounts. Personally, I can't seem to hug my children often enough. We are definitely a "touchy-feely" family with physical touch and quality time as primary love languages. I relish receiving touch from my husband, long hugs from friends, and hands-on healing services. But there was also a time when I had a love/hate relationship with touch; I didn't know how to receive it in a healthy way, let alone use it to bring forth more life and healing. Growing up, my father's hands, the same hands that provided strength in my early years, also became the hands I feared and that caused me so much pain.

My guess is that you've also felt the pain of touch misused or withheld in some way. It's said that "hurt people hurt people," and this is so very true. When we are full of unresolved, unprocessed anger or pain, we often lash out in the same manner, using touch to punish others. Slapping, hitting, slamming doors, using sex as a means of control, denying intimacy or hugs—these are some of the many ways we misuse this powerful weapon. Can you think of other ways the laying of hands has been misused in your own life? Where have you experienced it for healing and good?

The laying of hands is a super-natural weapon that goes way beyond physical touch. I urge you to upgrade the way you look at and use this gift in your life. Begin to use your hands and body to express love, not perpetuate pain. To transfer blessings, not withhold them. To soften a hardened or closed heart with a gentle hand; to be the one to lean in for a hug; or to diffuse a heated battle between yourself and your partner or children simply by pausing, relaxing your body, and hugging it out. The beautiful thing about touch is that it transfers love, healing, power, and so much more ... without you needing to say anything at all!

So, where have you been knowingly or unknowingly withholding touch from others? Where have you been harsh, rigid, or inflexible with your touch? Who needs to feel your touch and feel your love and blessings on their skin? Where can you practice the art of healing touch?

MOVE DIFFERENT

Shift your pace, Warrior.

Proverbs 19:2 (NIV) says, *"Desire without knowledge is not good— how much more will hasty feet miss the way!"* We live in a culture of instant gratification and dopamine addiction. We want what we want, we want it now, and we want it our way! Nothing could lead us to the path of folly and destruction faster.

Right timing is an art, and our pacing is a weapon to be mastered. When we go too fast, we easily get caught up in the moment, trapped in corners and sucked up into storms we could have easily avoided. Before we know it, we are saying yes to something that we never intended to engage in, find ourselves getting tossed around like a ship lost at sea! When we try to rush something like a relationship or business growth before its maturity, it often comes crashing down around us because it lacks the time to develop roots and infrastructure to support what we were trying to pile on. When team members are all forcing different timelines, it causes friction and dysfunction in the team. When you are hesitating in fear or self-doubt, the cost can take the form of lost opportunities and momentum.

We all have a pace that is familiar and natural to us, determined by our autonomic nervous system. We have a speed that we speak at, think at, write at, and move to. Even inside our relationships, there is a pacing. Have you noticed it?

One of the simplest ways to break a pattern or stop a battle in its tracks is to interrupt the speed of it. If your thoughts are running wild, begin to tune into your thoughts in slow motion. If you are speaking super-fast trying to get the last word in, try slowing down the pace of your words, and select fewer words to articulate your point. It's amazing what this one upgrade will do.

When working with clients, I often teach a concept I call the Sacred Pause—or, when working with women, the "Queen's Pause." In that split second before you want to speak up, take one slow breath, lean back, and relax your body. Then choose your words slowly and intentionally. This practice can completely change the atmosphere in conversations.

Powerful shifts happen when we begin to slow down, listen intently, and truly hear everything someone is telling us. How often are you rushing your spouse, your children, or your employees inside your head, only to toss out a response that exasperates all of you? The same thing goes for reading; we often get offended or panicked because we read a text message or email in a rush and completely miss the essence of what the other person was saying.

When you read, listen, and observe something with presence,

depth and potency is unleashed. We miss things when we rush. Not just details, but *big* things. Essential things. Moments we can never get back. The upgraded weapon here is about presence and pacing.

Last year I took a group of clients to Steamboat Springs, Colorado. We took a beautiful hike up the mountain to a clearing. I gave them an exercise of walking in silence—to complete the entire hike without speaking. The intention was to help them become fully aware of each step they took and move at their own pace, regardless of how fast or slow the group was going. At the top, we regrouped and shared our experience. It was such a powerful exercise to hear what everyone saw, heard, and felt. That opportunity would have been missed if they were rushing, trying to keep up, or talking the whole time.

For most warriors, the upgrade here is going to be all about slowing down. But sometimes, it can also be about speeding up—taking immediate action without hesitating and before you can talk yourself out of it. I often say, "Hesitation is disobedience to the Spirit." When God convicts us and calls us to move on something, we must take fast action. In those moments of divine inspiration, there are divine appointments, and those must be acted on!

The key to this, of course, is discernment. There will be times to slow things down, times to speed up, and times to establish a new pace and rhythm altogether. You will know which to choose based on the nature of the battlefield at hand. If you are battling chaos, confusion, disorder, or overwhelm, it's time to slow things down before something breaks and you are forced to slow down. If you are experiencing stagnation, lack of momentum, or your life force is slowly drying up, it's time to speed things up. When something is ripe and full of life in your world, it's time to move, *now*! And when things aren't working for you any longer, you have outgrown a process or tactic, or it's just time to mix things up, it's time for a new pace altogether.

I have discovered that my pace needs to be different from that of the rest of the world, otherwise I begin to sound, act, think, and feel like the rest of the world. When I am operating according to Kingdom timelines, as I will unpack shortly, my pace should match that of God's timeline, not the frenetic pacing of the world that is always behind, enslaved in a grind. And in order to understand Gods' timing, you must spend time with Him, immersed in His Word, His ways, His presence. This is how you will come to know whether it's your move or His.

So, what is requiring a completely different speed/pace in your life right now?

Be a pacesetter. Be a Warrior of the Heart who operates by a different timeline. Train yourself to *move different.*

THE ORIGIN OF TIME AND THE ART OF TIMING

The one who understands time, works with it, and chooses how to experience it is wise. The one who fears time and is always running from it, running toward it, fighting it, or trying to work around it is robbing himself.

The final weapon we'll examine in this chapter is time. But how can time—the thing in our world over which, some say, humans have the least control—be a weapon, let alone an ally?

I am a "quick start" type, and when I get an idea in my head, it's as though it's already happened. The gap between the point at which I have the vision and the point where physical reality catches up has left me frustrated and anxious many, many times. I also tend to make daily to-do lists that actually include a week's worth of projects and tasks. Are you with me here?

In order to move in accordance with God's design and plan for me, and stop fighting unnecessary or superficial battles, I had to become a student of time and timing—to understand and become at ease with my timing, God's timing, and nature's timing, and to respect the timing and rhythms of others.

I fought this one *hard.* Maybe you're fighting it, too.

But here's the thing. Time and space are constructs of the mind, so *we* can define how we will experience them. The upgrade here is our relationship with time itself. In much of the Western world, we believe that time is something we are constantly "up against" and "running out of," rather than something to be experienced as a divine gift and teacher. As I dove into my own relationship with time and how to work with it rather than against it, I was introduced to two distinct modes of time and timing as defined by the Ancient Greeks: Chronos and Kairos.

Chronos

The first construct of time is *Chronos time*—what we call chronological time. It is measured in seconds, minutes, hours, days, months, and years. This is where many of us get stuck. The slow ticking away of our lives becomes all we can see and react to. Sometimes it can feel as if nothing is happening, nothing is going according to plan, or we are drastically falling behind. In times of waiting, we grasp and struggle to see God's hand at work in our lives. We have become so conditioned to the incessant need to know, control, and plan everything *right now* that anything that is unknown, unanswered, or unpredictable becomes terrifying. This has created an obsessive drive for comfort and false security held together by this invented system of chronological time.

In basic terms, Chronos time is linear, strict in starting and ending. As one moves linearly along the timeline of life, events are passed, and then they are complete. Life is organized around a schedule—and the schedule, or the ticking of the clock, runs us. We don't run it.

People who struggle in their relationship with time usually place heavy value on the system of Chronos time. But time itself is not linear. The clock is merely a tool that was invented to help us organize ourselves better. The idea of a twenty-four-hour day and linear clock serves as a great reminder that our time is limited, so we should make the best use of it! It gives us an exact measure to reference specific moments so we can make appointments and connections. It also creates an interesting scenario where we are racing against the clock.

Stay with me for a minute.

When I was upgrading my own relationship with time, I found it interesting to discover that in Greek mythology, Chronos (also Cronus or Kronos) was the king of the Titans, who ate his own children because he had been warned that one of them would overthrow him. In the Roman version of the myth, Saturn ate each of his sons the moment they were born. The Sanskrit equivalent of Chronos is Kala, from which the goddess of destruction, Kali, takes her name. Isn't it interesting that the entire system upon which the world bases its relationship to time and success is named for forces of destruction? This made me realize that, when I am ruled by the clock (or by the idea of time born out of this Chronos system), I often feel like I'm being eaten alive—constantly pressured, overscheduled, overcommitted, with little to no room for unexpected miracles to drop into my days. Can you relate?

The clock itself is neither good nor bad. Like any weapon, it's a tool. But, as with so many tools, we have made time our master. Before we know it, time has weaponized us instead of the other way around.

Time and timing goes way beyond a twenty-four-hour clock or linear progression. In order to upgrade our weapon, we must understand the fabric of time beyond this one system.

Kairos

In the Bible, the term *Kairos* speaks to God-ordained times throughout history, sometimes called the "right time" or the "appointed season" (see Titus 1:3). Kairos is God's dimension and is not marked by the past, the present, or the future. In Christian theology, it is often defined as a moment of "ripeness" when, all of a sudden, it's *the* time we have been waiting for.

Interestingly, in the first Greek translations of the Bible, each use of the word "time" was delivered as Kairos, not Chronos. Many native and tribal cultures have a relationship with time that moves in cycles, seasons, timing, and super-natural moments that logic simply cannot explain. As a result, they did not trust Chronos timelines when they were first introduced. In Sanskrit, the word for this timing is *ritu*, which means "the correct time" or "the moment *for*," as in performing certain rituals or ceremonies.

While Kairos time is always present and operating in the heavenly domain, as humans we only tend to experience it in moments here and there, and only to the extent that we allow ourselves to live in connection with this concept of time. I like to call these moments "divine appointments"—moments where we tap into the heavenly realm and doors miraculously open (or close) for us outside of normal or established timelines. Kairos moments can change everything as we know it in an instant. As written in Ecclesiastes 3 (NIV), *"There is a time for everything, and a season for every activity under heaven."*

So how do we find these Kairos moments? They cannot be planned, predicted, or forced. Kairos is God's timeline, and only God knows when and how He will reveal things to us. Instead, Kairos shows itself to us when we are positioned for it. Divine moments are revealed when we slow down, are fully present to the moment, serve well where our feet are planted, and tune into the voice of the Holy Spirit. When you do this, He will direct your steps. Suddenly, you may notice things you have never noticed before. We must have our spiritual eyes and ears open to receive these divine moments when they arrive. This is the stuff an extraordinary life is made of!

Kairos also applies to seasons of life. Everything in nature operates in seasons and cycles—from nature's harvest, to the four seasons of the year, to our life's journey, to our relationships, to our businesses, to every project or creative endeavor we embark on. When we fail to honor the timing of the season we are in, we miss both the beauty and the lessons, and end up causing ourselves much grief in the process! The analogy I like to use is that of a farmer planting one crop versus another. The farmer knows the right time and exact month to plant each specific seed based on the growth cycle of that plant. Once a seed is planted, there is a season for nurturing, watering, and letting the seeds germinate below the surface. Then, there is a time to reap the harvest. We don't try to plant strawberries in the dead of winter. We also don't try to pull sweet potatoes out of the ground in spring! So it is with everything in our lives.

This has been one of the most powerful lessons for me with regard to how I run my business, engage in parenting my children, and navigate my marriage. If all things have a time and a season, why fight it? A few years ago, I began shifting my business onto "heavenly time," in sync with the divine order and flow of things. Whereas before I was constantly anxious about trying to "get something out in time," or grow it in a set amount of time, now I began tuning into the "right order" of projects and treating them like unique entities that wanted to be birthed into the world in their own time. I began to honor the planting of the seeds—or, in my feminine terms, the impregnation of the ideas. Then, I began to let them germinate or gestate, not forcing or rushing them, but instead giving them oxygen, nourishing them, and discovering what they wanted to become. Only then do I prepare to birth them into the world and get the back-end systems in place to support them. When launch time comes, it is just like birth: there is an inner sense of urgency that tells me it's "go time." A window opens, and I know it's time to push a little. At this point, it's natural to experience a few contractions, so when they come, I also know deep relaxation and trusting the process is the way forward. Once the product or program is birthed into the world, my primary order of business becomes nurturing it and allowing it to grow at its own pace so it can mature in the process.

This Kairos approach to timing has been a game-changer. It's so much less stressful. So much more enjoyable. So much more life-giving to everyone involved in the process as we drop into collaboration and co-creation with God, timing, divine order, and partnership with the very thing that wants to be created. It's really no different than allowing a new relationship to unfold. Yet, how many of us are impatiently forcing and rushing our creations into maturity? It's like trying to force a toddler to act like an adult in full bloom! It took a lot of growth and development to get to this season. What you force, you eventually break, and what comes prematurely often creates a lot of sleepless nights, anxiety, and worry.

So, can you imagine a life where you are working in God's perfect timing and order? A life where you are living in flow with the cycles and seasons, and optimizing them instead of swimming against the current? It is life-changing to grasp this and begin to move differently in time.

Moving in a new way has positioned me to see God moving in my life in every single arena—from the way I parent my children and show up as a wife to my husband, to the way I interact with my clients, launch new programs, and make investing decisions. Opening my eyes to the miraculous moments that I would have missed under the veil of Chronos has catapulted me onto a whole new playing field.

Below are some ways for you to begin to work with time.

- Open space in your schedule and become a fierce protector of it. This will not only give you a reprieve, but also create space for God and His universal intelligence to support you and surprise you. In his book *Seven Laws Which Govern Increase and Order*, Neil Kennedy presents the "50 percent rule," which states that if we want to operate in the place of increase, we must leave 50 percent of our schedule open for God to fill with the new. This doesn't mean we aren't working on things or doing things. It simply means we are not scheduled fourteen hours per day! So, schedule yourself for four to six hours, and allow the rest to be filled intentionally with what matters most.

- Ask and pray that your eyes open to see more divine moments and opportunities in your life. It's truly in the subtle moments that a door presents itself. Be aware of the opportunities that arise, even if they feel scary or vulnerable.

- Slow down, be present, and pay attention to what's happening around you. As you know from previous chapters, this will serve you in all kinds of ways—but it will also help you understand the season you are in right now, and what God is trying to show you.

- Stop trying to control every step. Decide how you want to experience time, and focus on that. The doing comes easier when you are clear on what matters most.

UPGRADE YOUR SPIRITUAL WEAPONS

Logos: The Sword of the Spirit

In the book of Ephesians, the Word of God is described as "The Sword of the Spirit." Hebrews 4:12 (KJV) tells us that the word is alive and active: *"Sharper than any double-edged sword, it penetrates even to dividing soul and spirit, joints and marrow; it judges the thoughts and attitudes of the heart."* Spoken with the right motive of heart, I believe that the Word of God is the most powerful and underutilized weapon in our arsenal.

A super-natural sword that is alive and active? Yes, please!

Let's consider the qualities of a sword for a moment. A sword pierces the heart. It cuts through things. It clears pathways. It guards and protects. It is both an offensive and a defensive tool. It is durable and at the same time incredibly resilient. It is multifaceted. It represents power, protection, strength, courage, and authority.

The text of the Bible holds so much power to heal and reveal. It is more than a collection of stories, rules, and laws—so much more than something to be read with the eyes and the mind. It is a multidimensional transmission, a gateway into the eternal realm, a blueprint for life, the constitution of heaven, a love letter to the people, an intimate conversation. It is medicine. It is *alive*. And, as with anything that holds unparalleled, indescribable power, it often gets manipulated, distorted, and misused by humans in their own attempts to control and claim power over others. Like any other weapon, it can protect and heal, or harm and destroy.

Let's just get it out there. For many of us, even the word "Bible" makes us cringe and roll our eyes a little. The idea of reading it, let alone having a relationship with it, can feel less than appealing. I get it. When I was young, I attended Catholic churches where the Bible was read in Latin in dark, gloomy places filled with stained glass windows portraying scenes that totally creeped me out. The Bible was something for priests and "special" higher-ups to read to us and translate for us—in other words, to tell us what it meant and how to behave. Yikes! Everything about this screamed a huge "No!" to every corner of my being. As I got older and we moved to the US, I was exposed to many new varieties and flavors of religion. Some hit me over the head with rules, laws, and judgments. It was all hellfire, fear, and guilt. So heavy. So unlike the pure messages of love and freedom contained in God's Word.

I fundamentally believe that our relationship with God—with the Holy Spirit, with Jesus—is so unique and so personal that it cannot possibly be explained, only experienced. So it is with truth.

When something is true, it just *is*. There is no logic, reason, or explanation for it. It is simply felt in deep resonance, as if every part of our being recognizes it and aligns with it.

When I felt called to come back to the Bible and read it on my own, everything began to look and sound different. This time, I was feeling the pull of Jesus calling me back to Him, wanting to know me and for me to know His heart. *This* was what drew me back to the Word—back to the *logos*. It wasn't a church service, a priest or pastor, or someone else's suggestion. It was simply a tug in my heart to cultivate a real relationship with a God I knew existed, but from whom I had felt distant for so long.

If you let it, the Word can be a vital weapon in the battle for your life force and the brilliant future God has designed for you.

Whether or not you have a relationship with God's Word at this time, there are three aspects of the Word that are necessary to unpack:

- The Word is the Plan of God.

- The Word is the "Rhema" of God.

- The Word is Him—the Father, Son, and Holy Spirit.

The Word is the Plan of God

In Greek, *logos* means "word, reason, or plan." In Greek philosophy and early Christian theology, *logos* is the divine reason, implicit in the cosmos, ordering it and giving it form and meaning. It is the mind of God revealed to us—His divine reasoning and the meaning behind His plan.

When you get to really know the mind of someone, you begin to understand them at a whole new level. The more I understand how my husband thinks, the more I know him. I can understand how he moves and begin to move with him, in harmony. As I have opened myself up to better understand the mind of God, I can better see and understand things beyond just the superficial explanations and reasoning before me. My own mind is refreshed and renewed as I begin to think with the mind of God, rather than my limited human perspective.

The Word is the "Rhema" of God

"Rhema" is defined as "God's Word spoken to you." In other words, it is the whisper or breath of the Holy Spirit, the very breath of life breathed into us. This is why when you re-engage with the Word of God from a different vantage point, the "spoken word" comes alive in you through the Holy Spirit.

There is no doubt that, when you begin to immerse yourself in the Word of God, a whisper moves in you and through you. Something stirs the waters within you. Grace washes over you as you experience more of His presence. There are no words to describe it. You can read the same exact passage a hundred different times, and the Holy Spirit will reveal something new to you and speak over a specific situation in your life each time. Again, because the Word is eternal and not linear, it not only applies to a specific linear moment of time or circumstance, but all time and all people. God's time is eternal. His words are always speaking to us, and always relevant.

The Word is Him—the Father, the Son, and the Holy Spirit

In Greek philosophy, *logos* remains an impersonal force, an abstract concept that is used to explain the purpose of things. It's an energy, like what many modern people refer to as "the universe." In Hebrew thought, however, *logos* is personal; He indeed is the Creator *of* the universe—the power of unity, coherence, harmony, perfection, and purpose. The distinctive point is that the biblical *logos* is a "He," not an "it."

To be honest, I don't know anyone who, in the midst of a life crisis, starts praying to the universe or to an energy. We work with energy and understand universal laws and intelligence, but how do you have a relationship with the whole universe? Intuitively, instinctively, something within us calls us back to God. Creator. Helper. Some*one*. We are designed for a relationship with a divine being, and that is why mankind since the beginning of time has been searching to "find" God.

There are many ways for us to experience the mind and Heart of God. The Bible, His Word, is one of the most powerful ways that leads us directly to Him, yet so many of us are not going there to harvest the treasure trove of wisdom, power, and life available to us! We are seeking answers everywhere else, often to find ourselves confused at best, and empty, unsatiated, and unsatisfied at worst.

If you are ready to unlock this super-natural "weapon" and get to know the wonder, mystery, heart, and soul that beats within it, here are a few tips to receive the *logos:*

- *Be still.* You cannot hear through the noise.

- *Be open.* Set aside what you "think" you know about God's Word and come with an open mind. Ask God to speak directly to you, to open the eyes of your heart.

- *Let go of expectations.* Don't get attached to what it should look like, sound like, or feel like when God speaks to you. Just let go and receive.

- *Let it marinate.* There are infinite layers to God's Word and He speaks to us based on the season we are in. Don't worry if you don't grasp the whole meaning of something right now. You will when the time is right.

Praying Powerful Prayers

Prayer can move mountains, welcome instantaneous healing and transformation, and elicit the perfect answer just when we need it—and yet, it's often the last resort for so many of us. We pray as a last resort once we've exhausted all other options and everything else has failed us. And, while it may work in the end, we often could have saved a lot of heartache, time, and energy if we had gone to God first.

Imagine walking into a store and having an issue with a purchase, and then talking to everyone except the key decision-maker who actually has the power and authority to do something about your problem. Prayer takes you straight to the highest authority, with no detours.

Upgrading my prayer life has been undoubtedly the biggest game-changer in my life. I used to think that meditation and prayer were the same thing. They are not. However, both are powerful and essential. Meditation allows us to disconnect from the external noise and drop within ourselves. It detaches us from the ego and the world, and we feel a sense of timelessness, suspended in the great possibility of all things. We may use meditation to contemplate a particular verse, examine a thought or experience, or observe something closely to see the intimate layers of it. Personally, I practice some form of meditation daily; often, it is after times of prayer, or during times of intense work where I need a break.

Unlike meditation, prayer is a two-way street; it is literally a conversation *with* God. Imagine being able to talk to someone who already knows everything about you—everything you are going through, every challenge, every dream, your future and your past. When we pray, we enter into conversation with the One who has been here from the beginning of time. Through the gift of the Holy Spirit, we have direct access to Him. So, when we need answers to our most pressing questions, why would we go anywhere else?

It is my belief that the resistance most people have to this most potent weapon in our Warrior arsenal stems from the fact that *we have not been taught how to pray*. For most of us, what we learned in church or from our families creates the opposite of a loving and trusting relationship with God.

Below are a few of the common problems with and blocks around prayer and its effectiveness in our lives.

Praying From Fear, Not Faith

Most people pray from a desperate stance of lack or fear, rather than from a heart of faith. This is especially common among people who grew up in dogmatic religious communities where the constant messaging was around fear, guilt, and shame. In such cases, we can become afraid of God rather than trusting Him. We view Him as a great punisher rather than a great provider and protector. I often work with leaders who are so overwhelmed by the topics of the world that fear is running their prayer life. Fear becomes the state they are consistently holding, and it bars them from establishing a true connection with God; as a result, they keep manifesting the very thing they fear.

Going Through the Motions

Reciting the same old prayers day in and day out without any real feeling behind them means you're praying with your head, not your heart. As you know from our previous discussions, when we are not present and are instead simply going through the motions, our relationships become distant. Prayer is no different. Where there is no presence or heart, there is no access to the transformative, collective power!

Asking From the Wrong Place

Selfish gain, status, and personal power are what the ego wants, not necessarily what the Spirit wants. "Follow your heart" can be terrible advice if our hearts are hardened, jealous, or chasing validation. Check the roots of your heart's desires before you present them to God, as He will always, only, and ever give you what you need to live the purpose He has designed for you. I am a firm believer that He will provide everything we need and so much more, as long as our hearts are pure and our intentions align with heavenly objectives.

Asking for the Wrong Things

When our minds are fixated on temporary solutions and Band-Aids, rather than fixing the root of the problem, we may feel unheard by God. This is often because we are asking for earthly solutions when God works in heavenly currency. An example of this could be a business owner who is in debt and praying for money to get him out of a hole, but who is not asking for help to fix the underlying problem—which could be the courage to let certain people go that he knows are misaligned, the faith to make that difficult decision he's been hiding from, or the wisdom to know which strategy to implement in the midst of conflicting information.

Admittedly, I used to pray like this a lot. "Fix the problem for me God," I would say. I used to pray for God to change my husband and his habits, controlling in-laws, or my financial situation. Needless to say, that didn't work out. However, when I began to upgrade my prayers and actually deal with the roots of my issues, I saw manifestation after manifestation in my life! Instead of praying for money, I began to pray for wisdom, favor, discernment, and economic strategies. Visions arrived to show me how to better manage the flow of resources in my life, including an instruction to "build rivers" or channels for money to flow more easily. Now, entire programs, courses, and structures are given to me during times of prayer. About six months ago, I was spontaneously healed from a chronic neck injury during a prayer session. The miracles just keep coming!

***

Today, I remain fascinated with sharpening my prayer tools. I'm always upgrading my prayers for provision, protection, wisdom, character development, insight, healing, and for spiritual warfare.

Here's how you can do the same:

- *Protect the sacred place* that is designated for you and the Spirit. I pray in my office early in the mornings. I put on quiet, instrumental music and prepare my heart and atmosphere. There are also times when I pray in the car, on the go, but there is a special kind of power that shows up when I eliminate all distractions and go into the place of solitude with the Holy Spirit. Just like any relationship, when we give all of us, we receive all of Him. (See Matthew 6:6, Psalm 91:1-2)

- *Enter with reverence, awe, and deep respect* for He with whom you are conversing. The King of all Kings, the Creator of All Things, deserves our utmost presence and respect. Bring *all* of you into the conversation. Show up intentionally, humbly, and prepared to be fully seen, heard, and held. (See Isaiah 40:28-31)

- *Check your heart. Check your motive.* Be honest about where you are. He already knows everything about you. You can't lie to the One who is all-knowing. Be open, be real, bear your heart and soul to Him and He will meet you there. He wants the real you, not some perfect or pretend version of you. (See Psalm 139, one of my favorite chapters of all time)

- *Pray expectantly and faithfully,* knowing that He is listening and will answer you. Do not mistake this for demanding. Make the shift from a child begging their father for a toy to a calm child filled with wonder and trust in your Father. (See Matthew 7:7-8)

- *Be specific.* Ask for what it is you long for, desire, and need. There is no thing too small or too large in God's Kingdom. Size is a man-made construct and so is most of the value we put on things. The value system of heaven is completely different from that of Earth. (See Philippians 4:6-7)

- *Receive it!* When we say, "Thank you. I know this is done," and we let it go, we receive it in the Spirit. We then release the timing of how it manifests in our physical world. Too many of us show up begging for the same thing day in and day out without ever expressing gratitude, expecting it to be done, and moving forward in faithful action accordingly!

- *Speak to the victories, blessings, and promises, not the defeats.* This looks like repeating the promises and blessings made to us through scripture. I am agreeing with what is written and spoken to my heart—His words—rather than what is coming at me from the outside. I believe what He says is true. I believe He is faithful till the end. I believe He will complete what He started. Why? Because He says so in His Word and He does not lie. The enemy lies. God commands victory and truth. This is especially important when you are facing constant battles in your life. Ask God to show you the victory. Start singing and praising long before the walls come crumbling down. Take one out of the pages of His book! That level of praise, worship, and obedience will make the enemy turns on itself. (See Joshua 6)

- *Be Bold.* Too many of us are whispering weak prayers, wishing and hoping for something to happen. When we pray with certainty, clarity, and boldness, we activate the super-natural. If you don't feel bold or confident, pray for those feelings! Where our strength ends, His begins. Pray that you are filled with His strength, confidence, trust, faith, clarity, kindness, patience … whatever it is that you need that surpasses your own ability. (See Joshua 1:9, 2 Timothy 1:7, Psalm 28:7, Isaiah 40:31)

Remember, your prayers are a declaration of your faith. They have the power to move mountains, mobilize armies, heal the sick, free the captives, and claim victory over your hardest challenges. Pray with that level of awareness and knowing, and you will have everything you require for the battles ahead!

PUT ON THE ARMOR OF GOD

I want to close out this chapter with Ephesians 6:10-18 for it pulls everything together better than any words I can offer. We must always remember that our battle is not only in the physical, but also the spiritual realms. We must shift our vantage point beyond what is in front of us. We must check the motives of our hearts and equip ourselves with truth, faith, personal integrity, peace, and solid footing. And we must begin each day by putting on the full armor of God.

We have been given everything we need to move forward victoriously.

In conclusion, be strong in the Lord and in the power of His might.

Put on the full armor of God so that you may be able to stand up against all the schemes and the strategies and the deceits of the devil.

For our struggle is not against flesh and blood [contending only with physical opponents], but against the rulers, against the powers, against the world forces of this [present] darkness, against the spiritual forces of wickedness in the heavenly [super-natural] places.

Therefore, put on the complete armor of God, so that you will be able to resist and stand your ground in the evil day [of danger], and having done everything [that the crisis demands], to stand firm [in your place, fully prepared, immovable, victorious].

So stand firm and hold your ground, having tightened the wide band of truth [personal integrity, moral courage] around your waist and having put on the breastplate of righteousness [an upright heart].

And having strapped on your feet the gospel of peace in preparation [to face the enemy with firm-footed stability and the readiness produced by the good news].

Above all, lift up the shield of faith with which you can extinguish all the flaming arrows of the evil one.

And take the helmet of salvation, and the sword of the Spirit, which is the Word of God.

With all prayer and petition pray [with specific requests] at all times [on every occasion and in every season] in the Spirit, and with this in view, stay alert with all perseverance and petition [interceding in prayer] for all God's people.

— Ephesians 6:1-18 (AMP)

WARRIOR INITIATION

- What new awareness have you gained about the weapons already available to you as a Warrior of the Heart?

- What are some ways in which you may have been misusing these weapons? How have you used them to harm, rather than build up?

- What is the one area you most need to upgrade, and why?

- How do you relate to the Word of God as a weapon in your arsenal?

- What does upgrading your prayer life get to look like moving forward?

CHAPTER TWELVE

Cultivate Faith
and Trust

"Blessed [with spiritual security] is the man who believes and trusts in and relies on the Lord and whose hope and confident expectation is the Lord.
For he will be [nourished] like a tree planted by the waters,
That spreads out its roots by the river;
And will not fear the heat when it comes;
But its leaves will be green and moist.
And it will not be anxious and concerned in a year of drought Nor stop bearing fruit."

— JEREMIAH 17:7-8 (AMP)

*I*n March of 2020, just before the world went into lockdown, I received my first vision from God. I was in a deep state of meditation, a dreamlike state. I saw myself in the car driving with what I initially perceived to be my soul, but I believe was actually an angel. I was in the passenger seat, the angel driving. We were flying down the highway, and it was obvious we were rushing to get to wherever we were going. Then, all of a sudden, the car took a sharp left turn that threw me into the door.

I remember thinking, *What on earth just happened? Where are we going?*

Bewildered, I looked at the driver, who at this point told me clearly, "We're not going that way anymore. We're going this way now!"

Wait a minute. *What?*

The next thing I remember was a slamming of the brakes, bringing the car to an abrupt stop. I crashed forward, bracing my hands on the dashboard so I wouldn't hit my head. I remember the feeling of my sweaty palms gripping the dashboard, head down, panting in shock. Then, slowly I lifted my head and looked out the front window.

Before me was a magnificent, glorious landscape. Lush and green, with light pouring in. It was rich, vibrant, and teeming with life.

I asked the driver, "What's the catch?"

"What do you mean?"

"What do I have to do so I can go there?" I asked, pointing out the window. It was just too beautiful. There had to be a catch. Something I had to do, some challenge to overcome. Something. *What was it?*

The driver said, "There's no catch. We are here. Step outside and enjoy it!"

I hesitated. Looked left again, then forward, and slowly took a breath, putting my hands on the door handle to open the door and step out.

That's when I woke up, and came back into my body.

At that moment, I realized something was about to take my life in a crazy new direction. This was not the agenda I had been planning and executing on at full speed. I took my heart and soul's message to heart. *There is no catch.* If I wanted to be in that beautiful place, there was nothing I needed to do other than *choose.* Get out. Enjoy it. There was no need for me to stay addicted to suffering in order to earn the right to that view.

I wasn't quite sure what to make of it all, but I captured the vision in my journal and carried on with life.

SUFFERING IS OPTIONAL

As I shared in Chapter Five, in May of 2020 Mark and I packed up and made the eighteen-hour drive to Phoenix for a few days' getaway, and also to begin to explore the possibility of a move there. On our first day in the city, we hiked Camelback Mountain and randomly found a painted rock tucked in a stone with a picture of an angel on it. I posted a picture with the rock on my social media, with the caption, "Angels always watch over us".

Then, I felt the urge to drive up to Sedona for a few days. After the first twenty-four hours, I knew I wasn't going back. The red rocks were calling, so I told Mark I would be staying on for an extra week, which (as you know) turned into a month.

That was when things got wild.

A few days later, I was on a long hike when I stopped to pray and meditate on a rock. I had my eyes closed for about twenty minutes. Just as I was opening them, I clearly heard the words, "You're here."

Where? I thought.

Then, I opened my eyes.

Here.

I was looking out over a vast, lush, golden landscape. Yes, lush, in *Sedona*. I was facing Oak Creek Canyon just as the sun was going down. A golden hue washed over the trees below. It was incredible. Beautiful.

It was the same landscape that I experienced in my vision two months prior. Immediately, I felt myself back in the car, looking out over the dashboard, and I knew: *this is the place where everything changes. I'm already here. I don't have to keep suffering like I have been. What if choosing to live in beauty, abundance, and the richness of life has always been here, right in front of me? What if I have been making it way more complicated and difficult than it needed to be?*

You are already there, dear Warrior. It—whatever you truly desire—is already here, right now. The love you have been longing for is here now. The joy you've been chasing is here now. The intimacy and connection with God is here now. The beauty to behold is here now.

Suffering is a crazy addiction. So many of us believe that we need to keep suffering to be worthy of the lives we want. Nothing could be further from the truth.

A photo of that landscape still hangs in my office. It reminds me that suffering is optional, and that the "beauty way" is always here if we are willing to let go of that old story, yield to the way of the Holy Spirit, surrender our need to be large and in charge 24/7, or jump to the next hard thing before we stop to celebrate, worship, connect, love each other, and enjoy the life before us.

I still get choked up every time I think back on that series of events and the divine orchestration that took place to make this happen. The hand of God was all over it: the gifts of visions and little reminders along the way; my and Mark's willingness to follow our inner impulse to travel, even when the world was panicking and shut down; the goodness of God to show me the same vision not once, but twice, in both dream and waking life.

We thought we were driving to Phoenix to check out neighborhoods and home values. But that was just another hard left that God took me on, unexpected and unplanned, which resulted in a confirmation of my vision (just in case I was starting to doubt it), and it continued with an entire month of dropping into solitude, prayer, devotion, rest, and intimacy with Him.

The Art of Surrender

There have been several "hard left" moments since then. The next one happened when I stopped holding on so tightly to my past identities and the success of my fitness studio. Through the Holy Spirit, I became convicted to close it down. I was also "told" in a vision to rebrand my entire online coaching business. *"We're not doing it that way anymore,"* whispered the Lord. With each step I took in trust, something more magnificent was born. Another door opened, and another.

Although it's not always easy, I now am able to understand and move in surrender with much more ease because I have witnessed the doors that open when I release control. The tighter my grip to the past, the more suffering I endure and the longer the suffering lasts. The sooner I am willing to open my hands and release the thing I need so badly back to God, the quicker I have seen doors open. Unexpected. Unplanned. Abundant blessings where I didn't think there were any.

I heard the whisper again when I came to North Carolina to visit my mentor and was clearly instructed to purchase land here. At the time, it didn't make sense, as we had no intention of moving to North Carolina. But I surrendered to the whisper in my heart and the signs dropping in front of me. A land auction email made its way to my inbox out of the blue (I had never signed up for or heard of land auctions) and, before I knew it, I was signing the purchase agreement. I had always wanted to move to the mountains or the ocean, and had held that vision in my heart for a long time, but moving now would mean Mark's ex-wife would have to agree to move as well, since they shared custody of their children. This seemed like an impossible feat to tackle, so we didn't even bring it up or address it.

Then, out of the blue, we got a phone call from Mark's ex asking if we would be open to considering a move to North Carolina. A dream job had opened up for her at the University of North Carolina and she wanted to take it, but that would require us agreeing to it.

Another coincidence? Not a chance. God keeps surprising us with these divine orchestrations.

The ultimate surrender, *letting go of needing to know the how and when*, happened before all this, back when Mark and I began dating. At the time, I was living in Canada with my three children, running my fitness studio. He was living in Nebraska, also with his three young children who he had shared custody of. It did not make sense to start a long-distance, long-term relationship with someone who lived in a different country. The odds of that working with any degree of ease are not good. Immediately, our well-meaning family members and friends began piling on the questions. "How are you going to make this work? How will you see each other? This is not going to work. Do you think you'll ever get married again?"

When? How? When? How? Those questions were on repeat. Our answer was always the same: "We're not even thinking about that." And truly, we weren't. There was no doubt we were brought together by divine orchestration. If this was going to work long term, it would also be through divine orchestration—through God's hand, His timing, and our faith to stay the course. We focused on the moments we had and made the most out of the times we had together. We did not spend our time together stressing about how we were going to make this happen. We did not put pressure on each other or our relationship. We gave it space to let it grow, unfold, and surprise us. We focused on building our communication and our connection regardless of distance. We shared our visions for our lives. We released the need to know and plan too far into the future or have every detail ironed out. Most of all, we enjoyed the process. As a result, things came together with so much ease. There were natural progressions that took place, and we just kept saying yes.

Now, we are living together in our beautiful home in North Carolina and experiencing a marriage that is so much more connected and fulfilling than anything I could ever have imagined in my previous life. The things that God is calling us to do, together, are way more powerful than anything we were attempting to accomplish on our own. It's bigger than each of us now because it's a God vision, not a "Mark or Christine" vision.

Lean on Faith, Build Trust

"Now faith is confidence in what we hope for and assurance about what we do not see." (Hebrews 11:1, NIV) Faith is believing in what we cannot see with our physical eyes. When we act from this place, we are making a choice to exercise faith in spite of current conditions. We *choose* to open our eyes to see that what we dream of, the victory we long for, the promises of God, already exist beyond the current reality. We *choose* to believe there is a power greater at play that can orchestrate and accomplish much more than we could ever do on our own. We place our confidence in Him and what He says He will do.

Trust is different than faith, and often more challenging to exercise. Trust is cultivated and developed over time when we have evidence to lean on. It is deepened and strengthened when we look back on our life and take note of all the moments when unexpected, unplanned, and yet perfect alignments showed up in our life. Recalling these moments where God was with us and for us, even when we didn't recognize it, increases our faith and ability to trust, and allows us to see His hand at work in every aspect of our lives today.

Divine presence is the all-encompassing, everlasting, eternal, and ever-present nature of God.

His Word says:

I look behind me and you're there, then up ahead and you're there, too—your reassuring presence, coming and going. Is there any place I can go to avoid your Spirit? to be out of your sight?

If I climb to the sky, you're there!

If I go underground, you're there!

If I flew on morning's wings to the far western horizon,

You'd find me in a minute—you're already there waiting!

(Psalm 139:5-10, The Message Translation)

Everywhere we are, there He is. In every situation, every moment, every detail, we can't hide or escape His presence. The one who created and holds this entire universe together is always here, within us and around us. When we recognize this, we recognize *Him*. And the more we recognize Him, the more we see His work in us and around us.

As one of my mentors, Staci Wallace, recently said, "When you see what you want to see more of, more of what you want to see shows up in the world around you!"

Our incessant need to control the process and plan every detail, without leaving room for spontaneity or unexpected "left turns," holds us back from what God has waiting for us, and ultimately keeps us in a place of suffering. We get so fixated on things going according to plan that we dismiss the possibility of better outcomes in the here and now. I see too many relationships ruined because one person is fretting and anxious about the future and ends up robbing both people of their joy and pushing the other person away because their attachment to their agenda is so intense.

We know the root of all control is fear. And, as we've learned, the antidote to fear is faith—aka, placing our trust or confidence—in something greater than ourselves. For me, faith is knowing that God's hand is in all things.

Some of us need to be completely broken down before we are willing to surrender. And unfortunately, some of us may need multiple breakdowns to really get it through our thick skulls because our pride is so invested in our current stories. Whether we have our wakeup call after the first, third, or twentieth time around, eventually we come to a place where we recognize that suffering is not required. We don't need to wait until everything we hold dear is destroyed yet again before we give God the reins.

At this point in your journey, you have shifted your allegiance. Your heart is open. You have woken up and reclaimed your true identity. Now is the moment of trust. Will you listen to His voice? Will you obey His call? Will you move where He wants to lead you? If you do, I guarantee He will deliver that which He has promised, and so much more.

Of course, for most of us, that's easier said than done. 99.9 percent of "surrender" moments do not make logical sense. They are not in our original plan. They're not even close to our original idea,. They simply arise once we release the need to control our every step. Sometimes, even in moments of surrender, things don't turn out as we expected, but looking back we can see that these were divine orchestrations, too; one thing needed to be removed so another, more glorious thing could enter. Often this "removal" has to do with relationships, money, things, or false identities. Jesus gives a beautiful parable about a vine that bears much fruit and what's required in order to do so. He says, *"I am the true Vine, and My Father is the vinedresser. Every branch in Me that does not bear fruit, He takes away; and every branch that continues to bear fruit, He [repeatedly] prunes, so that it will bear more fruit [even richer and finer fruit]."* (John 15:1-8, AMP)

This reminds me of my own rose garden. As the years pass, my rose bushes grow bigger and produce so many fresh cut flowers for our home. In my early gardening days, I used to feel bad going out there and pruning those bushes, especially when I was cutting back roses that looked just fine. Now I understand that the better job I do of pruning that bush—not too much, not too little—the better it will look and produce the next time around.

If we want to experience a life that yields abundant fruit year after year, we must remain attached to the vine and allow the gardener to prune those things in our lives that need to go! Sometimes we are the ones getting pruned, and sometimes we are the ones called to do the pruning in our business or our children's lives. This perspective has totally shifted my vantage point around releasing things that need to go to make room for what is to come.

The Pain of Attachment

Recently, I was on a call with an executive client who was experiencing an incredible amount of internal pressure and anxiousness about large clients canceling their contracts. This felt like a huge hit to the business. But, as we looked back, he realized that every time they had "lost" a major client in the past, it had opened the door to a new and better partnership. Some of those new, unexpected partnerships resulted in opportunities that vastly exceeded the original agreements. In fact, he said, it was "like some super-natural force came in and lined this whole thing up!" This was not a one-time thing. It was a pattern repeated throughout the history of the business.

So, were these "rejections" really God's protection and redirection? Clearly the answer was "yes." So why all the anxiety and anguish?

Attachment.

My client was attached to his current status. To the perception that others may have of him. To his current circumstances. To his current outcomes. To the things he thought he needed in order to move forward. To the familiar and predictable things in his life and business.

Unhealthy attachment is rooted in the fear of potential loss, and it will give you tunnel vision and leave you feeling stuck. To combat this, we shifted his focus as well as his language. No longer would he refer to these changes as "hits and losses"; rather, he'd call them "removals and restructuring." This subtle shift helped redirect his energy and expanded his vision so he could see solutions and opportunities to which he'd been blind when he was anxious and contracting.

If you are constantly battling for approval, love, significance, or worth, surrender can feel like failure. Who will they think you are if you are no longer driving that ultra-high-end car? What will you miss out on if you don't say yes to everything? How will others perceive your value if you don't look like you're always growing and advancing?

Do you see how ridiculous all of this is? Surrender *is* the place of power. It allows us to trade in our suffering and move into "the beauty way" where we can enjoy life *now*, regardless of what is happening around us, while also being open to what the future holds.

However, surrender can only happen when we are willing to submit to a greater power.

Submission Unifies and Multiplies

Submission. I resisted that word long and hard for most of my life. It was definitely a trigger word for me. Submission meant weakness and loss. It meant being a pushover, getting taken advantage of, and losing. I was a winner, not a loser! In my mind, if I "submitted" to authority, to my parents, to my husband, or to anyone or anything else, I would be giving them total control over me and lose any sense of influence, power, and control. Therefore, I was *not* going to surrender, submit, or obey anyone other than myself, thank you very much!

Submission can feel like ceding all control because, in many cases throughout history, this has been true. Nations "submit" to conquerors. Criminals "submit" to justice. Submission and the teachings around it have been distorted and misused by humans to control and dominate other humans, so of course we have unconscious trauma and resistance around it. You don't need to look far to see how churches, governments, power-hungry leaders, and ordinary men and women took something meant to unite and free us and completely twisted it for personal gain, making it utterly wicked.

All this is to say that, if the word "submission" makes your skin crawl, I get it. But we are past the old definitions now, Warrior. It's time for a different conversation and an upgraded view of getting under the *right* mission.

In *The Shack*, William Paul Young wrote, "Submission is not about authority, and it is not obedience; it is all about relationships of love and respect." When we submit to something or someone, we agree to place our trust in them and their vision, and follow their direction for the good of all. It's about unity above the individual.

One of the biggest hurdles we face—in marriages, in companies, and in families—is that of competing interests and division fueled by self-servitude. We may be physically grouped together, sharing a common space, but in reality we are fighting against each other over affection, significance, status, being right, or other superfluous matters because we lack a grander mission and purpose.

Ask a couple who is struggling, "What do you two stand for? What is the glue that holds you together?" and most will simply look puzzled. Sometimes they blurt out, "Our kids," or something of that nature. When I ask leadership teams, "What is your North Star? What is the one thing you all agree on?" the answers are vague, confused, and almost always different for each person. There is no one thing that everyone can agree to set aside their personal interests for.

Submission literally means, "to be under the same mission." As I picture this, I see an umbrella of both protection and direction. I see a North Star that guides. I see something greater than the sum of our individual parts that unifies us, ties us together, and multiplies us in strength, potential, and ability. Submission is a choice. It's what happens when we set our own agendas aside and come together in a relationship from a place of love, respect, and mutual agreement. This allows us to be part of something much greater than ourselves, and to be clear on our role within that greatness. With great submission (getting under the same mission) comes great unification. And with great unification comes exponential increase!

In the next chapter, we'll go deeper into the topic of vision and mission, but for now, I want you to consider the real mission you are fighting for—as a man, as a woman, as a couple, as a family, as a leader. What is the one thing that brings you together, multiplies you, blesses you, protects you, and increases your ability to multiply and prosper?

When we know what we are willing to submit to, we see our place in the bigger picture and can keep our gaze fixed on that, even in the midst of challenges and temporary problems. Instead of fighting over superficial things, we can redirect each other to the bigger picture. We are here for something bigger than us. We are *together*—in marriages, in families, in teams, and most of all, under God. As the African proverb tells us, "If you want to go fast, go alone. If you want to go far, go together."

We know that a house divided will fall. A company divided will eventually dissolve. The age-old trick of the enemy is to sneak its way into our territory, divide us, and eventually conquer our territory. To protect ourselves, we need to learn to submit to the Heart of God and dedicate ourselves to serving what truly gives us life.

For me, everything shifted once I truly *got* this in my body, soul, and spirit. When I was able to submit my heart to the Heart of God and refocus my gaze on that which gives life, I was able to learn to fully trust again. On my own, I always felt like I had to look out for myself, watch over my shoulder, check in on my partner (and everyone else), and keep tabs on everything to make sure no thread was out of place. I ran my own race—and, most of the time, I was anxious about running it. When I started to run the race that God had mapped out for me, when I saw where He was leading me and the immense amount of love that He has for me, I longed to submit to His love and guidance. Where I once resisted, I began to yield. I naturally wanted to come under His protection, guidance, and mission. Now I can't imagine stepping out from this incredible covering! Once you experience the feeling of operating from this place, you will never want to go back to the way things used to be.

This has impacted my marriage to Mark beyond words. Our marriage and our mission became possible because, ultimately, I submitted to something greater. I know what God intended our marriage for, so

I refuse to get caught up in the minutia or take every little thing personally. I refuse to look at my husband as my adversary or competition. Even when we disagree on how to do things, are butting heads, or have completely different views on how to tackle an issue, I know there is a way that is bigger than both of us. Because we are submitted to God and the vision we share for our marriage, we can take the "gaze" off each other and the thing that is baiting us, and instead look up and forward. This completely changes the discussion, and along with it, the outcomes! As we redirect our attention inward and upward, we come under the same guidance and protection. No longer divided, but united. No longer against each other, but for each other and for something greater than each of us. We can fight better together.

One of the best ways to get back on the same page and under the same mission is to ask potent questions, like these:

- God, this is your (marriage, business, money, situation). Give us your view of this situation.

- What do you see that we are missing?

- What needs to go so we can focus on the right thing?

- What are we focused on that is contracting us and robbing life from us?

- What matters most right now that we can both/all agree on?

- What is the thing we are both/all after here?

- What is the unified way forward?

When we ask questions that shift our gaze, we realize we have the ability, willingness, and choice to trust each other, to trust God, to trust the process, and to trust divine order and Kairos timing. From there, we can more easily know which battles are ours to fight.

Obedience Protects and Multiplies

Let's be honest: very few people *like* being told what to do. Warriors, in particular, are not order-takers. You have certain ways you like things done, certain habits and tactics that you can depend on, and certain ways you want other people to show up. You probably have people you pay to advise you, and you may or may not listen to them.

Obedience means "to comply with an order, request, or law, generally given by a higher authority." It's natural that this would be a struggle for us Warrior types. I resisted this even more than surrendering. My whole life had been spent trying to break out of restraints—from the harness my mom put on me as a kid after I got lost in a mall in Zurich, to the bonds of my own negative programming. The idea of letting someone or something else have dominance over me was ... not comfortable.

A headstrong attitude and ability to forge our own path regardless of external input is a great trait of many warriors. It can also become our downfall as the stakes increase. We do not like taking orders or direction from others—even those who know more than we do. Even the One who knows *everything*.

Here's what's interesting. The word for obedience in the Hebrew language is *Shama*. Shama is traditionally translated as "to hear, to listen, or give attention to." Obedience literally means "being able to *hear and listen* to God's voice." In the Hebrew there is a direct correlation between hearing and obeying. As with any great relationship, listening unifies us; it yokes us together. In a healthy and intimate relationship, we not only have the desire to listen to each other, but also the desire and willingness to respond to one another. Therefore, obedience is the act of listening and acting from a place of deep love, devotion, and utmost respect. There is a healthy "fear" of God which is a deep respect, reverence, and awe. It says, "I don't want to be away from you—from your protection, your guidance, and your blessing." It says, "I don't want any division, misunderstanding, or misalignment between us. Let's come together. Let me listen."

Obedience requires next-level trust. And for many of us, trust is the *last* thing we want to offer up to anyone, even God.

There's an interesting link I came to recognize in my own life patterns; now, it regularly shows up in the coaching sessions and workshops I host. More often than not, it is the wound of rejection and abandonment, unhealed or provoked, that continues to keep pride and fear running the show.

Don't get me wrong: a healthy sense of pride is required at times. Pride of ownership moves us to care for and respect the things we have been entrusted with. It's also generally anger and pride that get us to the place of reclaiming our power and self-worth, and move us to do something about the abuse we have endured. Fear, too, can be helpful. Fear of abuse helps us stay away from dangerous situations. Fear of getting sick helps us take steps to preserve our health.

But when pride or fear take over, especially when they partner up, they become destructive. Obedience and devotion go right out the window, and all trust goes with it. Our operating system switches to "lone wolf" mode, and we think, "I am the only one who can make this happen, do it right, find the solutions. I am the only one I can count on. It's all about me, *me, ME*." We are easily offended and easily put on the offensive. Fear always has us fixated on what we lost, what we are about to lose, or what we will not have access to in the future. It throws us right into survival and scarcity, and the costs of operating from that place are great. Many, many bad decisions are made from the place of pride and fear. Marriages are thrown away, families divided, great companies fall, and even the best intended church leaders have fallen prey to this merciless force. We must guard ourselves to stay humble in heart, grounded in the Love of the Father and obedient to the Spirit.

You know what happens when you are willing to obey?

God speaks.

You know what happens when you long for direction?

He gives it.

You know what happens when you show up? He shows up too, and as you see Him moving in your life, your desire to obey Him increases within you as an act of love and devotion. You're no longer listening because you are told to, or because you fear some crazy punishment. You listen because you have a relationship with Him. And the more intimate that relationship becomes, the more each of you want to show up for the other. I love this parallel and how relatable it is to our most intimate relationships! So, our ability to trust and obey (hear) Him begins with a willingness to hear His voice. He has something to say about every area of our lives. He has guidance for every little thing. And it's so liberating! No longer do we have to carry the weight of every decision on our own shoulders.

There are so many verses to dig into around this subject alone, but I want to share two here.

In Luke 11:28 (NLT), Jesus tells us, *"Even more blessed are those who hear the Word of God and put it into practice (obey it)."*

In James 1:25 (AMP), we read, *"But he who looks carefully into the perfect law, the law of liberty, and faithfully abides by it, not having become a [careless] listener who forgets but an active doer [who obeys], he will be blessed and favored by God in what he does [in his life of obedience]."*

Recently, my husband received word from God to shift his entire business model, just as I had a few years prior. Mark came to me one day after a season of struggling and said, "God told me to give away the events!"

What? I thought? I said, "Give *what* away, exactly?"

For the last thirteen years, he had been running live events and coaching programs. His signature program was an in-person event at a cost of $3,000 per attendee. Now we were going to be giving it away?

"Yes. Give the whole thing away and let people come to the event for free. Open it up. We will have companies sponsor it instead. I am not sure how this is going to pan out, but I'm clear I need to do this."

Mark obeyed, and shifted his entire business model. Where he had been struggling to fill seats at $3,000 per person, this new approach has opened the door for strategic sponsorships, companies collaborating to fill the events, and private event opportunities on the back end. With this one shift, he moved from addition to multiplication. From grinding one at a time to exponential increase. It was both an economic strategy and a directive. The financial gates opened up and he not only brought in several hundred thousand dollars in new business, but also an entirely new, more sustainable model that was in full alignment with the future vision for the company.

I would not be writing this book if I had not listened to and obeyed the voice of the Holy Spirit. I would not be doing the work I do with my clients. I would have remained doing what I felt confident in, what I had expertise in, what I knew and could rely on. God has stretched me so much further as I learned to listen and practiced trust.

Obedience shifts our dependence from ourselves onto God—in part because obedience usually involves us doing something we would not necessarily want to do or even think to do on our own. It takes our gifting and abilities and multiplies what we can do with them. How cool is that? Who on earth wouldn't want that level of support? And, while we don't obey just so we can get a reward, I have seen the blessings flow in this place. Obedience is the place of overflow, where we are held under divine protection and provision.

Obedience truly is a lifelong process of leaning further into the relationship, further into trust, further into devotion. There are days we will get it right, and days we will completely miss the mark. That's part of being human and part of any relationship. When we don't obey, we will pay a price—not because we are being punished by God, but because our actions always have equal and opposite reactions, and we reap what we sow.

There have been many times when I have blatantly disobeyed God. He clearly told me to rest, and I pushed Him away because I needed to get "one more" hard run in. As a result, I was forced to stop doing what I loved for eighteen months. I paid the price for my hubris. Other times, I clearly heard His voice telling me to let a client or program go, but I kept gripping on tightly because of fear and pride, thinking, *I don't know where else the funds are going to come from, and I worked so hard on that program!* That fearful grip caused an immediate block in the inflow of cash. I have held onto business partnerships and employees I was clearly instructed to let go of and even warned about, yet I held on out of fear, and it cost me the trust and respect of my team and clients. Disobedience will cost you so much more than the thing you are afraid to lose!

But here's the good news: God is a loving Father. He will let us learn from our mistakes. Yes, there are real consequences to our actions, and they almost always involve a radical humbling. Yet, He will be there for us when we truly ask for help, and He will show us a way out. I have found such comfort in Corinthians 10:13, which states: *"No temptation has overtaken you except what is common to mankind. And God is faithful; He will not let you be tempted beyond what you can bear. But when you are tempted, He will also provide a way out so that you can endure it."* This passage reminds me of the many situations in which my own children have come to me after messing up, often blatantly disobeying the very rules I had set out. I worked hard to create an atmosphere where they could come to me with the truth and know that I would not attack or shame them, but rather help them get things right again. They also knew there would be consequences—but that they wouldn't need to navigate the storm on their own. When we came into partnership, and there was a true change of heart on their part versus just lip service, there was always an incredible opportunity for growth.

I have worked with CEOs whose acts of disobedience cost them millions of dollars in lost or stolen revenue. The Holy Spirit directed them to remove certain people from their organization, but the fear of what others would say, the fear of not having someone to fill that role immediately, or their lack of trust in themselves because they had messed up in the past ultimately cost them an incredible amount of time and money in damage control, lost client relationships, and copious amounts of mental, physical, and emotional energy. With every day of hesitation, the cost was compounded.

Our small acts of defiance can seem like no big deal in the moment. But they have detrimental effects if we carry on in our rebellion. We will always pay the price. Our refusal to listen could cost us millions. It could cost us our marriages and family relationships. It could even cost us our lives. My father had everything a man could ask for, and he had so many opportunities to get back into obedience, but he was unwilling. With his rejection wound still unhealed, pride and fear took over. Today, he sits alone in his home in Florida, in a marriage full of tension and resentment, barely surviving, his health fragile, his spirit broken. My heart cries out for him. As a daughter, I would love to have a deeper relationship with him, but there are limits to the connection that is possible when someone lives in that state. Witnessing his life from a heavenly perspective has put a wildfire inside me to live fully and reach as many people as I can with this message: *Drop the armor.* Heal your heart. Walk in obedience to the Holy Spirit—the breath of God available in each of us. As is written in Isaiah 1:19 (KJV), *"If you are willing and obedient, you shall eat the good of the land."*

As we close out this chapter, I want to highlight a few key things around cultivating trust:

1. *Faith is leaning into the unseen.* Trust is exercised as you move in faith and is strengthened over time.

2. *Surrender is yielding to the Holy Spirit and releasing the need to control the outcome or know every step.* It is the act of surrender that frees us and opens doors.

3. *Submission means getting under the greater mission,* His mission, above our personal agenda. It is the very thing that unifies and multiplies.

4. *Obedience is a natural expression of our devotion.* The deeper we love, the more we desire to hear one another and move accordingly,

5. *Our experience of meeting God increases as we go where He calls us.* When we move toward where He is, we will naturally see more of Him working in our lives.

6. *God works through partnership.* He requires our obedience in order to fulfill His promises in our lives!

WARRIOR INITIATION

- Recall a time when your back was against the wall and you were forced to surrender. What was the result of releasing control of that situation?

- Recall a time when you chose to "let go and let God" before you were forced to do so. What was the result?

- Where in your current life are you resisting surrender?

- How do you feel about the concept of obedience? What does that word trigger inside you?

- When in your life have you obeyed the voice of the Holy Spirit, even when it didn't make sense? What was the result?

- Recall a time when you heard the voice of the Holy Spirit but refused to obey. What was the result?

- Where in your life are you receiving instruction from God to pause, move, let go, or reset your focus? Are you listening, or are you resisting?

WARRIOR LETTER #4

All In

Dear Warrior,

Another layer of God's Masculine Heart has been revealed to me.

This morning I was reminded once again with laser precision that God's heart is fierce, loving, passionate, and ...

Territorial.

Let me explain.

Lately, the Heart of God has been pursuing me like wildfire.

His words coming through me loud and clear.

I want to lead you.

I want to show up for you.

I want to come through for you.

I want to support you, provide for you, and be your rock.

Most importantly, I want you to trust Me.

His heart went on ....

I AM the fortress to your garden.

I AM the shelter to your storms,
I AM the direction in the midst of chaos,
I AM the structure that allows you to flow,
Like the banks of a river holding you firmly
when you roar wildly or move gracefully,
I AM the Lover, Leader, Protector you have been seeking.
AND
I want all of you.
Not part of you.
Not some of you,
Not some of the time.
I WANT your devotion, your presence.
I WANT intimacy with you.
I WANT to share my Kingdom and the wildest adventures with
you.
I WANT to experience ALL of your presence just as you crave to
experience ALL of mine.
I will love you fiercely.
I will provide for you consistently,
I will cherish you as the crown of creation you are.
But I will not share you.
I certainly will not share your devotion with other "Gods" and
useless distractions that pull you further away from me,
Just as your husband doesn't want to share you with other men,
I don't want to compete for your affection.

Ah, yes. There is something wild, fierce, and territorial about God's heart. In my soul, I can say this is refreshing, liberating, and incredibly life giving.

I can breathe again.

***

For years, I didn't fully get this.

I have not been all in.

I will admit: to be fully devoted to one God felt way too terrifying.

What if He didn't come through?

What if He hurt me?

Betrayed me?

Left me?

My entire life has been a reflection of my spiritual walk, half in, dabbling in many things that felt "kinda right" and "mostly good" but my soul has *not* been at rest.

> I remained a fiercely independent warrior,
> In relationships but truly feeling alone,
> Not fully trusting the Heart of God,
> Not allowing my own heart to be revealed.
> I am so grateful that He pursued me,
> Called me back to His own heart.
> And humbled me.
> To come back home.
> In love, In devotion, In service.

***

My Dear Warrior,

> Where have you been seeking deep love
> But showing up halfway?
> Where have you been flirting around
> With things that bring you moments
> Of superficial bliss
> Yet, no lasting depth?
> Where have you been robbing yourself
> Of this deep, rich love affair?
> I believe God is calling us back.
> He is pursuing our hearts to
> Come home to our original design
> To be *all in*

With Him
With each other
With the mission He has placed on our hearts
We are here to rise as Warriors of the Heart, Kings and Queens
Co-creating Kingdoms here on Earth as it is in heaven,
with Him at the center of it all.
Are you willing to unlock this wild, fierce, loving part of you?

CHAPTER THIRTEEN

Practice Discernment

"Discernment is not knowing the difference between right and wrong. It is knowing the difference between right and almost right."

— **CHARLES SPURGEON**

I once coached a couple who were really struggling to find peace in their home and clear communication in their marriage. They so badly wanted to be on the same page, to understand one another and come together—but no matter what they did, they would end up angry, confused, paralyzed with fear, and stuck at a standstill. Not moving toward one another, and certainly not moving forward together.

As we dug into what was going on, we discovered three things which were highly present in their marriage.

First, they had put each other on pedestals, and had unrealistic expectations of one another. Their entire sense of worth stemmed from the other person's approval or disapproval of them. As a result, they had lost their ability to tune inward and trust their own guidance. It's a dangerous game when you make mini-gods out of people in your life, because everything they whisper then becomes a "truth" (with a small "t") that you live by.

Second, they had so many well-intentioned people giving them advice about what they should do and how they should do it. They allowed so many open doors that family members, friends, and other people who had no business offering advice were now influencing them with their foolishness. Many of those people had not done the inner work themselves, and so were influencing this couple with their own fears and projections. With all the open doors (portals) came more confusion, grumbling, gossip, and division. The more they listened and entertained the outside voices, the more they invited those into their marriage and home, the more they found themselves running in circles, and the more exhausted and disheartened they became.

Third, and most importantly, they had stopped getting quiet and spending time with God. They were too busy listening to everyone else instead of getting still. They stopped communicating with and listening to the voice of their own inner man or woman, and to the voice of God speaking to them. They had become distant by the lack of attention to this; with so many fires to put out, they had become hardened by anger and pain, and deafened by all the noise.

Discernment requires us to get still and communicate directly with God. Not through someone else's opinions or a book, but through real-time communication, one to one. Reading His Word, praying, meditating, reflecting, writing, sitting with Him, waiting patiently to see what comes through, and then asking for clarification again and again. Over time, we get to know what His voice sounds like, and we begin to trust *that* voice over all the others.

DISCERNING DECEPTIVE SPIRITS

Years ago, I was in a season of spiritual exploration where I began going into deep, trance-like meditative states. Innocently and nonchalantly, I began pulling oracle cards from "angel" decks and things of the sort. I introduced other, similar practices that seemed innocent enough— and, in the beginning, I was getting a lot of "downloads." It was amazing at first. Every little thing was like bait, drawing me in, and many things revealed to me were, in fact, true. I started spending less time in prayer and more time in trance-like states. Less time in the Word of God, and more time looking for signs, wonders, mystery, and magic at every corner.

In the beginning, it was all love, light, and bliss, and signs were popping up everywhere. Little did I know I was treading in dangerous territory and opening all kinds of spiritual doors into my mind, heart, and home. It got to a point where there were so many different voices (literally, voices) talking inside my head, so many mixed messages, so many pings and dings and mixed signs, that I became completely disoriented and started to feel like I was losing my mind. I started to get paranoid about making decisions, and was second-guessing every little thing. My energy plummeted, and it got really dark inside.

This didn't happen all at once. But my subtle, innocent introduction to these tools opened a new portal. I was drawn into the beauty, light, and trance of it all. But once I was in deep, I could not get out, and things quickly became dark and distorted.

I remember vividly the moment when the hand of Jesus came in and quite literally *pulled* me out of the dark, confusing pit and back to Him. In the Spirit, I felt His hand reaching out for me. His whisper was clear and direct.

"That's enough. I am here. I am everything you need and more. You don't need any of those things any longer. You have direct access to me. You do not need intercessors, rituals, or objects to get to me. Get rid of all that. Free yourself, and come back to me. Let me be more than enough for you, Christine."

I was so convicted. I knew I needed to get rid of the books, cards, objects, and practices immediately; to clean up the atmosphere, cut ties with all those "intercessors," and get to know His voice intimately.

And I did. That week I burned or gave away bins of books, trinkets, and materials. Not all of it was spiritual in nature. Many were sales and business books that I had become obsessed over. I purged anything and everything that had become a "source" of answers that eventually created more confusion and stress for me. I began to pick up the Bible, and asked the Holy Spirit to breathe life into its words and pierce my heart with them. I asked Him to show me and train me in discerning wisdom from foolishness, how to discern His voice from all others, how to discern the different ways that He would speak to me and guide me to move forward, and how to discern spiritual forces at play in my atmosphere.

I read the book of Proverbs multiple times and ways. It is the Book of Wisdom, after all. I re-read the gospels to understand the heart of Jesus and what He was really saying in all those stories and parables. I came in with the renewed heart of a hungry student and lover ready to receive it all. I did not want to go back into that dark cloud of confusion and disorientation ever again.

Discernment allows us to gain direction on our next steps. It allows us to be aware of the truth without being afraid. It gives us the ability and confidence to move forward wisely, rather than making foolish decisions. It's both a gift and a skill, and it is the final (and perhaps most crucial) weapon in the arsenal of the Warrior of the Heart.

DEFINING DISCERNMENT

Discernment is one of those words I could not fully grasp or understand until I experienced it. Discernment is knowing *what* to do and *when* to do it. It's knowing the difference between the competing voices in your head, knowing which motives are pure versus adulterated, what is truth versus deception, and what is a clear direction versus another tempting distraction—or, worse, a dangerous or destructive path.

Discernment is *the thing* that gives us the ability to move confidently forward *in faith* when we can't see the tangible result or evidence in front of us. It is the companion and partner of trust and a skill to be cultivated. Our faith and ability to surrender in hard moments, to obey (hear) the call and submit to the inner voice of the Holy Spirit, is strengthened as we build trust in Him and develop our discernment. It's a muscle we must put to use daily.

In short, it's understanding and knowing what is *of* God and *from* God, and what is not. Proverbs 3:5-7 (AMP) reads: *"Trust in and rely confidently on the LORD with all your heart and do not rely on your own insight or understanding. In all your ways know and acknowledge and recognize Him, and He will make your paths straight and smooth [removing obstacles that block your way]."*

Let's go back to that obedience (hearing and following) thing for a moment. Our *inability* or *unwillingness* to trust His voice and obey (follow) ultimately comes from three things.

First, our trust muscle has not been developed. Perhaps we have failed to recognize and catalog all the ways in which He has already shown up in our lives, all the times He came through unexpected and unplanned, all the times we leaned forward in faith and He supplied our needs, opened doors, and protected us from our own destructive desires.

How many times has He been right there, but you've failed to acknowledge Him?

The more we move in faith to where God is active, the more of Him we see at work in our lives! The more we obey, or hear and follow His lead, the more we experience His blessings. The more we experience of Him, the more we trust that He will follow through on what He says He will do! Do you see the cycle?

Second, we may lack discernment. Sometimes, we quite literally cannot tell what is what. If we have not cultivated this skill, we will still operate from filters of fear, past wounding, doubt, judgment, envy, and pride. In other words, we will remain open to attack by the enemy. When we can't trust what we are seeing, hearing, or experiencing in our atmosphere, we will find ourselves adrift in a sea of confusion and self-doubt.

This confusion can happen when our reptilian brain is going wild trying to keep us alive. When we are hijacked by fear, we can't be a host to the Holy Spirit. We might be going too fast and need to slow down and pay attention. God is never in a hurry; He is always on time for what matters most. We might have *way* too many "doors" open in our minds, too many external inputs coming at us, too much noise and content, or too many spiritual practices and agreements with spirits that are not from God. In this case, slam those doors shut, and just listen. Finally, we might simply be unfamiliar with God's voice and the natural ways in which He speaks to us because we have never really invested time in getting to know Him in all His ways.

Is it any surprise that we are confused, doubtful, or even paranoid at times?

The third and final reason why we may lack discernment is that we simply have not asked for this gift. Simply put, if we don't receive and acknowledge a gift, there is no way we can actually use it. Jesus said,

"You desire but do not have, so you kill. You covet but you cannot get what you want, so you quarrel and fight. You do not have because you do not ask God. When you ask, you do not receive, because you ask with wrong motives, that you may spend what you get on your pleasures." (James 4:2, NIV) The key to receiving anything that we ask for is: first, to actually ask for it; and second, to check our motives for asking. Why do we actually want this money, relationship, opportunity, or blessing? How will we put it to use? It's wild how simple this is, but how few of us put this step into practice—and, when we're done, say, "Thank you."

Discernment is a spiritual gift. It comes from God, from the Spirit. Therefore, if we want to receive true discernment, we must receive this gift from the Spirit of God. Ask from the right place. Then, accept the gift in faith, knowing that you have received it, and be grateful.

Whose Voices Are You Entertaining?

I would be remiss if I didn't include this here.

Not every voice is wise, not every opinion counts, not every well-intentioned person has the right answer. Deeper than that, not every "spirit" that reveals something to you is from God. Often, we are so desperate to get that one piece of insight, that one sign that gets us a little closer to what we want, that we consciously or unconsciously open ourselves up to deceptive spirits. I believe this is what happened to me during my meditative trances.

I have many great teachers, coaches, pastors, and mentors in my world, not all of whom are faith-based. I am incredibly grateful for them all, and graciously invite their counsel into my life. At the same time, I never move on their guidance until I test it through the lens of the Spirit. Just because something is for others does not mean it is for us. As John 4:1 (NIV) states, *"Dear friends, do not believe every spirit, but test the spirits to see whether they are from God, because many false prophets have gone out into the world."* As mentioned earlier, some of those spirits may be coming from or working through the most well-intended people we know. We must learn to discern what is at play in every situation. Is it Truth? Does it bring you spiritual peace, rather than strife? Does it support life, not death? Does it align with God's Word? For He will never contradict himself.

Any source that is not God is not the ultimate Source. And while there may be many wise teachers, coaches, mentors, and guides out there, we must test everything against the Truth and His Word.

Scripture tells us that the Holy Spirit does not speak on His own accord, but only repeats what the Father speaks. The Holy Spirit is literally God's Word being spoken right into us, into our very essence. In John 8:28 (NIV), Jesus says, *"I do nothing on my own but speak just what the Father has taught me."* Jesus emphasizes His complete obedience to the Father's will. He declares that He does nothing on His own but only speaks what the Father has taught Him. This statement underscores the intimate relationship between Jesus and the Father, and highlights Jesus' role as the obedient Son who fulfills the Father's purposes. Later, as Jesus speaks to the disciples about a time he will no longer be with them in the physical sense, He continues, *"And I will ask the Father, and He will give you another advocate to help you and be with you forever— the Spirit of Truth. The world cannot accept Him because it neither sees Him nor knows Him. But you know Him, for He lives with you and will be in you."* (John 14:16-17, NIV)

Isn't that amazing?! He sent the Spirit of Truth, the Holy Spirit— the breath and Word of God himself—to live in us and be with us forever. When we give our lives to Him, and choose to no longer live according to our own agenda, we invite the Spirit of Truth to be with us.

He is always here, always waiting for us to connect to Him. When we do, He reveals things to us, He goes before us. His direction is unlike any other you will ever experience. You will know it because you will know Him intimately. This can only be experienced. There are no words to describe it other than an internal sense of certainty, knowing, and peace.

And isn't that really what we are all seeking, in the end?

Once you receive the gift of discernment, it's up to you to learn how to cultivate and use this new gift. How do we do this, exactly? We begin to slow down (again) and notice the different ways that God speaks to us. There are an infinite number of ways the Spirit speaks, moves, and guides us.

Below are several of the most prominent ways I and my clients have experienced discernment.

- Through Creation itself
- Through the body
- Through the "super-natural"
- Through His Word
- Through His wonders

In the following sections, we'll unpack each of these in depth so you can begin to recognize how God speaks to you and how you might begin to cultivate your own practice of discernment.

GOD SPEAKS THROUGH CREATION ITSELF

As is written in Romans 1:20 (AMP), *"For ever since the creation of the world His invisible attributes, His eternal power and divine nature, have been clearly seen, being understood through His workmanship [all His creation, the wonderful things that He has made], so that they [who fail to believe and trust in Him] are without excuse and without defense."*

Have you ever noticed how much clarity and peace emerges when you are immersed in nature? Have you felt the almost-immediate shift in your body—from being tense and fearful to being relaxed, open, and held—when you are close to the mountains, near a river, or at the beach? When I'm observing wildlife, it's as if I am observing God himself at work and play.

Any time I feel overwhelmed, mentally congested, or too caught up in the noise of the world, I pull back and retreat into nature. Most of my greatest insights, breakthroughs, problem-solving, and new ideas have come on solo hikes in the forest. The more time you spend in nature, the more it begins to reveal to you.

The opposite is also true. The further we get *away* from nature and its organic elements—including natural foods, fibers, scents, and even natural light—the further away we get from the Creator Himself. The one who created all things and knows all things. As we fuel our bodies with clean, organic foods, we stop polluting our temple. As we quiet our minds in a forest, we see and hear more clearly the natural ways in which our Creator speaks. I can't even begin to count the times that God spoke to me in these places—not only as an internal whisper or inspiration, but literally by showing me a specific animal or opening up a new path in the woods that led me to a beautiful new location, thus revealing the right direction to move on another situation in my life.

A few years ago, I was in Colorado in February with the kids and I needed to make some big, scary business decisions. I was terrified of making the wrong move and ending up unprotected financially, and afraid of putting my children in a compromising situation. I also knew I was holding onto the past, struggling with trusting the next move.

Early one cold morning, I was kneeling by the river in my snowsuit, praying for guidance. When I opened my eyes, I saw a massive moose right across the river from me. She was maybe twenty feet away. Next to her, between me and her, was her calf.

The sight was something spectacular: an incredibly strong mother watching over her calf. Moose are highly protective, especially if you get between a momma and her baby—so I froze up and just watched. She stared at me for a few minutes. It was so quiet. So peaceful.

At that moment, I knew her appearance was an answer to my request. I had a clear direction. I slowly stood up and backed away from the river, thanking God for the glimpse of natural splendor, His majestic presence, and the overwhelming sense of strength and protection I felt in that moment. I felt Him say, "*I've got you. You are mine. Your children are my children. I am here with you, protecting you. Move forward and know that I am going with you.*"

From there, it was just a matter of obedience and faith.

When was the last time you immersed yourself in nature without AirPods in your ears? When was the last time you took a slow walk on the beach or sat by a stream and simply observed what was happening around you? I encourage you to make time in nature a habit. Get outside daily. Bathe in the forest. Soak in the ocean. Relish the sunshine, and allow God to speak to you through His marvelous creation.

GOD SPEAKS THROUGH THE BODY

I feel fortunate to have spent nearly three decades of my life working with the human body as an athlete, trainer, and holistic health practitioner. Our bodies are miraculous in the way they heal themselves, the way they store information and speak to us second by second. The more I worked with the body to help people optimize their mental and physical performance as well as overcome health challenges, the more I realized how perfectly designed and intricate this vessel is.

The body holds so much information and wisdom. Not only is it keeping a tally of everything we've experienced in our lifetimes, but it also processes our trauma, our emotions, our waste, and gives us constant feedback as to whether something is adding harmony to our life or working against us. God designed these miraculous vessels to support us, to house His spirit within us, to nourish us, and to be vessels for not only physical multiplication and replication but also creative vessels to multiply everything around us! It's no coincidence that the better we feel in our bodies—the healthier, stronger, and cleaner our bodies are—the more joy, peace, clarity, and abundance is created in us and around us.

In scripture, the body is referred to as a temple of the Holy Spirit. When I took this to heart, things really shifted for me with regard to discernment. It only makes sense that, if the place my spirit calls home is a temple not only for my soul but also for the Spirit of God, I should honor it and keep it pure so I will be able to experience, recognize, and meet God there.

When we are in harmony with God and lead our lives from a place of wisdom, we often experience that same harmony within our body! Proverbs 3:7-8 is one of my favorite passages that speaks the blessings of wisdom with relation to health. When we live in alignment with God's will and lead from a place of wisdom, we will experience longevity and quality of life, health in our body, and refreshment to our bones!

When we are out of harmony with the God-given design for our bodies, we experience heightened levels of dis-ease or the body being out of ease. This manifests as all types of dysfunction and disease—including, but not limited to: mental fog, chronic anxiety, high blood pressure, cardiovascular issues, fatigue, sleep issues, chronic pain, musculoskeletal (structural) problems, auto-immune diseases, cancer, and inflammation. The costs of being out of harmony are exorbitant.

If we are honest with ourselves, much of our dis-ease comes from living out of harmony. Eating fake foods, stressing over things we cannot control, engaging in behaviors and patterns that rob us of life force ... these things can cost us years of our lives.

We know our capacity to handle stress and navigate life's challenges with resilience increases as we take better care of our bodies. And yet, when we get squeezed, care for our bodies seems to be one of the first things that goes right out the window.

However, there's more to our bodies than just physical health.

There are natural ways that our bodies speak to us that I believe are God speaking *in* us. If we are tuned into our bodies, in a grounded, pure, and rested state, we can discern the signs more clearly. Again, our bodies are vessels and channels. When the vessel is clear we can move more efficiently, and when our channel is clean/pure we have the ability to tune in to receive clear messages. If we are full of toxic chemicals, hungover, congested with mental fog, or inflamed from a poor diet and mismanaged stress loads, it becomes harder to discern what the body is telling us. We will remain disconnected from this beautiful way we are designed to know with ease which way to move.

Let's explore a few of the ways in which the body speaks.

Our Instincts

At some point in your life, you made a split-second decision that did not make any logical sense but ended up saving you tons of money, time, energy, or heartache. Maybe an instinctual decision even saved your life!

There are times when you just *know* what move to make, where to go, or what to do. Those are your instincts at work.

We hear it all the time: "What does your gut tell you?"
It's a great question ... for someone who is tuned into their body and has a clean gut. It's not such a great question to someone who doesn't know or trust their body, whose trauma body is highly active, or who has a gut full of inflammation. For that person, the answer will most often be, *"I have no idea!"* or *"Everything feels like a threat!"*

While our "gut instinct" extends beyond the physical form, we do experience physical reactions in our gut when something is off. Indigestion, nausea, stomachaches, or an "uneasy feeling" are just some of the ways our body speaks to us. I can't possibly begin to unpack the mechanics of this here, but if you're curious, there are many wonderful books on the subject (see my recommended reading list at www.dropthearmorbook.com). When it comes to tapping into the gut instinct, I'm a big believer in asking yes or no questions. These tap into my gut instinct and allow my body to generate feedback as to whether I am on the right path or completely off course. This is just one of the areas I check whenever I am needing to trust and lean in.

Our Heart

The heart is the gateway to the soul, and our soul has a unique calling and mission in this lifetime. We often hear the advice, "Follow your heart. It will never lead you astray!" I disagree. In fact, I feel this can be downright dangerous. This is great advice *if* our heart is aligned to the Heart of God and His will for our lives, and we are operating from a place of love and God-given desire. But, as you know from our earlier discussion, our hearts can also become hardened, closed, traumatized, or hijacked by egoic desires and old stories. If our wounds are still running the show, our hearts may not be the best place to go for wisdom. In fact, they will give some downright foolish direction (see Proverbs 12:15).

The good news is, we can always ask the Holy Spirit to stir up our hearts and reveal the truth. We can find much wisdom and guidance through this portal. Some questions I ask when searching my heart are: "Does this create more expansion and openness in my chest, or more pressure? Is this bringing excitement (swelling, conviction, clarity) in my heart as well as peace in my spirit? Is what my heart is saying aligned with God's Word?"

Our Intuition

Intuition is often described as the ability to understand or know something instantaneously, without the need for conscious reasoning or analysis. It is a nonlinear way of processing information that is often seen as a form of inner awareness or insight that arises from a deep, unconscious level of awareness. Also known as our "trustworthy inner voice" or "inner compass," it feels like something you can't quite put your finger on until it's happening.

Our brains are constantly assessing and gathering information. That information is stored in our bodies and subconscious minds as both individual experiences and patterns of information and behavior. This is collected throughout our lifetime and also passed down through generations.

The depth and breadth of our information is determined by our awareness. When awareness is broad, more data is captured, and bias is removed. With a broader and unbiased data set, intuition can flourish as it flows in the background of your consciousness—as your subconscious mind makes sense of all the data and spits out insights and ideas to guide your way forward. The development of, and trust in, such a capability is especially vital in high-stakes and uncertain circumstances. The intellect, the thinking mind, can only work so fast and crunch so much data, but the intuitive intelligence within the mind can see more, and therefore respond more appropriately to the present moment, be it chaotic or clear.

Some people say intuition is the same as the voice of the Holy Spirit. I disagree. I believe our intuition, like God-given gut instinct, is there to assist us and guide us on the battlefield of life. It's part of God's intelligent and brilliant design, our own internal steering system. When we live in harmony with our internal ecosystem—meaning, we are clear and clean in body and mind—we are better tuned into it and able to assimilate information that ultimately informs our decisions and movements.

While God can certainly speak to us through our intuition, the Holy Spirit is a distinct part of the Godhead speaking in us and through us. The Holy Spirit always glorifies God, speaks wisdom into us, points us back to Jesus, and manifests in very clear ways, as we will unpack later in this chapter.

Your Energy

Have you ever felt like you had the weight of the world on your shoulders? Have you ever walked into a room and felt the "energy" was just off—as if the atmospheric pressure was increasing and squeezing you or pushing you back? Have you ever felt constricted or suffocated, like you can't breathe fully, and you know it's not something you ate or a respiratory issue?

Or, on the other hand, have you ever felt yourself so buoyant and light that you knew you could take on the world? Have you ever walked into a space and felt immediately safe and welcomed? Have you ever felt like your whole body was set on fire by an idea?

Our energy—the amount of life force within and around our body, our perceived level of energy for our tasks, and the feeling of energy within our bodies in relation to certain feelings or situations—is another way that God can speak to us through our bodies.

Whenever it feels like I have a copious amount of weight sitting on my shoulders or back, or weight begins to accumulate on my body, that's my sign to pause and take a look at what I am carrying that is not mine to carry. This could be many things: worrying about things that are out of my control, taking on roles and responsibilities that are no longer a fit for me, or simply trying to do too much in a day. Often, when I feel "heavy" it's because I am trying to energetically carry or do the emotional work for others—feeling everything they feel, helping them feel what they need to feel, overexplaining, or wanting to shift/save them from their "negative" emotions. This is common in highly empathic people who feel everything around them.

A few years ago, I was speaking with a client who was stressed out and on the verge of depression. She was feeling weighed down, and as a result the physical weight was also piling on. She was waking up anxious, going to bed exhausted, and generally unhappy. When we began to unpack what was going on, we found that she was *so* over-extended! In addition to her day job as the general manager of a large organization, she was also trying to be at all her kids' competitive hockey games/tournaments, run a side hustle, and serve as the chair of a nonprofit committee. That last one was throwing her right over the edge. She was feeling the weight of obligation. The weight of guilt. The weight of other people's opinions and letting others down. The fear of failing as a mother, wife, and leader. The weight was crushing her.

Once she realized the weight of staying on as chair of the organization was an anchor keeping her tied to an old version of her identity, she decided to cut the cord. That took faith and courage, but once she did, she was able to breathe again.

Like our intuition, heart, and gut instincts, our energy levels deliver messages to us from God. When something isn't right, we will feel it, and it will be reflected in the amount of life force we can access and have available. We can do all things, but we were never designed to be in all places at once. That is called *omnipresence*, and there is only one who can fill those shoes. We can say yes to all things, but not everything is the right thing or appointed assignment for us. We can care for others deeply while also not carrying the weight of their actions and feelings. Learning the power of loving and clear boundaries are critical skills to better manage our energy and keep our focus on the things that matter most.

God Speaks Through the Super-Natural

Just as God speaks to us through the natural world—through both nature and our own bodies—He also speaks through the "super-natural," or the etheric.

The Holy Spirit is the very Spirit of God. It exists beyond the realm of our five senses. We have been gifted with super-natural channels of communication as well as natural ones, and God speaks through them all. He speaks to us through messages, sights, wonders, the miraculous (unexplainable), internal whispers, visions, dreams, angels, and more.

You may have noticed that I've chosen to write "super-natural" instead of "supernatural" throughout this book. This differentiates the way God speaks beyond our senses from the usual use of the term, which is often connected to ghosts, evil spirits, horror movies, and fear-based stories.

Spiritual Sight

Scripturally, the word "vision" is often used to describe an encounter with God where He imparts special revelation, often in dreams or visions that may or may not involve seeing something in the physical realm. Your spirit sees what your physical eyes cannot. Visions are a means through which God communicates His will, messages, or future events to individuals. They are often used by God to convey important instructions, warnings, assurance, confirmation, or promises over our future.

Spiritual sight may appear as an insight or revelation into a situation or circumstance that goes beyond what the eye of the beholder can recognize. Wisdom often presents itself as this form of knowledge or spiritual sight. It's through the Holy Spirit that we are given eyes to see and ears to hear (see John 14:26, 1 Corinthians 2:14). God gives us super-natural sight so we can perceive beyond the limitations of our physical form into the spiritual, into the promises of the future He has for us, and into what He sees in the current moment that we cannot.

Everything we see with our physical eyes is a manifestation of what was created in the past. On top of that, situations and circumstances have many realities going on simultaneously; the lens we see them through will determine what we see, and ultimately how we engage with them. Staying stuck in the three-dimensional, physical realm can lead us to react rather than respond and keep us stuck in a limited perspective. Moving into the spiritual realm allows us to see things as God sees them, which completely changes our encounter with them.

Ultimately, visions are a manifestation of God's sovereignty and His desire to communicate with His people. They highlight God's power, wisdom, and ability to reveal Himself in super-natural ways. As is written in Proverbs 20:12, *"Vision, then, like love and wisdom, is not something to be lost but the constant gift of God to be fully used."*

The closer I have come into intimacy with God, the more He shows me. Visions, dreams, insights, and revelations are now regular occurrences rather than rare encounters. I've shared several with you throughout this book. Sometimes, I receive something in a dream; other times, it's a revelation or picture revealed during prayer times. Still other times, a vision can come smack in the middle of a conversation, or while looking at something completely unrelated. The more I embrace the gift of spiritual sight and honor it, the more this gift is realized and normalized in my life.

I want to note that there is no right or wrong way to receive a vision from God. Visions are highly personal. Spiritual sight is a gift, and I believe it's available to all of us if we are willing to ask for it. As with all gifts, it requires us to ask from the right place with the right intentions. I asked for the gift of super-natural sight so I might see things through God's eyes. It has been such a healing gift for me to see others, past situations, and current moments through a different set of eyes—an all-knowing, unconditionally loving set of eyes.

In those hard-to-trust moments, regardless of what's happening on the surface level, we can cultivate the gift of our spiritual sight to see beyond the ordinary into the extra-ordinary. It is not something we force into existence. It's something we yield to, surrender to, and open ourselves to. We invite the Holy Spirit to come in and give us fresh eyes. We ask for a vision to see what we were blind to before. We honor the vision without distorting it to match our agendas. We sit with it. We ask the Holy Spirit to reveal its meaning to us.

Spiritual Hearing

"My sheep hear my voice, and I know them, and they follow me." (John, 10:27, KJV)

God's voice can sound like a whisper in the wind or a murmur in our innermost being or heart. Sometimes, we may even experience an audible sound. Other times, we may be sitting right in front of someone who is speaking and yet hear something totally different than what they are saying.

People and things in the world are constantly screaming and competing for our attention, but the voice of the Holy Spirit often whispers. Most of the things we hear are intended to distract us and take life from us with subtle temptations and shiny promises. They are clickbait: loud, obnoxious, interfering, and adding more friction in the atmosphere. Those are not God, and God is not in them.

God wants intimacy with me, intimacy with you. He is not going to compete for your attention. Rather, He will wait until you are ready to be still, and *listen.*

Consider this passage from I Kings 19:11-13: *"And, behold, the Lord passed by, and a great and strong wind rent the mountains, and brake in pieces the rocks before the Lord; but the Lord was not in the wind: and after the wind an earthquake; but the Lord was not in the earthquake: and after the earthquake a fire; but the Lord was not in the fire: and after the fire a still small voice. When Elijah heard it, he wrapped his face in his cloak and went out and stood at the mouth of the cave. Suddenly a voice came to him and said, 'What are you doing here, Elijah?'"*

I get chills every time I read this. I have personally experienced this many times over, and there are no words to explain it well. Most often, the Holy Spirit shows up as a whisper, tugging at my innermost being. Calling my name to pay attention, saying, *"Listen."* God will not scream for my attention. He knows my address—and yours. He is available now, inviting us to go right to the Source.

There have been multiple occasions when I was dreaming and heard His voice loud and clear—an audible noise, usually one word or one sentence that had an entirely different timbre and sense to it than everything else in my dream. When that happens, I wake up and quickly write down the words I heard, then pray over them to discern what the Holy Spirit was trying to communicate. At this point of my life, I dismiss nothing, but I also take everything directly to the Spirit in prayer and back to the Word to affirm and confirm what has been spoken.

Spiritual "Knowing"

The more we spend time with someone, the more we feel and know their presence. We know what it's like to be in their atmosphere. Like its Hebrew counterpart, *yada*, the Aramaic word for "know," *yida*, can convey both intellectual understanding and experiential knowledge, as well as personal acquaintance or intimacy (including sexual intimacy), depending on the context. To know someone is to have experienced intimacy with them, such as a husband "knows" his wife. So it is with this relationship.

Sometimes, we can sense Him in the atmosphere; we may even feel a warmth in the air or on our skin. Sometimes, it's as if a flood of unexplainable love washes over us. While this is different for everyone, one thing is clear: when we can *feel* Him, we *know* that He is there with us. There is a knowing, and a certainty when the wisdom we seek is granted.

Some confuse spiritual knowing with intuition or even a flood of emotions or chemical reactions (such as excitement), but they are not the same. There is a difference between our intuitive sense within our body, which is a God-given sense and ability, and the Holy Spirit of God Himself. There is also a clear difference between an emotional rush, which is mostly chemical, and an internal spiritual knowing, which is beyond the physical—although our bodies may respond similarly in both cases.

Webster's Dictionary defines wisdom as "the ability to discern inner qualities and relationships; insight; good sense; judgment; generally accepted belief." The Bible explains wisdom as a state of omniscience; of having infinite awareness, understanding, and insight.

God is pure love. Pure grace. When His love and grace washes over us, it's unlike anything we have experienced before. There is an overwhelming sense of being held, fully seen, fully loved. We are invited to yield to an unconditional love that even in our wildest dreams we have not experienced.

This is not a blissed-out, transcendental state. It is not "nirvana," as some spiritual communities call it. It's not a place where you are suspended in timelessness, consciousness, or the ether. I spent many years learning and practicing yoga, transcendental meditation, and other spiritual and New-Age practices in search of spiritual enlightenment. I drew tarot cards in search of answers. I experimented extensively with plant medicine and spent multiple days at a time in altered states of consciousness under the influence of ayahuasca. That was not God. It was an altered state of consciousness. It *felt* like God at first. It was definitely a spiritual experience. But it is nothing like the spiritual knowing, certainty, and clarity that comes from being in the presence of God Himself, and connected to the knowledge that can only come from the Holy Spirit.

When you experience His presence regularly, you will never want or need anything else. You have direct access to the one True God and Holy Spirit. The One who created all things. The One who is all-knowing, all-powerful, all-encompassing. It's a grounding place that is so pure, so rich; so secure, safe, and steadfast. It's unending. It's as real as it gets. I have never looked back or needed to seek anything else. He has supplied every need, every desire, everything I could ever ask for.

GOD SPEAKS THROUGH HIS WORD

Ultimate discernment comes from knowing His character intimately, and we discover this through His Word.

We get to know how He speaks and what He stands for by spending time in His Word. We get to know His character by studying Him, by observing Him, and by allowing Him to speak directly to us through this living text.

"*In the beginning the Word already existed. The Word was with God, and the Word was God. He existed in the beginning with God. God created everything through him, and nothing was created except through him. The Word gave life to everything that was created, and his life brought light to everyone. The light shines in the darkness, and the darkness can never extinguish it.*" (John 1:1-5, NLT)

The Holy Spirit will never contradict His own Word, and through it all things are created. So many people are resistant to reading scripture with a fresh heart and mind because of something that happened in their past, or because the think they know it all already. There's nothing new to discover.

I urge you: don't make the mistake of thinking you "know" God's Word already. As you pick up the Bible and dive into His Word with fresh eyes and ears, He will reveal more and more of Himself to you. As you cultivate and develop a relationship with Him through His Word, just like in conversation and listening, you will have an intimate first-hand ability to recognize Him at work.

The more I show up with an open and willing heart, the more it is revealed to me. The more I pick up the Bible as a love letter and access point into my Spiritual Father's heart and mind, the more insight and wisdom I gain, the clearer things become, and the hungrier I become for it and for Him. The more I use it as a playbook for life, the more I see blessings flowing into all areas of my life—relationships, finances, health, business, and family. In each passage, there is real-time practical and tactical strategy and endless wisdom to help me in any situation I am facing. At this point, the last thing I want to do is confuse my mind and heart with other "interpreters" and intercessors. In fact, I cannot imagine a life where I don't have this level of direct access, intimacy, and direction from Him at every moment. What a gift! What a blessing!

Whatever your past experiences with the Bible, religion, or even God Himself, I encourage you to pick up and open this gift today and watch as it begins to reveal a whole new world of insight to you.

GOD SPEAKS THROUGH HIS WONDERS

I would be remiss if I didn't include this here, and I put it last on purpose. Miracles and wonders are often the *first* thing people look for when they look for God at work, but they are not the most common, the most reliable, or the most obvious ways in which He works. When we get distracted by looking for wonders, it is also very easy to start taking everything as a sign and getting totally disoriented.

God is a God of wonders, and as the ultimate Creator of all life and everything that supports it, God has the power to suspend natural laws in order to fulfill His purposes. This is what a miracle is, essentially.

Who doesn't love a spectacular display of the miraculous? I have seen and heard of many miraculous and spontaneous healings in my lifetime. Humans have forever been trying to tap into the super-natural world and experience more of the power, insight, vision, and wisdom of the spiritual realm. Miracles were a part of the ministries of many prophets, and of course of Jesus and the apostles. Miracles primarily served the purpose of confirming their message as being from God.

If you ask for signs from God, you will receive them. If you ask for miracles, you may also receive them. But you will observe far more of the miraculous in the subtle ways God speaks to you, loves you, and supports you. And, when your eyes are fully opened, you will begin to notice Him moving in all things, big and small.

HOW TO PRACTICE DISCERNMENT

Do we really need more people taking selfies in front of mansions and Maseratis, telling the world how great they are and how they got to the top? Do we really need to watch more TikTok videos of people dancing to grab attention, or plastering their faces with a dozen filters to try and look more beautiful? Do we really need to get in on some secret society that has the keys to success and wealth that no one else does? What does this accomplish?

Sounds ridiculous, but we are falling for these things—or for similar tactics—every day. We need to start asking, "What is the *motive* and *heart* behind this?"

What gives you full confidence in God's presence and direction so you can actually surrender, obey, and move forward in faith? I can guarantee it's not chasing superficial things or shiny objects. That's already been proven a million times over. It's certainly not going to be the thing our pride jumps up and dances over. When we are seeking discernment and want to know who to trust, we need to be able to see clearly the motives and heart behind the information. This is where discernment begins.

In Matthew 23:12 (KJV), Jesus says, *"Whoever exalts himself shall be humbled; and whoever humbles himself shall be exalted."* The Holy Spirit will always direct us back to Jesus and to our Father's Heart. In the end, it's so that He, not man, may be glorified—so that we may fix our eyes on Him and His ways, and not be obsessed with our own status, significance, or platform. I have had mentors in my life who claimed to be spiritual and "faith-filled," but every single thing they taught or sought was to build up *their* world, not the Kingdom. All the business strategies and "intuitive" guidance was fueled by deepening their pockets rather than deepening their impact. I've been there, too, albeit unknowingly—but even then, something inside me was restless and uneasy about it. Something felt off, but I went along because I lacked discernment and conviction. I didn't trust the Spirit or my ability to discern because I hadn't built that muscle up yet. The result was turmoil in my business and turmoil in my soul.

We are blessed beyond measure when our hearts are in the right place. I love how God shows up abundantly, giving us well beyond what we ask for or need, when our focus is on building others up, being conduits of His love, and bringing more life to this planet. When we seek first the Kingdom of God, all things truly are added unto us. We get the platforms, the relationships, the positions, and the resources to support the vision. We get the favor—not because of who we are or what we made happen, but because of who He is, and because we moved in tandem with Him (obeyed) and allowed Him to position us for growth, increase, and responsibility. When we operate from a place of discernment, we no longer have to carry the weight of the world on our shoulders. We can sleep in peace about the present and the future.

When we begin to move into discernment, there are a couple of questions to ask that can quickly shift your perspective on a relationship or situation and bring you into greater clarity. They are:

- Does this show the "fruits" of the Spirit?
- Who or what is being exalted and glorified?
- Do you have spiritual peace about it?
- Does this lead with and produce more love?
- Does it align with His Word?

"But the fruit of the Spirit is love, joy, peace, patience, kindness, good-ness, faithfulness, gentleness, self-control." (Galatians 5:22-23, NASB) If whatever we are engaging with does not show signs of the fruit of the Spirit, then it is not of God. It is a counterfeit spirit acting as God. If the information at hand, the decision at hand, or the action at hand is ini-tiated from or produces anger, fear, evil, mistrust, aggression, a lack of self-control (impulsive drive), impatience, chronic guilt, or shame, rest assured it is not of the Spirit. The Holy Spirit will always produce more love, more joy, more patience, more kindness, more goodness, more faith, more ability to control the 'self' or superficial desires (delayed gratification) in exchange for true, lasting, life-giving reward. When you are aligned with God's will and desire for you , you will feel a depth of peace, even if the choice before you is uncomfortable or scary.

And, if you are ever unsure, look for the answers in His Word. You will always find them. *"He will glorify and honor Me, because He [the Holy Spirit] will take from what is Mine and will disclose it to you."* (John 16:14, AMP)

Trust and discernment are the keys which unlock the heart, the possibilities, and the next season. Without them, it is impossible to move forward, to surrender, to move—to obey. With discernment, your life will transform. Trust and faith are a choice, but they are not blind. You cultivate trust. You also cultivate faith and act in it.

From this point forward, I invite you to bring the Holy Spirit into every decision. He wants to be involved, and is available. Start with the easy things. Ask for guidance, then listen. When you get information, gut-check it. Heart-check it. Intuition-check it. Energy-check it. Then, check it above all in the Spirit and in the scriptures. The more you prac-tice with the little things and follow through, the more faith and trust you will have in the bigger moments where more is at stake.

WARRIOR INITIATION

- How has your view of discernment shifted or grown by reading this chapter?

- In what areas of your life have you been lacking discernment?

- How can you become more intentional about getting quiet, clean, and clear in your body vessel?

- How can you become more intentional about checking the motives of your heart?

- What have your energy levels been telling you? What gets to stay? What must go or be drastically reduced?

- Can you recall any times that God has clearly spoken to you through a vision, dream, or otherwise? How did you know without a doubt that it was Him?

- Are there any areas of your life right now that the Spirit is speaking to you about?

- Are there specific areas of your life where you need to be asking for insight, revelation, or wisdom? (And, if you aren't asking, then ask with the right motive and be ready to receive!)

CHAPTER FOURTEEN

Rise, Warrior! (The Manifesto)

"The purpose of your life is far greater than your own personal fulfillment, your peace of mind, or even your happiness. It's far greater than your family, your career, or even your wildest dreams and ambitions. If you want to know why you were placed on this planet, you must begin with God. You were born by His purpose and for His purpose."

— FROM *THE PURPOSE DRIVEN LIFE* BY RICK WARREN

When my children were younger, there was a book series we would read together called *The Magic Treehouse*. In this series, Jack and Annie would go on incredible adventures. There was always a mission at hand, but no one knew how the story would go, or how it would end. At the end of each chapter, Jack and Annie would find themselves at an intersection where they had to make a decision. That one decision could change the course of the whole story. Every stage and every ending hinged on the decision made at the end of the chapter before. The books were so much fun, and so exciting to read.

What a beautiful parallel for life!

One of the reasons I and my children (and millions of children around the world) loved these books was because they contained the element of adventure for which we are all designed. As we learned in Chapter Five, a longing to be in the unknown is ingrained in our DNA. As children, we let our imaginations run wild, travel into foreign places with mystical creatures and guides, and face seemingly insurmountable obstacles, always knowing we will come home safe in the end.

As we grow older, we crave deeper purpose inside our adventure. We are drawn to stories that test the characters we love to the core, and have deeper lessons and morals. We are drawn to defining moments of sacrifice, courage, and a mission to fulfill. The unknown territory now has greater stakes: lives, nations, and entire future generations are at stake! These epic stories become turning points for humanity, with one person or a small group of people stepping forward in courageous leadership and defying the odds stacked against them.

The problem is, for the majority, the adventure stops there: with stories. These adventures are fantasies and escapes only experienced through movies or books. Caught in the drift of daily obligations and unrealized expectations, our willingness to lean into the adventure right here and now diminishes, and we lose our faith to forge forward.

In King Arthur's legend, Arthur pulls the sword out of the stone long before he is willing to use it in the way it was intended. First, he doubts who he is. Once he has been given his clear calling and his mission, as well as the tool (the sword) that was specifically made for him, he still runs from his responsibility and tries to use the "gift" for his own personal gain. It's not until he experiences even more hardship, loses more people he loves, and sees the extreme "darkness" at play through a vision that he finally wakes up to his calling and purpose, begins to wield the sword the right way, and ultimately wins the battle against the dark kingdom.

This chapter is an invitation back into the calling, the mission, the gift, and the life-giving adventure you are created for.

Throughout this book, I have shared stories of "leaps of faith," where one decision I made, in a specific Kairos moment, became the first domino that tipped all the others. With that one decision, that one domino—even though I didn't realize it or see it at the time—I began writing a new chapter, with new characters, new discoveries, and new gifts, ultimately leading to a new ending.

However, in those moments of decision, and for a little while afterward, very little transformed or transpired in the physical world. In the moment, it all actually felt quite uneventful; like I was still plodding along, one step at a time. Sometimes, it even felt as if I was running in the total opposite direction of what I had said yes to! But what was happening behind the scenes that I couldn't see with my physical eyes was a spiritual realignment. With that powerful acknowledgment and decision, an energetic recalibration began to reorganize everything in my field of awareness. Those moments of decisiveness were me pulling the sword from the stone.

I believe that something happened just before those moments presented themselves to me. As I reflect back on my life, a pattern is forming. The pattern: that the "divine intersection" always showed up *after I claimed my new identity.* It was my new identity that made the decision in those moments, not my old one.

When I was thirteen, I decided I was an athlete, and then the opportunity showed up to try out for a team.

When I was fifteen, I decided I was a leader, and then the opportunity showed up to become captain of the team.

When I was eighteen, I decided I was capable and fully able to support myself. Then the opportunity to work at Disney and become one of the top trainers at my job came along.

When I was twenty-eight, I decided I was a world-class athlete. Then the opportunity to qualify for World Championships showed up. I made the team and got to travel to Vancouver and Australia the next two years representing Team Canada.

When I was thirty-one, I decided I was worthy of following my dream to open my own studio. Then, the opportunity to sublet a dance studio showed up which would later become the launching pad for my next endeavor.

In my forties, I decided I was an investor and an owner, not just an operator. Then, the opportunity to invest in commercial real estate presented itself—as did the opportunity to take my family on a month-long holiday in Italy while my team ran my business back home.

And then, there was one that changed the game forever: when I decided I was a woman who was willing to be loved. To be cherished. To be supported. To have a partnership where we could dream together, build something meaningful of service together and have amazing life experiences, and travel the world together. When I announced, in front of thousands of people at Tony Robbins' event, that *"I AM beautifully inter-dependent and I do need others".*

Just three weeks later, I made the crazy and illogical decision to get on a plane to South America with "some guy I met at Unleash the Power Within."

That guy, of course, was Mark.

That one decision to stand up and make that vulnerable and awkward declaration was the first domino. The second domino was my decision to get on a plane with someone I barely knew, but whom my gut and intuition were saying "yes" to. At the time of this writing, we've been married for two years and together for four, and have experienced what feels like multiple lifetimes of adventure, love, and blessings. We have done, seen, created, and experienced so much more than we could have ever asked for or imagined. Our old lives seem foreign, distant, like another planet altogether.

Today, we live in a completely "upgraded' and rebirthed reality designed for us by God. Both of us have launched completely new businesses and are fully in alignment in our calling and work in this world. We work together and play together every day. We have been blessed beyond imagination with our dream home in North Carolina (on that land I bought during another Kairos moment). I am beyond words to share how good God is when we receive what He is trying to give us.

CLAIM WHAT IS PROMISED

I believe that receiving God's gifts begins with us *claiming* the identity that's been ours all along, and then *deciding* we are not only worthy of it, but also that we will commit to taking aligned action to become it. The identity we long to embody has always been ours—it has always been in us. The Warrior of the Heart. The Lover. The Leader. The King. The Queen. The Abundant One. The Chosen One. The One Who Says Yes. We are already all of these, and more.

Our soul knows its time. We feel the nudge, and there is a calling inside of us to rise up! To come out of hiding, and embody more of who we were created to be all along. There is a yearning we cannot deny. God is calling us, but it's up to us to claim and receive this identity and take the journey to fully embody it in our character and every cell of our being.

That is what I am inviting you to do in this final chapter.

We have already learned and begun to embody the truth of who we are—the "us" that God sees. However, claiming that identity is not something that He will do for you. It is up to you to step forward and receive what was promised.

What changes when you shift your identity? Everything! But one of the most important is your everyday decision-making.

Humans make about 35,000 conscious decisions per day. If you take out the time we are sleeping, that is roughly 2,000 micro-decisions per hour. Research indicates that, for founders and CEOs, that number is much higher. Within that range, 90 to 95 percent of those decisions are automated—meaning, they are rooted in habits, beliefs, reflexes, reactions, and our instincts. So much is run by who we believe we are, and our current sense of identity! So, can you imagine what could happen if you could shift your identity and begin to make different decisions even 10 percent of the time? That would equate to 3,500 different decisions per day. What if you could shift by just 1 percent? That would still be 350 different decisions! Imagine how what you eat, what you read, who you reach out to, or what you write in your next proposal could change if you made those decisions from a place of being a whole, beloved Child and Heir of God!

The reality is, you don't need to change 3,500 decisions a day. All it takes is *one*—one moment, one choice. Because you repeat what you experience, once you make that one decision, it gets easier and easier to make that decision again. Before you know it, you've retrained your habits, beliefs, and operating systems, and a complete renewing of your mind and heart has taken place simply by bringing awareness to a few potent things each day. By redirecting your thoughts, your actions, and your identity, you orient toward that which is life-giving and expands you. The moment you do so, you begin to have new results and new experiences; this ultimately creates a "new normal" in your life. Where once your normal was angry and anxious, your new normal is open and curious. Where once the normal was unlovable, the new normal is loved.

The Word of God is clear on this. If you want to truly transform yourself, it begins by renewing your mind, body, and spirit daily in alignment with your chosen identity—not once, but daily. As is written in Romans 12:2 (NIV), *"Do not conform to the pattern of this world, but be transformed by the renewing of your mind."*

Unfortunately, I feel this passage has been misunderstood on so many levels. Instead of inspiring and moving us to renew ourselves daily so we can be a light in the world, it often has people feeling afraid of the world. In my opinion, this verse has a deeper context and meaning to it. The world is a collective of our past experiences and those of others. Unfortunately, what is seen is a world of trouble—a world of threats and dark stories that replay over and over again; a world of distorted definitions of success, beauty, love, and happiness; a world of betrayals, hurts, rejection, and loneliness. A world where most people cannot be trusted, and you must constantly watch your back.

The world that most of humanity lives in is the fallen world. In that world, we are separate from God, and therefore from our God-given calling. Separate from our own heart and soul, and therefore our divine gifts and essence. That's what happens when you conform to and abide by the world's standards, beliefs, and identities.

But what if you could make the leap into a new world? What if you could have a renewed mindset each and every day? What if you could tap into new thoughts, create new experiences, which create new memories and therefore new unconscious habits?

The good news is, we can. However, as the passage above reminds us, such a transformation will require us to unplug from the familiar world as we know it, and plug into a new world: God's eternal Kingdom.

For me, this is what it means to come home to the place we belong. The Kingdom of God and the Kingdom of Heaven that is here on Earth, now. It is our calling as Warriors of the Heart to get to know the operating systems and principles of *this* world, and embrace the Kingdom reality that is already at hand.

By the way, by "at hand," Jesus meant "right here." Right in front of our faces. In our midst.

The Kingdom of Heaven was the central theme of Jesus' preaching ministry while he was on Earth. Since his death and resurrection, one of the most critical spiritual mistakes and distortions propagated by humanity has been the failure to understand the concept of the Kingdom of Heaven. Many Christians have adopted the idea that the Kingdom of Heaven is somewhere out there, far away—that you can only get there once you die, and only then if you have accomplished enough good deeds. They are completely separate from the idea that by accepting Christ and receiving Him, the healing is here *now*. The love is here *now*. The joy is here *now*. The light, the freedom from our past— it's all here, right now, available to us should we choose to claim it.

If we are still attached to our old identities, opting into the systems of the fallen world each and every day, letting others or our own false beliefs rule our decisions, we will remain blind to the Kingdom.

In total honesty, I did not understand the depth or significance of this concept for most of my life. It only clicked once I realized that the message of Christ is, "I am here, walking among you now. I am in your midst now. I am available to you now. I am here to support you now. I am here to hold you in all your imperfections, as you are, where you are, and guide you now. I am calling you now. Follow me now. I will open doors you never knew existed now. I will equip you now."

Now, not someday. Here, not somewhere.

This level of awareness has empowered me to embrace my full identity, the woman I am created to be. It has given me the faith to make the decisions that seem totally illogical but give my spirit such peace. It has made me anew as a Warrior of the Heart.

In a moment, I am going to walk you through a simple framework that I use to help me digest this, break this down, and make it practical in day-to-day life. This framework is designed to help you make a bold declaration and reclaim what is yours. It's a Manifesto—an acknowledgment to yourself, to God, and to others—that you are choosing to rise to the occasion. That you are no longer a slave to the past, no longer caught up in the drift, no longer stuck or stagnant. That you are stepping out of the daily skirmishes and into the true battle.

Use this framework any time you begin to feel the longing—the *calling* on your heart and soul to step into the life God is calling you to lead. Come back to it anytime you begin to feel stagnant or stuck. Once you complete this process, I invite you to write it out on a clean page, and then declare it out loud daily. Back it up with scriptures or other evidence presented to you by God through your various channels of discernment. And then, watch how quickly your new reality will come to pass.

But first, remember: *it is all here now*. The visions placed deep in your heart are seeds that are ready to be watered now. The dreams are not distant; they are alive in you once you give them oxygen, not one day or someday, but now. Whatever you are being called to, it's already done.

The Holy Spirit is here and available now. He dwells in you now. Allow Him to guide you in this process.

Before we begin composing your Warrior Manifesto, I invite you to pray this simple prayer. We begin with prayer to set our agenda, ego, and pride aside. To quiet the inputs of the external and the predisposed ideas of the mind, and allow the Holy Spirit to speak in us and through us, through the gateway of the heart.

Dear Holy Spirit,

I invite you into this space. I open myself up to you. I ask that you open the eyes and ears of my heart and speak to me now. Thank you for calling me by name. Your Word says you formed me and knew me even before I was in my mother's womb. That I am fearfully and wonderfully made. That you know every intimate detail about me and have plans and hopes and a future for me. Thank you for placing a God-sized vision, dreams, and desires inside my heart. Thank you for the gifts and talents given to me. I am committed to acknowledging them, cultivating them, and pouring them into the world. Thank you for revealing what I am being called to leave behind, and what I am being called to embrace in this season. Thank you for speaking a clear mission into my heart. Thank you for giving me the faith and courage to step boldly into the identity you are speaking into me. Reveal to me with clarity the answers I am seeking.

Your Word says, "Ask, and it will be given to you. Seek, and you will find. Knock, and it will be opened for you." I ask that you guide me in this process. I am open and willing to hear the whisper of your voice.

In your name I pray,

Amen

DISCOVER YOUR CALLING

There are two kinds of callings we experience in our lives. The first is the general calling for all of us: a call to humanity to come back into unity with the Father and with one another, and to reflect the Grace of God. It is the calling to be filled with the Spirit and be a reflection of Christ in all things. To be a light in the dark places, a blessing unto others. To exhibit the fruits of the Spirit by being loving, joyful, peaceful, patient, kind, good to one another, faithful in all things, gentle, compassionate, and exercising self-control over our pride.

Paul articulates this so well in Ephesians: *"Therefore I, a prisoner for serving the Lord, beg you to lead a life worthy of your calling, for you have been called by God. Always be humble and gentle. Be patient with each other, making allowance for each other's faults because of your love. Make every effort to keep yourselves united in the Spirit, binding yourselves together with peace. For there is one body and one Spirit, just as you have been called to one glorious hope for the future."* (Ephesians 4:1-4, NLT)

The kind of love described above is "Agape love," the kind of love that Christ exhibited. It is unconditional, selfless, and not dependent on someone's worth or performance. It is freely given out of the purity of someone's heart to serve others and benefit the whole.

Our character is continually developed and refined in each season as we fulfill the calling at hand—meaning, whatever it is we are working on at the moment. Wherever our feet are planted. Every day, we are invited to wake up, show up, and love others this way. To contribute by sharing whatever gifts, talents, and skills we have acquired up to this point without grumbling, complaining, wishing we were somewhere else, or lamenting that we are not further ahead. We are commanded to love others out of a pure heart in order to advance unity and hope for the future.

The most depressed people are those without purpose. They are waiting on purpose to come to them instead of moving on purpose each day. So, the question becomes: whatever work environment we are in, whatever relationship, whatever economic situation, can we still move with purpose and serve well in this season with exactly what we have? Can we be trusted to respect, honor, and take care of what we've been entrusted with, regardless of how big or small it is in our eyes?

Jesus tells us in the parable of the shrewd manager found in Luke 16:11 (NASB), *"He who is faithful in a very little thing is faithful also in much; and the one who is unrighteous in a very little thing is also unrighteous in much. Therefore if you have not been faithful in the use of unrighteous wealth, who will entrust the true wealth to you?"*

Gut punch.

Wherever we go, there we are. And until we clean up the inner house, strengthen our character, and restructure the ways in which we operate where we are at, we will remain exactly where we are (if we are lucky), or worse, we will lose it all.

This is a key point because, often, the very thing that blocks us from receiving our next assignment or position is our inability and unwillingness to heed the call *where we are.* Our lack of presence literally blocks the flow of the larger things God has planned for us! This has been a place of deep reflection and humbling for me. I often need to rein myself in when I begin to look sideways at what others in my field are doing and compare myself to them—or, worse, compare myself to the vision He gave me for my life which has not yet manifested. There I am, impatient and frustrated, anxious and dissatisfied with where I am and what I am not doing. Before long, that has become my familiar "emotional home," and once again I am totally missing the point.

My husband Mark and I have recently been going through another season of refinement that has been painful but necessary for the next thing God is bringing our way. We knew God had brought us together as a couple for a reason. There was way too much divine orchestration required to make it possible. We also know He has something more in store for us to teach together and create together. We had clarity on what we are here to build together. We felt more alive and aligned than ever. But at the same, it was as if something was working against us. Every time we made gains on what seemed like the "next level" of income growth, team growth or business growth, we hit some sort of pushback.

As we were busy "getting to work" on the growth, the Holy Spirit revealed to us and convicted us both on all the ways we have been sloppy with what He had already entrusted us with. It was coming at us from every angle! It began with little things around the house breaking because we had neglected to deal with them. Little fixes that, ignored over time, became expensive to clean up. Then, it was a missed bill payment here or there because we were sloppy with our record-keeping. Insignificant, nonchalant attitudes toward little things started costing us thousands of dollars in late fees and accumulated interest charges. At the same time, poor financial decisions we'd made in the past showed up for both of us and hit us over the head. It felt like one thing after another!

I quickly realized that we were being called to pay attention to the details—to slow down, read the fine print, get organized, keep things clean and in order, and build the inner infrastructure and scaffolding both in our character and our financial systems. This is essential if we are going to steward anything greater! We both got to eat some humble pie, have a lot of tough conversations, and upgrade our relationships with stewardship, structure, order, money, and more.

Both Mark and I have gotten pretty far on our talents and charisma (and maybe a little on our good looks). But now, we were being called to upgrade across the board. From keeping the cars clean, to a streamlined system for paying bills, to making sure we honored God with the first fruits of everything (time, money, energy), to upgrading the lines of communication inside our home and in our teams, to raising our standards of excellence, there was work to do before we could be entrusted with the next outpouring of blessing.

Being purposeful right here, right now, is humbling. It's eye-opening. It's the essential next step you have been looking for. And if you are still waiting for your true calling to be revealed, this step is even more essential, because it will reveal the wisdom and guidance you have been waiting for all along.

So, I urge you to ask God and the Holy Spirit to reveal:

- "What am I missing?"
- "What do you see that I can't see?"
- "What have I been dismissing that you want me to give attention and time to?"
- "What do I need to do to prepare for what will be bestowed upon me?"

Start there.

When we shift our gaze or focus from being fixated on ourselves and the future we have yet to see happen, and instead refocus our attention on where we are called right now, we begin to witness a shift both within us and externally in our environment. When we are willing to show up *now*, in service wherever we are, and pour our gifts into *this* place, following the inner lead of the Holy Spirit within us, we invite God back in. We open the doors for Him to work in our lives and through us in unexpected ways. Often, we can't even notice it's happening. We simply show up, do the thing, and move on. But there are seeds planted in this season. Things begin moving below the surface and reorganizing themselves in the atmosphere. We are influencing and leaving an impact in ways we cannot fully see yet.

This is the preparation; this is the divine testing and fire of refinement. This is what positions us for our next chapter, and the point where we are finally ready to receive the next assignment. By following the calling which is common to all of us, we are building the infrastructure that will receive the future vision and also cultivating the character to hold that vision intact.

Your Unique Calling

Why does your collective calling come before your personal calling? Because you cannot and will not be able to sustain and execute your specific calling if you don't have the foundations in place. You can chase it all you want, but it won't stick until both you and God's divine timing are aligned.

There is work for us to do while we are here on Earth. We have been given gifts to pour out into the world, and while it may look different through different seasons of life, there is often an underlying thread in all positions we find ourselves in, either by His doing or our own.

One of my favorite comments on this subject in the Bible was spoken by Mordecai to Esther when he said to her, *"Perhaps you were born for a time such as this"* (see Esther 4:14).

Esther had found herself at an impasse. She lived with the Jewish people and was comfortable in her home with her uncle. She was loving and kind, devoted to leading a life of peace. But God had something else in store for her. She had been chosen as the one who would save her people by winning the heart of King Xerxes. But first, she had to leave her home, against her wishes, in order to be selected as a *potential* bride for the king. She didn't know at the time that that was the assignment God had for her. All she knew was that she didn't want to go; she wanted to stay where she was comfortable and felt protected. Going to the palace would require a whole season of preparation before she would even have the opportunity to be presented before the King. What if he ended up rejecting her, and this was all for nothing?

As the story goes, Esther ended up being one of the most influential and wise women in Biblical history. She not only won favor in the King's eyes, but ended up being the very one to save the Jewish people from genocide.

Repeatedly throughout scripture, whenever someone is called into a position of influence, they are called by God to leave their old, familiar life and move into a new place. A new land. To leave behind their old identity and embrace their God-given identity and role. Often, they are hesitant about going but move in faith as an act of obedience. And with that, they are also often even given a new name which matches their "renewed" identity and reflects not only who they are called to be, but also the blessing and promise God has spoken over their lives.

God chose you. He calls you by name. He knew you in your mother's womb long before you were born, and He has plans for your life. He has been preparing you all along for your specific calling, and will continue to do so, refining you at each stage. It's up to you to heed the call when the pull is strong, the whisper undeniable, reminding you, "It's time."

Your *unique calling* is divinely influenced and divinely orchestrated. It shows up as an inner impulse, a strong and unexplainable pull toward a particular course or path. It's a *must do*, even more than a dream or desire. You can't really explain it. You just know that you are *meant to do* this thing. You are *built* to do this thing. And once you do it, I guarantee that you will begin to see yourself through different eyes. You will no longer view yourself as you used to be—as your physical mother or father sees you, as your old friends or colleagues see you. A new identity is birthed as you remember who you really are created to be.

You are a son. You are a daughter. You belong to your Father.

You are called. You are equipped. You are supported.

You must do this *now*.

When you are called by God, "purpose" is no longer some fluffy affirmation or positive thinking, but a deep resonance of truth ringing through your body, soul, and spirit.

So, if each of us are called this way—if each of us have a divine purpose and are called to it by God, why do so many humans feel so purposeless?

What blocks our ability to clearly hear the calling over our lives is that we have not yet fully walked the path of the Warrior of the Heart. We are still attached to external opinions and ideas about what we should be doing. We are still putting what our parents, spouses, or our social media "friends" say above what God is saying to us. We are still chasing shiny invitations to become someone other than who we are, rather than returning to our true nature as God's child. We are unwilling to go to God as our Source with our questions, fears, dreams, and desires.

Neglecting going to the Source of our calling is the very thing that keeps us wandering wildly off course and our souls slowly withering away. It is the very thing that keeps us fighting the wrong battles, at the wrong times, for the wrong masters. When we are walking *outside* of our specific calling, it's as if we are rowing a boat in the wrong direction but we don't know how to change course. Everything feels forced and difficult; each task takes much longer to accomplish and requires all of our energy to keep it alive. Every day is an uphill battle. Just as when we deny our general calling, life slowly starts to have less meaning, as though our joy is being robbed from us—because it is! We are missing the fruits of this season of our lives.

Our calling is not to be dismissed. It is the reason we are here.

When we begin to walk in our specific calling, life itself explodes inside of us. We sense an urgency coupled with a heartfelt desire to serve and fulfill. A new confidence rises in us, and we are filled with a conviction to *move* that just was not there before—at least, not like this.

Suddenly, we are not putting out the fires of our problems; instead, a holy fire is ignited within us. We are recharged, refreshed, motivated, and inspired to take action. When we walk in our calling, we are blessed in so many ways. This is where we begin to experience the blessings that truly come from above. These blessings take on many shapes. Joy increases. Inner peace washes over us. We may discover that we have unexplainable favor or support, even when it doesn't make logical sense. We may see financial blessings, relational blessings, spiritual gifts and blessings, showing up in our lives in new and unlimited ways.

We find ourselves being poured into, instead of drained. And isn't that exactly what we are all seeking, in the end?

Right here, right now, without overthinking, get out a piece of paper and finish the following statement: *"I am called, right now, in this moment, in this season, to ..."*

THE VISION

Visions and dreams are seeds planted in our hearts, minds, and souls. Seeds must be watered, tended to, nourished, and given oxygen. They must be given the time and space to grow, and to do what only they can do in each moment and season. We do our part, and let the seed do its part. We let things work below the ground, in the unseen, for a while before we expect to see those first sprouts.

What dreams have you had for your life? How long have those dreams been locked up inside of you? Have you been watering them? Can you find the common "thread" in those dreams?

As we begin to pay attention to our dreams, those dreams turn into clearer visions.

We are all visionaries at some level. While some of us may be more gifted in this area—the ability to see visions or be the visionary of a company or movement—we are all designed with this innate ability. We can imagine all sorts of things, and tap into all sorts of visions for our lives. I have found that the more time I spend in solitude, quiet reflection in nature, meditation, prayer, or journaling—in other words, the more time I spend in conversation with God—the more I can see and acknowledge the God-shaped vision or dream on my heart, talk about it, and take action in accordance with it.

I have been keeping a dream and vision journal for years now. It is incredible to look back at the visions and dreams that were brought to me (rather than the ones I forced) and see how they actually came to pass once I acknowledged them. Also interesting to me is how, when the visions or goals I was chasing were *not* from God, I was either unable to hit them, or they took so much out of me that they were ultimately unfulfilling.

The more I sit with God and thank Him for the vision He is placing in my heart and consciousness, the more it grows. So, how do we know if a vision is from God, or created by our own ego?

Here are a few questions for consideration:

- "Is this vision born out of something that deeply broke my heart or moved me?" A God vision is usually born out of some kind of heartache we have experienced or witnessed. We are called to be agents of change!

- "Does this vision excite me, stir up a fire within me, and light me up?" A God vision will always be fueled by holy fire, so it should inspire and breathe life into you.

- "Does it challenge and stretch me beyond my current abilities?" Remember, He doesn't call the experts. He equips those He calls. Does it require you to develop your character, operate in your gifting, and serve others?

- "Will fulfilling this vision require me to depend on God more than ever, and to trust that the right resources, answers, divine opportunities, timing, and favor will come together?"

- Is this vision *way* bigger than me?

If the answers to all of the above are a resounding yes, then you are on the right track.

On the other hand, if the "vision" you see is one of fear, contraction, worry, competition, or vengeance; if it sucks the life out of you, moves you into a state of obligatory action, or creates win/lose situations, I can guarantee you that it is *not* a heavenly vision.

If your vision is God-given, it's time to set aside all excuses and run with it. If it is not God-given, it's time to set aside all attachments and lean into what God actually desires for you.

Once you have begun to connect with your God-given vision, *acknowledge* that you have been given a vision. You may or may not have acted on it before now, but deep down, the seeds have been planted. What you acknowledge begins to show up more and more. So, acknowledge and receive this beautiful vision, instead of rejecting it. Thank God for planting it in your heart.

Secondly, if it's been a while since you have felt clear enough to dream, invite God to come in and dream with you. One of my favorite ways to do this is to imagine that I am sitting with my Father (because I am) and sharing with Him what I have been dreaming about and envisioning. However, I am not only speaking to Him. I am sharing with Him and listening to Him! When our children share their dreams with us, we want to enlarge what they see is possible for them, encourage them, and affirm them. Imagine how much more our Heavenly Father wants to do this with us! "'And it shall be in the last days,' God says, 'That I will pour out My Spirit on all mankind; And your sons and your daughters will prophesy, And your young men will see visions, And your old men will have dreams.'" (Acts 2:17)

This has been a beautiful practice for me. I am no longer alone in my dreams. No longer is it "my vision." It's His vision planted in me. A gift and picture of the future I receive. A promise of what is to come into my life and the lives of others, should I heed the call. (Note: to support you with this process, I have included a free guided visualization at www.dropthearmorbook.com.)

At this point, when we have seen the whole (or even a small part) of what God has planned for us, it's time to decide. We either trust the vision and follow Him, or cast it aside and follow what we think is "realistic."

For so long, I was afraid to fully acknowledge my dreams and visions for fear that I would fall short—I would not know how to make it happen, or that the resources to make it happen would not be there. Again, that's all about *me* having to *make* something happen on my own, by my own strength and resources. But we are not playing in that space, are we?

If God gave you the vision, He will also provide the *provision*. "Provision" is the resources to carry out the vision. If you invite God into your heart, and allow Him to walk with you along your journey, you will always be provided for.

So, what is the vision for your life that God has placed in your heart? Who is in the picture with you? What are you doing? What else is happening around you? What is the energy of the atmosphere? Get specific and clear on as many details as you can, and enjoy the process of dreaming with your Heavenly Father!

Now, consider which aspects of your vision you have been denying or not giving attention to because they feel unrealistic or unattainable based on your current circumstances. If you truly believed that God would supply the provision for the vision He gave you, how would you be showing up differently?

THE MISSION AT HAND

"But now that I have the vision, what do I focus on?"

That seems to be the never-ending question. I can't count the number of times my clients have said, "I don't know what to do," when in fact they know exactly what to do, but they are running from it, distracting themselves from it, or doing everything else but the *one thing* that matters and will make everything else open up.

That one thing you don't want to do, but will change everything when you do it? I call this "the mission at hand."

Once you have received a vision or a picture of what you are here to create, and have made the decision to move in that direction, there is always a mission that presents itself. That mission is a project or something that must be completed in order for the next piece of the puzzle to drop in.

God does not give us the entire blueprint, strategy, and plan all at once. That would overwhelm us. He gives us pieces so we can walk intimately with Him through each step of the process. Each mission (or assignment) is handed to us by Him; as we receive it, He continues to reveal the how step-by-step. We can opt out at any time—that's the beauty and power of free will. And to be honest, the mission at hand is most often something we don't want to do or don't quite feel prepared to do. It can be downright terrifying, and as a result we will avoid it, run from it, or dig in our heels.

But, when we finally complete the mission, everything else starts to make sense.

Initially, when I received the mission to rebrand my entire coaching business, I cringed. "Stop. We are doing something different now." Seriously? By this point, I had spent tens of thousands of dollars to attain High Performance Coaching Certifications. I had also invested well over six figures in mentorship and masterminds that told me to structure my business a certain way. Yet, here I was, grappling with an urgent need to *stop* promoting all of my old programs, *stop* teaching all that old content, *stop* trying to follow others' frameworks, and do this other thing instead. To create a new business and brand titled, "Warriors of the Heart."

God told me, "Launch this new program. Take the people I send you through an initiation. I will guide you." As soon as I pulled the trigger and put it out there, I downloaded the entire program with clarity.

Because I accepted that mission, you are here, with me, having walked through your own Warrior's journey and deeper into God's grace and the heart of your own mission. But there was no way for me to see that far ahead at the time. I was simply called to trust God, accept this assignment, and birth the initiation.

I had two men sign up for the initial program. Then, a handful of women. Slowly, over the next two years, I kept delivering the messages. The community grew slowly, but God was blessing me and others in so many ways. Spiritually, relationally, financially.

My obedience to that mission opened me up to receive the next assignment, which was to launch my podcast, originally titled *The Untamed Life* and recently relaunched as *The Breaking Chains Podcast*. When the call came, it sounded like this: *"Go and share the message I give you."* I had always wanted to host a podcast, but before, when it was "my" idea and was intended to showcase my expertise in the fitness world and elevate my brand (and my ego), it just didn't work out. Launching *this* podcast was a pure act of obedience because I surrendered the whole thing to God. Again, like the program, it was a slow start, but it gained momentum. Now, as we close in on over 150 episodes, I feel like I'm just getting warmed up and ready for what He *really* wants me to share. Everything up to this point was planting seeds, putting in the reps, showing up consistently, and letting go of my attachment to a particular result.

Shortly after, in the early winter of 2022, I received the mission to write this book. God showed me the picture you now see on the cover of the book you're holding. I saw copies being distributed and I heard the words, *"Go. Write the book."* Not *a* book, but *this* book. Then, one of my clients, Denise, spoke up in our coaching group, "Christine, last night I had a dream that we were all sitting around in your kitchen, and you were signing copies of your book for us!"

Okay, Lord, I thought. *I will do it.*

But I didn't have a clue where to begin.

I shared this with a mentor of mine, and within weeks, he had introduced me to his publisher and the book writing was underway.

And here's the thing: although it has taken me well over a year to complete this manuscript, the whole book was already "written" in my journal entries over the past twenty-four months as I went through my own Warrior Initiation. The raw content and the process of the Initiation was documented. The book essentially wrote itself. I did not need to "figure out" what I was supposed to say. My job was simply to put all the notes in order, and be the vessel for the words that God wanted me to birth into the world. How cool is that?

So, why did it take me over a year? My attention wandered. God kept reminding me, "Stop everything and finish this." But I didn't always do that. There were other key projects, program launches, clients to serve, conferences to attend, etc. And, you know what happened?

Nothing.

I did not make progress on the book during those times. And the other projects that I thought I needed to focus on that were taking so much of my attention? They failed or got little traction. I grew frustrated, but I also knew exactly why they weren't fruitful. It wasn't that I was doing something wrong. I was just not focused on the mission at hand. It wasn't time for those other missions. I was trying to fulfill the mission He gave me while also doing all the other things I thought I needed or wanted to do. In reality, what I needed to do was finish the assignment that I had already been given!

There is a lesson in this for you, too, Warrior. Every day is an opportunity and a decision to try and do it all, or to do the *right* thing, in the right timing and order. When we are clear on the mission at hand and in full trust and obedience, we move through these missions and succeed more quickly. When we hesitate, delay, get distracted, or fail to trust the process, things stop flowing. It becomes hard to complete the mission, and we may actually feel resentful toward it.

There are so many reasons why we avoid doing the thing we are called to do. Insecurities and doubts creep in. We wonder, *Will anyone even notice? Will it matter? Will it be successful?* But the work while on mission is to remain devoted to the mission. This, too, is a divine opportunity, and a testing ground for obedience, devotion, trust, and discipline.

I want to end this section by saying that, sometimes, the mission at hand or current assignment to fulfill is not a specific project, but rather a situation that needs to get cleaned up. There may be a few things that you need to put in order so that you can receive the next assignment. I often see that, when someone hits a block or goes through a dry season in their business, it is because they are avoiding taking care of something that they've been told to do by God.

Perhaps you already know exactly what the mission at hand is for you. If so, it's time to take action! And if not, it's time to get still and ask God to reveal what it is He is calling you to do.

Below, I have put a chart that reflects the way God calls us and His promises if we obey. As we outlined at the beginning of this chapter, God usually works in steps. That means He gives us one move at a time. When He sees us move toward that which He calls us to do, He meets us there. There is most always a call or command, followed by a promise of how He will come through. We go, He goes. We go, He goes. That's how He works.

So, take a look at the list below and tune into the left column. This is our work. The right column reflects His promises to us when we move in obedience. For a full reference, I encourage you to look up any Bible verses where there is a command, and then read the promises directly following. The two usually go hand in hand.

OUR PART (What He commands/calls us to do)	**HIS PART** (What He promises He will do)
Listen	I will be with you
Go! Move	I will protect you. I will show you
Come	I will guide you
Say this/speak	I will put words in your mouth/give you words
Obey	I will bless you

Have faith/trust	I will equip you, I will bless you
Move!	I will build you, extend favor
Shout, sing, worship, march	I will tear down your enemies, hand them over to you, turn them against themselves (handle your enemies)
Prepare	I will give you, bless you, multiply you
Give	I will pour out on you, fill you, redeem you
Release, let go!	I will replace, I will free, I will extend
Pick up	I will love you, I will come with you
Honor, seek, ask	I will give you, show you
Do not fear	I will strengthen you, give you faith, embolden, make you a great nation
Pray	I will answer, I will provide

NEW WARRIOR, NEW STANDARDS

I trust that, by now, you are beginning to see the pieces coming together with more clarity. With your vision and the mission at hand identified, we can move to the next step—the place where your vision begins to manifest, and your reality begins to reorganize to match your vision.

But first, we need to tune into the *atmosphere* that you hold as a standard.

By "atmosphere," I mean the air, the ambiance, the vibration or current energetic temperature in a place. You know what I mean. Unless you're completely aloof or disconnected from your body and spirit, you can sense it. You can feel it. It's what holds the whole thing together. Have you ever walked into someone's home and immediately felt tension in the air? What about walking into a shop or office space and immediately feeling lighter and inspired. A great deal of intention and marketing dollars go into curating environments for people to shop in, work in, or work out in, but how intentional are we in curating the atmosphere of our own environment every day?

We are always either being influenced by the atmosphere and environment or influencing it. We are always adapting to our environments or creating the environments we want to be in.

So, as you go back to the vision that God shared with you, what is the *atmosphere* of that vision? Is it bold, steady, calm? Is it spacious and expansive? Is it lively and energizing? Close your eyes if you need to. Connect to that vision now. Once you see and feel that atmosphere, write down one to three words that best describe it.

Next, ask yourself, "What is the current atmosphere I have been holding in this arena?" If you have a future vision of your family, for example, what is the current family environment? If you have a vision of your future work or contribution, what is the current atmosphere around your office or work environment? This is super important, because the current reality you are experiencing is a direct result of the standard you've held in any area up to this point.

That is your gap. It's super simple, and super powerful.

The key here is choosing to move by faith and not by sight. To hold the vision in your heart and spirit, and begin to cultivate that same atmosphere that your vision holds *right now*, today. If the atmosphere of your vision is calm and you've been operating in chaos, then you get to raise the standard for what you allow. You have to become the calm you see, bring the calm you desire, and put things in place to protect that calm. That may mean that you have some "cleanup" to do in terms of what you allow or tolerate in your life. You can no longer continue to allow the same old behaviors while expecting a different result. It's upgrade time. What standards will you uphold and live by in this new vision?

Mark and I have had a vision of our home base being a place of gravity for our people. We saw a beautiful home where family could gather—where our kids, clients, and friends can come and feel safe, loved, and seen. A place where people can come to rest, heal, and grow. There are many layers to this vision—but as a home, it's a place of grounding, acceptance, and safety. We call this "Gravitas." That means we get to uphold the atmosphere and instill certain standards of behavior for ourselves and those we invite into our space.

These standards are:

- We respect each other.
- We are responsible for the energy we each bring to the room.
- We address problems and resentments as they are arise and don't allow them to build or fester.
- We value each other and recognize that everyone has something to contribute.
- We leave each room, day, or conversation better than we found it.

Of course, my husband and I are the leaders of the vision. Therefore, we are called to set and hold the standards that support that vision. To meet some of them, we have had to upgrade and retrain everyone inside our household, starting with ourselves! These standards allow us to maintain the atmosphere in our home so that Gravitas remains intact and multiplies.

As you look upon your vision and the atmosphere you are called to create and hold as the new normal, what are the standards you see yourself implementing? What must you change, let go, or reinforce? Make a list of your upgraded standards and the behaviors that match them. Write them down on a piece of paper in a clean, bulleted list so they are easy to identify. Then, write out the following statement:

"Effective immediately, this is the new normal! I am fiercely committed to upholding and protecting this standard for myself and others."

RISE, WARRIOR, RISE!

Each season requires a new version of us to surface. Each challenge, dream, and opportunity requires new versions of us to step up and take action. It is a constant process of remembering more of who we are, drawing closer to our true identity in God, and revealing and receiving more of the gifts, desires, and dreams planted within us by His grace.

Warrior, it is time. Time to step into your God-given identity , and fully embody it. Time to say "yes!" to the vision God has placed in your heart and accept your current mission. Now, we will take everything you have learned along this journey and put it all into one concise, powerful statement—your Warrior Manifesto—which is one or two pages that clearly and succinctly outline your calling in this season, what the vision is, the mission at hand, the atmosphere you will hold, your upgraded weapons and standards, and the new identity you have chosen.

Below is an example of the Manifesto framework I use for myself. I do this exercise at least once a year, and it's one of the most powerful in my arsenal. I can't wait to see what emerges for you when you're finished!

The Warrior Manifesto Framework

Finish the declarations below in your own words, feeling free to add any other statements that feel clear and true to you in this season.

The specific calling in my life right now is to ...

The clear vision I have been given is ...

The mission at hand is to ...

*The atmosphere I am committed to creating and holding as the
new normal is one of ...*

I no longer tolerate in myself or others the following behaviors: [list them].

I no longer distract or concern myself with ...

Instead, I commit to leading with and holding the following standards: [list your standards and what they look like].

I choose to put my faith in ...

I choose to trust ...

And release the need to control ...

My identity comes from within, from God, and not from the external.

[Back it up with scripture or evidence that is true.]

I AM [Insert your new identity/name]

Agreement

Once you have completed your Manifesto, read aloud the Agreement below to solidify your commitment in your own eyes and those of God. Again, feel free to add or change anything that feels relevant to you. Make this your own Agreement with God.

Father God, I thank you for creating me uniquely in your own image.

I thank you for the unique calling and divine gifting over my life.

I commit to honoring the gifts you have given me and will not waste them any longer.

I commit to putting them to use in the world to serve and bless others in the ways you are calling me to.

Thank you for speaking to me, for giving me the strength and ability to fulfill my calling through your Grace.

I commit to showing up and doing my part, and I trust you to do what only you can do.

I release any need to control the outcome and trust your promises over my life.

Let me be the vessel you work in and through.

In Jesus' name, Amen.

It is done.

Signed, [insert your name here]

When you are ready to complete your Warrior Manifesto, set the tone with deep prayer and reverence. Ask God to guide you as you write out your Manifesto and sign it.

Then, place your Manifesto where you can see and read it regularly. As you are learning this new way of being, having good protocols in place is essential. Personally, I like to make my Manifesto into a visually appealing PDF and use it as a screensaver. That way, I will read it and see it multiple times a day. Or, you can print out your Manifesto and hang it in a place where you will see it every day—like your refrigerator, your bathroom mirror, or your office wall.

Ignite Your Transformation

Below are some ways to add fuel to the fire of your Warrior Manifesto and stay in the energy of your new commitment to yourself and to God.

Back it with Truth

Research a handful of scriptures that affirm what you wrote in your Manifesto. For me, having verses to confirm what God has shared with me is like rocket fuel. Not only does my mind hear this, but my spirit and heart receive the deep resonance of His Truth. I incorporate these scriptures into my daily prayers or meditations.

You can also choose powerful quotes from other bodies of work that resonate with you.

Stack the Evidence

Anywhere you have had or begin to experience evidence of the new identity showing up, the new atmosphere being felt, the new standards at play, write that win down. Anywhere you see God moving in your life (or have seen Him in the past). Anywhere past dreams have already been realized. Anywhere you see evidence of new doors opening, new opportunities showing up, or new alignments taking place.

It's important for us to see progress and continue to affirm life over our visions and identities. When we begin to recognize the work working, our eyes become more and more open to the new world and timelines really do seem to collapse right before our eyes!

Share and Declare!

Too many great visions and ideas die because they get set aside in a journal or on the shelf. You must keep this front and center, daily. It is important to speak life over your Manifesto by declaring your new identity daily and sharing the vision wisely.

First and foremost, you are always declaring and sharing *in* the spirit and *with* the Spirit before anyone else. He is the One who placed this in you, who will equip you and fulfill this mission with you.

Second, make it a habit to read your Manifesto out loud daily. Speaking the words aloud gives them weight. The resonance of your voice serves to anchor them into your being at all levels. When you do so, you are moving from just having ideas and thoughts to active creation. The Lord spoke, and it was so. Speak truth over your life. Speak victory over your circumstances. Speak light into the dark place. Speak beyond the current form. Speak the future vision into the present moment, declaring, "Effective immediately, this is my new reality!"

Finally, share your vision and Manifesto with other Kingdom Warriors—men and women who can rally alongside you, pray with you, fight with you, encourage you, and celebrate you along the way. Share it with those who will steer you back on course if you get distracted. Those who can see the vision beyond the day-to-day. I would love to be one of those Kingdom Warriors for you. I want to hear from you. Email your Manifesto to me at christinejewell@warriorsoftheheart.io. I read every single one that comes in, and will come into agreement with you that it is done and becomes embodied within you!

Be intentional. Be wise. Be discerning. Be fiercely protective of this sacred mission and move forward faithfully.

WARRIOR INITIATION

- What was revealed to you as you explored claiming your new identity?

- What is the promise on the other side of God's mission for you?

- What will change starting today, now that you have declared your "new normal"?

- How did it feel to write your Warrior Manifesto and speak it out loud?

- What are you most excited about now that you have been initiated as a Warrior of the Heart?

Afterword
(A Blessing)

Dear Warrior,

It's been a full journey. We've traveled to the beginning of your wounding, released old identities, and burned old belief systems. We've forgiven and rewritten the stories in your heart. We've explored the possibility of what life can look like on the other side. I've done my best to pour my own heart and stories into you as inspiration. We've redefined who you are in Christ, and established who you are not. We have addressed the enemy that wants to divide you and rob you of the riches God has for you, and upgraded your arsenal with tools to overcome it. We've pressed into deeper faith, building trust and learning how to discern the Holy Spirit at work.

You are ready. You are equipped.

Thank you for being here to the end—which is really the beginning of a brand new world for you. I honor you and everything you have been through. I pray that, as you put these pages into practice and make this real in your life, you will be abundantly blessed. I have no doubt that it will be far greater than anything you could ask for, dream of, or imagine.

A few reminders for you as you move this work off the page and into your life:

- Not everyone will understand your new journey, new vision, and upgraded identity. In fact, very few will understand ... until they do.

- Remember that your God-given calling and mission isn't for them. It's for *you*.

- Your new identity and role isn't theirs. It's *yours*. Receive it, own it, and multiply it!

Everyone dies. Not everyone fully lives.

So go forth, Warrior of the Heart. Go forth and *live*. Love fiercely, lead courageously, and be a beacon of God's light in this world.

In love and faith,
Christine

Resources

To access the **downloads, resources, and audio recordings**
mentioned throughout this book, go to
www.dropthearmorbook.com
or scan the QR code below.

To **book Christine to speak**, please visit
www.thechristinejewell.com/in-the-media

To apply to **work with Christine or
join the Round Table Mastermind**, visit
www.thechristinejewell.com

Acknowledgments

*T*o my father, my first hero, who has served as the greatest inspiration for this body of work.

To my mother, who has always shown up in unconditional love, planting seeds of love in me that today are coming into full bloom. I would not be the woman I am today without your steadfast prayers and modeling of faith.

To my children, Bailey, Christiane, and Grayson, my greatest teachers and number one reason for pursuing the healing of our hearts and restoration inside families.

To my husband, Mark. You have been a rock and my greatest supporter through this entire journey. Thank you for believing in me, and for believing God's ability to get this message out through me, long before I ever did. I love you.

To all my clients who trusted me along the way, poured your hearts and stories into this book, and continue faithfully to press into your own growth as Kingdom leaders, I am so honored to be on the journey with you.

To my editor and publisher, Bryna Haynes. Without your support, I would have not been able to structure my thoughts, follow through on this mission, and birth this book into the world.

And of course, all Glory goes to the King of Kings. Thank you, Jesus, for pursuing me like wildfire in my darkest moments and taking me through this process of Initiation. Thank you, Holy Spirit, for filling me with the words to form the pages of this book!

My heart is so full to witness the birth of this message. I am beyond grateful and blessed.

About the Author

*C*hristine Jewell is a faith-based Executive Coach, author, and speaker with over twenty-five years of combined experience in the fields of holistic health, human performance, and leadership development. She is a mother of six through her blended family, an avid athlete, and a lifelong entrepreneur. She specializes in helping C-suite executives and impact-driven leaders reclaim their marriages, redefine what's next, and create lives of freedom and fulfillment by putting God first.

Christine is the host of the *Breaking Chains Podcast*. Together with her husband, Mark, she leads transformational retreats and leadership workshops worldwide.

Learn more at www.thechristinejewell.com.

About the Publisher

Founded in 2021 by Bryna Haynes, WorldChangers Media is a boutique publishing company focused on "Ideas for Impact." We know that great books change lives, topple outdated paradigms, and build movements. Our commitment is to deliver superior-quality transformational nonfiction by, and for, the next generation of thought leaders.

Ready to write and publish your thought leadership book? Learn more at www.WorldChangers.Media.

pg 20 - Mindset is everythg —
link to Molly's episode.

pg 44 gonta Read at intro

page 70 - Mastered vs Stuure to

I want to know what she's doy now to
avoid the control — once a high achiev
always a high achiever —